Brazil Is the
New America

Brazil Is the New America

How Brazil Offers Upward Mobility in a Collapsing World

James Dale Davidson

WILEY

John Wiley & Sons Inc.

Published by John Wiley & Sons, Inc., Hoboken, New Jersey.
Published simultaneously in Canada.

For general information on our other products and services or for technical support, please contact our Customer Care Department within the United States at (800) 762-2974, outside the United States at (317) 572-3993 or fax (317) 572-4002.

Wiley also publishes its books in a variety of electronic formats. Some content that appears in print may not be available in electronic books. For more information about Wiley products, visit our web site at www.wiley.com.

Library of Congress Cataloging-in-Publication Data:

Davidson, James Dale.
    Brazil is the new America : how Brazil offers upward mobility in a collapsing world / James Dale Davidson.
       p. cm.
    Includes index.
    ISBN 978-1-118-00663-4 (cloth); ISBN 978-1-118-22175-4 (ebk);
    ISBN 978-1-118-26041-8 (ebk); ISBN 978-1-118-23556-0 (ebk)
       1. Economic development—Brazil.   2. Economic development—United States.   3. Economic forecasting—Brazil.   4. Economic forecasting—United States.   5. Brazil—Economic conditions—21st century.   6. United States—Economic conditions—21st century.   7. Brazil—Social conditions—21st century.   8. United States—Social conditions—21st century.   I. Title.
    HC187.D38 2012
    330.981—dc23
                                                                              2012010364

Printed in the United States of America

10 9 8 7 6 5 4 3 2 1

To my Brazilian son,
Arthur Leonardo
DeClare Davidson

Contents

Preface

The first decade of the twenty-first century has taught me a lesson. I now realize that I was hasty to be cocky half a lifetime ago about having been born in the United States.

When I was a young man, the American Dream was alive and well. I took advantage of it to invent my own work as a serial entrepreneur. I have had a hand in launching and building three billion dollar-plus companies, two companies that attained a market cap of half a billion dollars or more, and about a dozen others that became worth $100 million or more. I enjoyed the adventure and the high standard of living that went with it. But I don't see the same opportunities ahead for my children, especially my two older children who are entirely American as I was.

By no means am I selling them short. They are both bright and energetic. They will need all the energy they can muster to succeed in the world in which they will live.

My youngest child has better prospects. He is a Brazilian citizen who speaks fluent Portuguese and is already learning Mandarin, to go with Spanish, French, and English in his language repertoire. Touch wood, he seems to have a bright future as a global citizen, more because his mother's family includes some well-connected and successful Brazilians than because of his connections to the United States.

Most Americans are ignorant of Brazil. Many might be inclined to consider it an Hispanic country. Or guess that its capital is Buenos Aires. Equally, many would be inclined to suppose that Brazil is a small, poor country. I remember my astonishment several years ago when a very wealthy Brazilian woman of my acquaintance took a fancy to a house in McLean, Virginia, that was for sale by its owner. When the owner learned that the proposed buyer was Brazilian, he arrogantly announced that he would take the discussion no further because "a Brazilian could not possibly afford" his house. What an idiot. Now I live in South Florida, where newspapers report that up to half of all real property transactions in Miami in 2011 were conducted with Brazilians for cash.

We Americans believe ourselves to be rich. For our entire lives, we have been told that the United States is the richest country on earth. Many of us who cast uneasy glances into the future anticipated that sometime in the by-and-by the unrealistic promises made to pay Social Security and Medicare benefits would come to grief. We were optimists. That someday is not decades away, but the day after tomorrow. Thinking superficially, we have supposed as Americans that we were far richer than Brazilians. No longer.

A little-noted report from the United States Treasury in August 2011 showed that the U.S. government owes $210 billion or approximately $1,034 per capita to Brazilians ($4,138 per Brazilian household). How many American households bear this burden could be debated. According to the U.S. Census Bureau, there are approximately 113,000,000 U.S. households, but only 97 million households are above the poverty line. Those who are already destitute have no capacity to pay the government's vast obligations. Another 18 million households are retired and no longer producing goods and services that can be used to support the government's obligations. That leaves approximately 79 million, nonretired, apparently solvent households to pay the staggering burdens left behind by economic collapse. On average, therefore, each productive household in the United States will owe the average Brazilian $2,658. The world is changing faster than we think.

This book is an attempt to explain how and why the world is changing, with respect to the other great, continental American economy, Brazil.

Acknowledgments

I thank the many persons whose thoughts entertained and provoked me as I got to know Brazil. The works of many of the published authorities are cited in the text. In particular, I found Austrian novelist Stefan Zweig's classic, *Brazil: A Land of the Future*, to be far-seeing and informative.

I was especially lucky in having the support and encouragement of Romualdo Concado, who graciously allowed me to roost in the guest room of his home in Belvedere, Belo Horizonte. He is not only a great host; he is also a well-informed observer of the Brazilian economy. He entertained me with stories about why "Brazil is no country for beginners." He generously read early drafts of some of the chapters and saved me from embarrassing mistakes. I also thank Cristina Barbosa for her spirit-lifting encouragement and her perspectives on the trials of dealing with Brazilian bureaucracy. I also thank my sometimes co-author, Lord William Rees-Mogg, for his encouragement. And cheers to my personal assistant, Laurie Geller, for braving tottering stacks of notes, books, and drafts to keep me organized in the writing process.

Arthur's mother, Taciana Davidson, helped set this whole enterprise in motion. I am grateful for the good years we spent together. She welcomed me into her Brazilian family, and went far to educate me on the ways of her country. I also thank my colleague Charles Del Valle for his intelligent comments on early drafts; my agent, Theron Raines, for finding a publisher; Jennifer MacDonald, at John Wiley & Sons, for her unfailing, good humor and constructive edits; and Debra Englander, for thinking I have an important thesis about Brazil and for publishing this book.

I thank Senator Joseph Tydings for providing me with a crucial education in the problem of water deficiency that faces so many countries across the globe. I also thank Donald Trump for taking the time to confirm his good-humored illustration of the logic of double-entry bookkeeping. Bill Bonner and Chris Ruddy are innocent of any faults in this book, but much appreciated for their encouragement. Chris traveled with me to São Paulo and shared his always shrewd observations about the dynamic heart of Brazil's economy. Thanks.

It has been a chronic drawback of thank-you notes through the ages that they are inadequate, and often, not posted to the right people. In this case, any number of people I have met along the way, both in Brazil and elsewhere, have engaged me in conversations about this dynamic, rising economy. I learned from many of these conversations and thank everyone.

As usual, the responsibility for errors, misjudgments, and dangling prepositions lies with me.

Chapter 1

The World in 2050

There is no evidence that God ever intended the U.S. to have a higher per capita income than the rest of the world for eternity.

Robert Solow, *Financial Times*, January 15, 2011

Half a lifetime ago, when I was a Yank at Oxford, I wondered why my English contemporaries were not all packing their bags to leave the country. In those days, before Margaret Thatcher, maximum tax rates on incomes above £20,000 were 98 percent. It seemed to me then that having been born in the United States at mid-century was a terrific advantage.

At that time, it probably was. But just because an economy is rich when you are born does not guarantee that it will stay that way. In 1901, when Queen Victoria died, Great Britain had the world's highest per capita GDP, more than $4,600 in 1990 dollars, 10 percent higher than the United States at that time, and four times that of Japan, the second-biggest economy at the end of the twentieth century. But after the UK was dethroned as the world's dominant economy, real growth rates slowed to a crawl—just 0.8 percent from World War I through 1950. By that year, British per capita GDP had gone up less than 50 percent from Queen Victoria's time, while U.S. GDP per capita had surged by more than 230 percent over the same period.

A Preview of the Future

Much of the great accumulation of British capital that financed world growth in the nineteenth century was dissipated in wars, nationalized, and taxed away, contributing to stagnation that persisted for decades. Note that at 0.8 percent real growth, it would take an economy more than 87 years to double. By contrast, at China's recent growth rates (10.3 percent in 2010 and ranging as high as 11.9 percent in 2008)—its real GDP will double in less than seven years. No wonder economists speak of "the magic of compound interest." Rapid growth can make a poor country rich in short order, while sluggish growth makes even a rich country poor over time.

When you gaze into your crystal ball to estimate where the United States will stand in the future in the hierarchy of world prosperity, you may be tempted to rely on forecasts of econometric models, which for all their mathematical razzle-dazzle, are actually fairly simple-minded constructs. Basically, they tend to extrapolate long-term growth rates, with allowances for expected changes in population. If you look at the leading forecasts for 2050, almost all of them project that real U.S. GDP per capita will more than double in 40 years.

You'll see estimates of U.S. GDP per capita ranging from $35,165 (Goldman Sachs), to more than $38,000 (Carnegie and PricewaterhouseCoopers). This presupposes that U.S. growth will far exceed recent experience. But will it?

Over the longest time scale, from 1889 to 2009, annual average real U.S. GDP growth was 3.4 percent. During the 70-year span from 1939 to 2009 annual average GDP growth actually perked up to 3.6 percent. However, most of the good news was in the past, when the United States had a freer and more soundly based economy. Averaged over shorter time scales, the U.S. growth rate has been steadily decelerating:

- Over 60 years, it is 3.3 percent.
- Over 50 years, it is 3.1 percent.
- The 40-year rate is 2.8 percent.
- The 30-year rate is 2.7 percent.
- Over 20 years, the average growth rate is 2.5 percent.
- The 10-year rate (from 1999 to 2009) is 1.9 percent.

- The current 5-year average annual growth rate is just 0.9 percent.
- The current 3-year growth is zero.

Talk about a slowdown. U.S. growth has decelerated as much as it possibly could without turning negative. The question is, why has there been a sharp deterioration in U.S. economic growth over time? Several explanations come to mind.

Economic historians Carmen Reinhart and Kenneth Rogoff argue that high debt levels, per se, hamper growth.[1] Indeed, there is little precedent for any country becoming great or staying great because of all the money it owes.

This is pertinent because the United States has accumulated the greatest pile of debts in the history of the world. According to Professor Laurence Kotlikoff, the current sum of explicit debts and unfunded promises nets out at $202 trillion—an amount greater than all the wealth of the world. He says,

I calculate a fiscal gap of $202 trillion, which is more than 15 times the official debt. This gargantuan discrepancy between our "official" debt and our actual net indebtedness isn't surprising. It reflects what economists call the labeling problem. Congress has been very careful over the years to label most of its liabilities "unofficial" to keep them off the books and far in the future.

For example, our Social Security FICA contributions are called taxes and our future Social Security benefits are called transfer payments. The government could equally well have labeled our contributions "loans" and called our future benefits "repayment of these loans less an old age tax," with the old age

---

[1] See Carmen M. Reinhart and Kenneth S. Rogoff, *This Time is Different: Eight Centuries of Financial Folly* (Princeton, NJ: Princeton University Press), 2010; Carmen M. Reinhart and Kenneth S. Rogoff, "Growth in a Time of Debt," January 7, 2010, www.economics.harvard.edu/files/faculty/51_Growth_in _Time_Debt.pdf; and Carmen M. Reinhart amd Kenneth S. Rogoff, "Too Much Debt Means the Economy Can't Grow: Reinhart and Rogoff," Bloomberg, July 14, 2011, www.bloomberg.com/news/2011-07-14/too-much-debt-means -economy-can-t-grow-commentary-by-reinhart-and-rogoff.html.

tax making up for any difference between the benefits promised and principal plus interest on the contributions. . . .

The fiscal gap isn't affected by fiscal labeling. It's the only theoretically correct measure of our long-run fiscal condition. . . .[2]

Thinking people have realized for many years that Social Security, Medicare, and other entitlement spending were based on the smile of a Cheshire Cat. Everyone knew the numbers didn't add up. Everyone knew there would be a crisis some day; we hoped that it would come long after we were gone. The unpleasant surprise is that the fiscal crisis of the welfare state is not just some smudge on a distant horizon; it is a looming problem now. Like most advanced economies, the United States is circling the drain of sovereign insolvency.

Another contributing factor to the slowing of growth has been a collapse in productive investment in the United States. Partly this reflects the far higher costs of doing business in the United States than in other jurisdictions. Yes, U.S. labor costs are generally higher than in other countries. But U.S. regulatory costs and the uncertainty associated with greater exposure to lawsuits also make the United States an unfavorable jurisdiction for business. So does the U.S. tax regime. U.S. corporate tax rates are the highest in the world.

I argue in the next chapter that a major factor contributing to the slowdown in U.S. growth was the advent of peak oil production in the United States in the early 1970s and its association with a perverse reorganization of the U.S. monetary system by Richard Nixon in 1971. Subsequently, not only did debt skyrocket, but the rise in BTUs per capita associated with the surge in U.S. prosperity came to an end in 1979. With U.S. oil production dwindling, the cost of energy-dense oil to fuel the United States rose faster than the rate of GDP growth.

With the stimulus provided by windfalls of high-density energy from oil dwindling U.S. authorities tried unsuccessfully to stimulate growth by artificial credit expansion. A big diversion of resources into

---

[2] Laurence Kotlikoff, "U.S. Is Bankrupt and We Don't Even Know It," Bloomberg, August 11, 2010, www.bloomberg.com/news/2010-08-11/u-s-is-bankrupt-and-we-don-t-even-know-commentary-by-laurence-kotlikoff.html.

malinvestment stimulated by credit bubbles was a factor informing the collapse of productive investment. Artificial credit bubbles financed by fiat money, which was counterfeited out of thin air, distort the price signals in capital markets. This distortion induces investors to crowd resources into unproductive sectors because of the artificially high returns they temporarily earn there.

Such was the case with U.S. real estate for more than a decade. During the subprime boom, U.S. housing prices exploded into what Yale economist Robert Shiller called, "the biggest bubble in history."[3] In 1995, inflation-adjusted U.S. home prices were only 10 percent higher than they had been in 1890. But by 2006, prices had jumped by 100 percent over prices in the 1890s. This temporary, unsustainable surge in housing prices lead to trillions of dollars in malinvestments to build more houses, which now sit empty or have lapsed into foreclosure as housing prices have plunged by more than they did in the Great Depression.

A Decrease in Productive Capacity

Unfortunately, the trillions invested to build houses with more bath-rooms and larger kitchens for subprime borrowers did little or nothing to enhance productive capacity in the American economy. While money poured into housing counts as "investment" in the national income accounts, it should not be confused with fixed investment in plant and equipment that actually creates productive capacity.

As John Ross (visiting professor at Antai College of Economics and Management, Jiao Tong University, Shanghai) has pointed out, the long-term slump in U.S. savings has created such a pronounced slowdown in fixed investment in the United States that the U.S. economy now consumes more capital than it creates. Ross directs your attention to:

> . . . the continuation of the long term downward trend of US savings, with inevitable oscillations in business cycles, since 1981.

---

[3] "Hard to forecast end to U.S. housing crisis: Shiller," Reuters, February 20, 2009, www.reuters.com/article/2009/02/20/businesspro-us-usa-economy-shiller-idUS TRE51J5SO20090220.

Each cyclical savings peak was lower than the previous one—21.4 percent of GDP in 1981, 19.0 percent in 1998, and 16.4 percent in 2006. Each cyclical trough was also lower than the one before—14.2 percent in 1992, 13.6 percent in 2003, 10.2 percent in 2009.

A small cyclical recovery in U.S. saving took place, from the 10.2 percent of GDP trough in the third quarter of 2009 until the second quarter of 2010 at 11.8 percent, and it is this which stalled in the third quarter of 2010.

Even more striking is that the third quarter of 2010 is the 10th consecutive three-month period in which U.S. net domestic savings (i.e., gross domestic savings minus capital consumption), has been negative. The last time U.S. net savings were negative was during the Great Depression in 1931–1934.

To put it in deliberately provocative, but accurate, language, this means that the world's number 1 capitalist economy has for the last 10 quarters not produced net capital—U.S. capital creation is less than U.S. capital consumption.[4]

Ross underscores two implications of the drop in the U.S. savings rate:

Rapid U.S. growth cannot take place without a sharp recovery in fixed investment—which in turn must be financed by savings. If U.S. domestic savings remain depressed, then either U.S. fixed investment will remain low, which implies a slow U.S. upturn, or the United States must finance a new higher level of investment from abroad; that is, there must be a new widening of the U.S. balance of payments deficit.[5]

In light of the collapse in U.S. savings and fixed investment, which is apparent even in heavily gamed official statistics, the U.S. economy is destined for stagnation, or even long-term decline in the future.

---

[4] John Ross, "New deterioration in the US savings rate and its implications," Key Trends in Globalisation, January 3, 2011, http://ablog.typepad.com/keytrendsinglobalisation/2011/01/new-deterioration-in-the-us-savings-rate.html.
[5] Ibid.

Far from expecting the U.S. economy to double within the next 40 years, I expect it to perform no better than Great Britain did after it was unseated as the world's leading economy early in the last century.

In other words, if the United States stays on its current path, (probably a bright scenario compared to what will happen), in 40 years' time, it will no longer be the world's richest large economy. The estimate for U.S. GDP in 2010 is $13.1915 trillion. Far from ballooning to $38 trillion in 2050, the U.S. economy will be lucky to attain half that level. If the United States follows in the footsteps of the UK, which more or less extends the current five-year growth rate for 40 years, that would make for real U.S. GDP of about $19 trillion in 2050. Half of the conventional projection. I think even that is optimistic.

John Ross points out that the relatively rosy predictions of near-term economic growth put forth by conventional economists would still leave the average U.S. growth for the current business cycle stuck below 1 percent annually:

> A recent *Wall Street Journal* survey of economists revealed an average prediction of 3.2 percent U.S. GDP growth in each quarter of 2011. . . . The implications of 3.2 percent growth to the end of 2011 are that U.S. GDP would have grown at an average of only 0.9 percent in 4 years of the current business cycle—substantially below trend to an equivalent point in previous post–World War II cycles. Such a 3.2 percent growth rate, even maintained for a 4 year period, would not reverse the U.S. economy's long term deceleration.
>
> Therefore, unless there is a sharp acceleration of U.S. growth above current projections, the trend of long term slowdown of the U.S. economy will continue.[6]

Indeed, the situation is even grimmer than Ross suggests. First, actual U.S. GDP growth in 2011 was not 3.2 percent, but barely half

---

[6] John Ross, "Average economist predictions for US GDP would mean only 0.9% annual average growth over business cycle to end 2011," Key Trends in the World Economy, January 17, 2011, http://ablog.typepad.com/key_trends_in _the_world_e/2011/01/average-economist-predictions-for-us-gdp-would-mean- only-09-annual-average-growth-over-business-cycle-to-end-2011.html.

Table 1.1   Private Sector GDP (in millions)

Year	GDP	Government Spending	Net GDP
2001	11,371.3	2,056.4	9,314.9
2002	11,538.8	2,188.6	9,350.2
2003	11,738.7	2,303.3	9,435.4
2004	12,213.8	2,377.7	9,836.1
2005	12,587.5	2,486.0	10,101.5
2006	12,962.5	2,578.5	10,384.0
2007	13,194.1	2,570.1	10,624.0
2008	13,359.0	2,753.3	10,605.7
2009	12,810.0	3,210.8	9,599.2
2010	13,191.5	3,470.0	9,721.5

Source: From a reader submission to Mish's "Global Economic Trend Analysis," http://globaleconomicanalysis.blogspot.com/2010/09/why-statistical-recovery-feels-bad.html. Posted September 29, 2010.

that: 1.7 percent. Even worse the private-sector component of U.S. GDP has deteriorated significantly in recent years. Table 1.1 tells the tale. You can see that, net of increases in federal spending, today's U.S. economy has actually shrunk below where it was in 2004.

Table 1.1 shows the GDP numbers chained to 2005 dollars (in millions).

The only reason that the U.S. GDP has not fallen more than it has is that the federal government has raised its annual spending by more than $1.3 trillion since 2004. It almost goes without saying that this surge in government spending, financed out of an empty pocket, cannot continue indefinitely for decades into the future. With the private sector getting skinnier and government getting bigger, another amber light is flashing a caution about future U.S. growth prospects.

Not only is a bigger government a negative for economic growth, but even the overdue effort to trim excess government spending will weigh on growth, as we have seen in Europe. The unwelcome requirement to avoid an insolvency trap with austerity may compound the long-term slowdown in U.S. real growth.

The picture would appear even more grim if you tracked the advance in poverty in the United States, as measured in growing chronic unemployment and food stamp use, much of it due to the impact of surging energy prices on suburbs designed in the 1950s when gasoline cost 30 cents a gallon. One in every seven Americans now participates in the food stamp program. Neither austerity nor Keynesianism will cure what ails us, as the twin pincers of debt-deflation and rising energy costs are destined to impoverish the former middle class.

Squandering Prosperity

Decades of remorseless fiscal and monetary profligacy have squandered most of America's inheritance of prosperity. My generation and the older ones that held power failed to heed the prophetic warning delivered more than half a century ago in President Dwight Eisenhower's farewell speech on January 17, 1961:

> As we peer into society's future, we—you and I, and our government—must avoid the impulse to live only for today, plundering, for our own ease and convenience, the precious resources of tomorrow. We cannot mortgage the material assets of our grandchildren without risking the loss also of their political and spiritual heritage.[7]

Unhappily, we did precisely what Eisenhower warned against. We "plundered the precious resources of tomorrow" for "our own ease and convenience." Now, tomorrow is dawning.

The trailing generations of Americans, who came along too late to enjoy the boom financed by easy money, inherit the diminished prospects and the unpaid debts that will weigh upon economic growth and living standards in the United States during their lifetimes.

Up next, we delve into the American Dream and how it is—and will soon be even more so—alive and well in Brazil.

---

[7] Dwight Eisenhower, "Farewell Address" (1961), www.ourdocuments.gov/doc.php?flash=true&doc=90&page=transcript.

Chapter 2

The Original America Is
the New Brazil

*Thus in the beginning all the World was America, and more so than
that is now; for no such thing as Money was any where known. . . .
All the World was for the taking.*
— John Locke, *The Second Treatise on Civil Government* (1690)

The controversial thesis of this book is that the relative advantages
of two richly endowed countries, Brazil and the United States,
will reverse in the twenty-first century. One of the more
fundamental developments of our time is the progressive slowdown in
growth rates of the leading advanced economies and the increasing
dynamism of what were once known as "underdeveloped" countries.
While we don't often look at it this way, today's advanced economies
are those that were well-suited to prosper in the conditions prevailing
during the nineteenth and twentieth centuries.

Even though the United States emerged as the world's foremost
economy in the middle of the twentieth century, Brazil's growth rate
substantially exceeded that of the United States during most of that

century. But the twentieth century was not Brazil's century for at least three reasons:

1. Brazil was growing from a very low base, as its economy had stagnated during the colonial period.[1] As John H. Coatsworth, author of the *Cambridge Economic History of Latin America* put it, "At the time of independence (1822) Brazil had one of the least productive economies in the Western Hemisphere, with a per capita GDP lower than any other New World colony for which we have estimates."[2] Growth rates doubled during the imperial period, to a still meager 0.3 percent per annum. After the republic was declared in 1889, growth trebled, and Brazil went on to post some of the world's highest GDP growth rates until the growth collapsed in the wake of the oil shock around 1980.[3]

2. Brazil grew in spite of being encumbered with numerous counterproductive economic policies, including recurring runaway inflation that totaled more than 1 quadrillion percent, through the twentieth century.

3. The global economy had not yet outgrown its reserve of readily available natural resources, including food, water, and cheap energy.

A key to understanding the economic transformation just described is recognizing that U.S. growth was launched around natural advantages (including incorporation of copious amounts of cheap energy and cheap water transportation) that enabled Americans to grab most of the "low hanging fruit of modern history."[4] These advantages supported the

---

[1] Armando Castelar Pinheiro, Indermit S. Gill, Luis Servén, and Mark Roland Thomas, "Brazilian Economic Growth, 1900–2000: Lessons and Policy Implications" (Washington, DC: Inter-American Development Bank, 2004), 5.

[2] John H. Coatsworth, "Why Is Brazil 'Underdeveloped'?" *Harvard Review of Latin America* (Spring 2007).

[3] Pinheiro et al., "Brazilian Economic Growth, 1900–2000," 4. See also Angus Maddison, "Monitoring the World Economy: 1920–1992" (Paris: OECD Development Center Study, 1995).

[4] For a different account of how the United States came to eat "the low hanging fruit of prosperity," see Tyler Cowen, *The Great Stagnation: How America Ate All the Low Hanging Fruit of Modern History, Got Sick, and Will (Eventually) Feel Better* (New York: Dutton), 2011.

growth of middle-class incomes as annual energy input per capita shot up from one-twentieth of one horsepower before the Industrial Revolution to more than 131,000 horsepower lately.

The commonplace observation that U.S. prosperity depends upon cheap energy implies a downside. As energy becomes more expensive, U.S. prosperity falters. It is not entirely a coincidence that the peak in American incomes compared to the rest of the world occurred around 1950, when U.S. domination of world oil production peaked. The subsequent slowdown in world energy output per capita has closely correlated with a slowdown in U.S. economic growth. Median family income in the United States more than doubled between 1947 and 1973 but rose by less than one quarter between 1973 and 2004. Economist Robert Gordon has shown that the growth of multifactor productivity in the United States collapsed in the fourth quarter of the twentieth century, just as the growth of energy inputs faltered.[5] The meager income gains that did materialize were mostly wiped away in the ensuing financial crisis. The real median wage in the United States has been stagnant for a quarter of a century, despite a near doubling of GDP per capita.[6]

The extraordinary and unrepeatable success the United States enjoyed in achieving superior incomes for most Americans has now become a cause of instability as downward mobility bites.

It is little appreciated that as of 2011, according to Branko Milanovich's *The Haves and the Have-Nots*, "the poorest 5 percent of Americans are among the richest people in the world (richer than nearly 70 percent of other people in the world). The poorest 5 percent of Americans, for example, are richer than the richest 5 percent of Indians." The "middle class" in the United States is competing with the middle class in India and China. If U.S. middle-class incomes must fall until they match those in India and China, the bottom is a long way down. (As of this writing, an income in rupees that equates to $85 per month qualifies as "middle class" in India.)

---

[5] Robert Gordon, "Revisiting U.S. Productivity Growth over the Past Century with a View of the Future," NBER Working Paper No. 15834, March 2010, www.nber.org/papers/w15834.

[6] Branko Milanovic, *The Haves and the Have-Nots A Brief and Idiosyncratic History of Global Inequality* (New York: Basic Books, 2011), 228.

The Country of the Future

Brazil, by contrast, is already more nearly a microcosm of the whole earth: "The bottom 5 percent of Brazilians are among the poorest people in the world but the top 5 percent are among the richest."[7]

Brazilians are accustomed to a yawning wealth gap between the plutocrats and the very poor. Partly, this reflects Brazil's natural endowments, which have always required high capital investment to exploit. There was less low hanging fruit in Brazil. Brazil's early history involved plantation farming that necessarily required extensive farm labor. Unlike the United States, where yeoman farmers could expect to earn an independent livelihood on relatively small plots, Brazil in its early days was dominated by grantees on large plantations secured from the Portuguese crown, initially in a system of "captaincies" over gigantic tracts of land larger than European countries. Later, the dimensions of land holdings by the elite shrank to the merely vast. Still the investment requirements to develop these properties were enormous. As distinguished historian Thomas Skidmore summarized, "the risks were too great and the rewards too uncertain to persuade most of the grantees to make the investments required to be successful."[8]

The tradition of a dominant plutocracy reflects circumstances that have necessitated high capital requirements for economic development in Brazil from its beginnings. More on those later.

As Brazil has developed, wealth disparities have not been narrowed significantly by politically inspired income redistribution within the democratic process. This is at least partly due to the fact that the Brazilian state has heretofore lacked the credit to support debt democracy, the expedient policy that has dominated politics among the world's richest democracies. In debt democracy, the illusion of consensus over subsidies, handouts, and welfare support is achieved by borrowing on the credit of the state. The long indulgence of the world in according AAA credit

---

[7] Alex Tabarrok, "World Income Inequality," Marginal Revolution, January 31, 2011, http://marginalrevolution.com/marginalrevolution/2011/01/world-income -inequality.html.

[8] Thomas E. Skidmore, *Brazil: Five Centuries of Change*, 2nd ed. (New York: Oxford University Press, 2010), 15.

standing to the debt of OECD governments permitted the spending of vast sums out of an empty pocket. In the United States, the government chronically spends money to disguise declining private incomes. But unfortunately for the United States, the United Kingdom, Japan, Greece, Ireland, Portugal, Italy, Spain, and soon, other countries, the stimulative effect of new debt is waning along with the growth potential of the advanced economies.

If anything, the pressure for income redistribution in Brazil may have lessened as the incomes of the poorest Brazilians rose. While American incomes sink, almost 40 million Brazilians have risen from poverty to middle-class status in the eight years prior to May 2011. Brazil has grown rapidly while its energy inputs soared.

Although U.S. investment in scientific and technical research has yielded new products and profitable companies, it has failed to duplicate the kind of comparative productivity advantage necessary to reproduce the gap in incomes that Americans enjoyed over everyone else half a century ago. Figuratively, no one knows where to find the ladder to enable average Americans to reach the higher fruit.

Whereas the United States enjoyed favorable access to cheap energy from the nineteenth century through the first three-quarters of the twentieth century, Brazil is becoming an energy superpower at a time when oil and other energy-dense fuels are becoming increasingly scarce and expensive. As we will explore, Brazil is better situated to prosper in a world of expensive energy where the cost of BTUs soars as global oil production wanes.

Brazil is also the Saudi Arabia of water in a parched world, where "to produce a single pound of wheat requires half a ton, or nearly 125 gallons of water."[9] Brazil comprises just 5.7 percent of the world's landmass, but about 20 percent of the world's freshwater flows through the Amazon basin alone. Few other countries can rival Brazil's freshwater resources. Water authority, Steven Solomon, places Brazil foremost among the "super Water Have countries . . . with far more water than their populations can ever use."[10]

---

[9] Steven Solomon, *Water: The Epic Struggle for Wealth, Power, and Civilization* (New York: HarperCollins), 373.

[10] Ibid., 375.

Water, per se, is too heavy to economically transport over long distances, but in a water-scarce era, "virtual" water exports in the form of food will be of growing importance. Discussing Brazil's preeminence in biofuels, Henry Mance wrote in the *Financial Times*, "No other country has the land, water and the know-how to increase production so easily."[11]

This is just part of Brazil's story as a richly endowed country that was poorly situated to exploit its natural wealth when its resources were cheap, but will be better placed as those resources grow more expensive.

The redoubtable Amerigo Vespucci, who first reached Brazil in 1501, famously said, "If paradise on earth exists anywhere in the world, it cannot lie very far from here."[12] Brazil is lush like no other place. In a sense, the difficulty of accessing and exploiting Brazil's vast resources has served to make Brazil a reserve for humanity's future.

Brazil is widely agreed to have the greatest biodiversity of any country on the planet, with the most known species of plants, freshwater fish, and mammals. It has high numbers of amphibian, butterfly, bird, and reptile populations, and is thought to lead the world in number of insect species, with 10 to 15 million.[13]

As I explore in Chapter Three, Brazil's development was hampered for centuries for geopolitical reasons. Unlike the United States, Brazil lacked a favorable "specific coastline" in the terms set out by Nicolas Rashevsky in *Looking at History through Mathematics*. Rashevsky argued that Europe led the way in economic development because its "specific coastline," the ratio of coastline to its surface area, was almost 10 times higher than that of China, for example.[14] That made for much cheaper transport of goods and more profitable trade. Through most of history, shipping cargo via water was up to 30 times cheaper than hauling it overland. In that sense, the configuration of the land itself helped determine the difficulty and the

---

[11] Henry Manse, "Crop and Ore Riches Skew Economy," *Financial Times*, December 21, 2011.

[12] Stefan Zweig, *Brazil: A Land of the Future*, trans. Lowell A. Bangerter (Riverside, CA: Ariadne Press, 2000), 19.

[13] See "Brazil," www.lonelyplanet.com/brazil.

[14] Nicolas Rashevsky, *Looking at History through Mathematics* (Cambridge, MA: MIT Press, 1968), 133.

capital intensity required to exploit its riches. This is why much of Brazil remains thinly populated and unexploited. By point of comparison, Brazil's landmass is almost three times larger than that of India, with less than one-sixth of India's population.

What was not obvious to Amerigo Vespucci and other early explorers of Brazil was that while it may have been "paradise on earth," Brazil was not paradise on the cheap. Development came with remarkably high capital requirements. Seen superficially, Brazil would have appeared to be favorably endowed with specific coastline, as its ocean shore extends for 4,650 miles, and Brazil also contains the greatest part of the world's largest river basin, the Amazon. Yet other than the Amazon, which drains an area of tropical jungle, most of Brazil's rivers flow north and west and are better suited to hydropower generation than navigation, given their passage through deep valleys with rapids unsuitable for cargo vessels.

Brazil is the world's largest tropical country. For most of its history, Brazil's tropical environment has been seen as a drawback. Tropical jungle is a difficult setting to adapt for economic activity. Clearing the land alone requires much more work than clearing temperate forest. Jungle soils tend to be poor; the climate too humid for grain to ripen and too infested with pathogens to avoid large losses from crops that do grow.

Even planting a crop in a jungle area like the Amazon basin entails discomfiting encounters with all manner of hazards, from killer caterpillars (*Lonomia oblique*) and the deadly marble-coned snail (one drop of snail venom can kill 20 humans) to the tiny and beautiful but deadly poison dart frogs. The jungle and the rivers are full of thousands of exotic species of animals; ferocious piranha fish, snakes, spiders, and insects that would like to taste the blood of humans. Disease-bearing mosquitoes (carrying malaria and dengue fever), along with venomous spiders and tarantulas abound, including the most dangerous spider in the world: gigantic Brazilian wandering spider. Possessing leg spans of up to 5 inches, it is listed in the 2012 Guinness Book of World Records as the world's most venomous spider, so toxic that it has practically become a cliché that 0.006 mg of its venom can kill a mouse.

Far from encouraging low-cost exploitation of Brazil's bountiful resources, the jungle environment (along with other geographic features, such as Brazil's mostly unnavigable waterways) helped preserve them. Brazil's topography and climate were obstacles hampering development—or rather delaying it—until returns could repay a high cost of exploitation.

While in the nineteenth and twentieth centuries, the natural endowments of the United States seemed almost ideally conducive to prosperity, the tide is now turning in Brazil's favor. As the era of cheap energy expires, Brazil's natural advantages are growing in relative importance while those in the United States decline. Brazil is already one of the world's largest generators of hydroelectric power. Some 82 percent of Brazil's electricity is produced through clean renewable sources compared to 11 percent in the United States. Brazilian energy demand is growing 10 times faster than that of the United States, principally because it has the scope to grow. On a per capita basis, Americans devote more energy to heating their homes than Brazilians do for all uses.

As the world grows colder (talk of global warming notwithstanding, I argue that it is growing colder), Brazil's relative advantages will compound. To the extent that I'm right, Brazil's much warmer climate will give it a comparative advantage over cold latitude economies.

Brazil enjoys another distinct advantage in a bankrupt world. Its government is not insolvent. The multitrillion-dollar bailout and stimulus packages in the United States lavished on efforts to relaunch consumer spending are unaffordable in an era of slow growth or stagnation. As U.S. deficit spending is inevitably curtailed as a result of a growing solvency crisis, Brazil's comparative advantage will increase.

As a result of what I've just described, you will see Brazil trade places with the United States in the decades to come as the foremost haven of economic opportunity and of upward mobility in the world. As American actress Karen Allen famously said, "Someone born in Brazil is an American." This is a long-established belief, but it represents an important permutation of James Truslow Adams's concept of the American Dream. Adams wrote of:

> that American Dream of a better, richer, and happier life for all our citizens of every rank, which is the greatest contribution we have made to the thought and welfare of the world. That dream or hope has been present from the start. Ever since we became

an independent nation, each generation has seen an uprising of ordinary Americans to save that dream from the forces which appeared to be overwhelming it.

Writing in the depths of the Great Depression, Adams went on to say,

> possibly the greatest of these struggles lies just ahead of us at this present time—not a struggle of revolutionists against the established order, but of the ordinary man to hold fast to "life, liberty, and the pursuit of happiness" which were vouchsafed to us in the past in vision and on parchment.[15]

This concept of the American Dream, which now seems such a crucial component in the self-image of residents of the United States, was in fact a phrase first articulated by Adams and popularized in his *The Epic of America* published in 1931. "The pursuit of happiness" may seem uniquely Jeffersonian, but it did not begin in Philadelphia with the Declaration of Independence. Its origins lie at least as far back as Aristotle, teacher of Alexander the Great. Aristotle wrote, "Happiness is the meaning and the purpose of life, the whole aim and end of human existence."

In that sense, the American Dream of upward mobility manifests a universal, human longing. It is no less present among the displaced farm workers crowded into windowless air raid shelters under the streets of Beijing, among the shop girls of Moscow, the samosa vendors of Delhi, or in the favelas of Rio de Janeiro than in small town America. The magic that associated it so closely with the United States was rapid economic growth fueled to a large degree by access to abundant, cheap energy. Of course, the time when the United States enjoyed that energy advantage has come and gone. With it went much of the success in upward striving that earlier generations considered a birthright of life in the United States. As reported in Investors.com, the web site of *Investor's Business Daily*: "Over the past decade, real private-sector wage

---

[15] Quoted in Jim Cullen, *The American Dream: A Short History of an Idea That Shaped a Nation* (New York: Oxford University Press, 2003), 4.

growth has scraped bottom at 4 percent, just below the 5 percent increase from 1929 to 1939, government data show."[16]

In other words, real wage growth in the United States over the first decade of the twenty-first century was even slower than in the Great Depression.

An unspoken assumption in this analysis of the American Dream is that it consists of an expectation of ever-rising material consumption, as compared to relational goods like social status. Horace Kallen observed in 1936 that "the American Dream is a vision of men as consumers, and the American story is the story of an inveterate struggle to embody this dream in the institutions of American life."[17]

The question for the next generation is whether the eclipse of upward mobility in the United States represents the effective end of the American Dream. Or can this widely appealing idea take hold and find expression elsewhere? Of course, for such a migration to occur, it must not only entail the prospect of upward mobility, it must also take place in a venue that could reasonably be construed as "American." A case could easily be made that the rapid economic growth in China entails the prospect of upward mobility. But it would be an abuse of language to describe the Chinese economy as "American." The same could be said of India and Russia. But the fourth of the rapidly growing BRIC economies, Brazil has an important characteristic that the other BRICs lack. Brazil alone is a rapidly growing New World economy that is every bit as "American" as the United States. Indeed as a matter of pedigree, Brazil can lay a better claim to the word "America" than does the United States.

The Origins of America

Those of us who live in the United States tend to forget the obscure, mythic origins of the concept of "America" and treat it more as a specific

---

[16] Jed Graham, "10-Year Real Wage Gains Worse than the Depression," Investors .com, June 2, 2011, http://news.investors.com/article/573982/201106020800 /10-year-real-wage-gains-worse-than-during-depression.htm.

[17] Quoted in *Consumer Society in American History: A Reader*, Lawrence B. Glickman, ed. (Ithaca, NY and London: Cornell University Press, 1990), 1.

geographic reference to the territory of the United States than it initially was and may be in the future. Long after Waldseemüller's world map of 1507 had appended the name "America" to Brazil, the territory now known as North America was identified on maps as "Indies." Or in Waldseemüller's map, North America was *Terra Ulteria Incognita*. The earliest designation of "the Indies" as "North America," came in 1538 more than three decades after Brazil was the original America.

Perspective on this momentous development begins with an examination of the somewhat elastic meaning of "America," which has signified so much for so many people the world over.

Note that the origin of both "America" and "Brazil" are shrouded in ambiguity. It is far from conclusively proven that America took its name from the Christian name of Albercius, also known as "Amerigo" Vespucci, a ship chandler who did not sail to America until seven years after Columbus. Jules Marcou of the Academy of Sciences in Paris pointed out back in 1875 that Amerigo was not the name by which Vespucci would have been known to the German cartographer Martin Waldseemüller. He refers to a map first published by Waldseemüller in 1507 in which "America" is the name given to a country in the New World. We know that country today as Brazil.

Waldseemüller deepened rather than resolved the mystery of why he attached the name "America" to Brazil in his 1507 world map when he wrote,

> But now these parts [Europe, Asia, and Africa, the three continents of the Ptolemaic geography] have been extensively explored and a fourth part has been discovered by Americus Vespuccius [a Latin form of Vespucci's name]: I do not see what right any one would have to object to calling this part after Americus, who discovered it and who is a man of intelligence, [and so to name it] Amerige, that is, the Land of Americus, or America: since both Europa and Asia got their names from women.[18]

His comment encompasses a triple puzzle. Firstly, Vespucci was in no sense the discoverer of Brazil or the continents of the New World. As

---

[18] Martin Waldseemüller, *Cosmographiae Introductio*, April 25, 1507.

an explorer, he did discover the Rio de la Plata. But his biggest contribution was to realize that Columbus, contrary to his lifelong belief, had not found a westerly route to Asia, but rather a "fourth part," a New World previously unknown to Ptolemaic geography.

Secondly, it is extraordinary that Waldseemüller would have chosen to name a continent after the first name of a commoner. Cartographers of the time normally would have employed the last name of an explorer to naming a land or region, while using the first name of a king or queen to designate a territory in his or her honor.

Thirdly, even assuming that Waldseemüller deemed Vespucci worthy of the honor of having the New World christened with his first name, the question arises why the new continent was not known as "Albercia?" Waldseemüller would initially have known Vespucci's first name as Albericus or Alberico. Vespucci published his 1504 work *Mundus Novus* (New World) under the Latinized name, Albercius Vesputius. To get "America" out of that seemed like a stretch to Marcou. I agree.

The fact that Martin Waldseemüller reconstrued the Latinized version of Vespucci's first name may not indicate, as is usually assumed, that Waldseemüller was indulging his prerogative as a cartographer to christen the continents of the New World in honor of Vespucci. To the contrary, he may merely have been offering an explanation for the otherwise mysterious designation of the New World as "America." On the other hand, he explicitly states, "for instance, in the west, America, named after its discoverer. . . . " And Waldseemüller also "prominently placed stylized portraits of Claudius Ptolemy and Amerigo Vespucci" on his map," underscoring the fact that he thought America had been named for Vespucci, whether or not Waldseemüller himself had bestowed this honor.

Marcou argued that the name "America" was not an honorific tribute to Vespucci but a name that was brought back from the New World by early visitors there. In particular, Marcou suggested that the name derived from the name of an Indian tribe that inhabited a district purportedly rich in gold in Nicaragua called "Amerrique." Both Columbus and Vespucci visited the area in Nicaragua inhabited by the Amerrique Indians. According to Ricardo Palma's *Tradiciones Peruanas*

(*Peruvian Traditions*, 1949), the ending of the word "America" indicates this origin:

> The ending ic (ica, ique, ico made Spanish) is found frequently in the names of places, in the languages and native dialects of Central America and even of the Antilles. It seems to mean "great, high, prominent" and is applied to mountains and peaks in which there are no volcanoes.[19]

An informing feature of the story is that the Caribe Indians, whom the explorers beginning with Columbus all met, referred to the mainland of Central America as "Amerrique" due to a vocabulary deficiency. The mountain range that was home to the Amerrique Indians was visible from a distance, and the Caribe Indians apparently employed the name of the mountains as a short hand for the whole landmass. As Jonathan Cohen suggested in *The Naming of America: Fragments We've Shored against Ourselves*, "The Caribs, traveling far from their Carib or Cariay coast, could see the Amerriques in the distance, and these mountains for them could have signified the mainland."[20]

Thus "America" may have been a native name for the continental landmass in the region where the Iberian explorers first encountered it. Its only connection to Vespucci's first name may be a linguistic coincidence amplified in an ill-informed attempt by Waldseemüller to explain why "America" was called by that name.

Of course, there have been other attempts to identify a source for the name "America." Some have suggested that it is a corruption of an old Norse word, Ommerike (oh-MEH-ric-eh), meaning "farthest outland." Another version that stipulates a North Atlantic origin of "America" ties it to the 1497 voyage by John Cabot to the Labrador coast of Newfoundland. An early twentieth-century account claimed that the New World was named after a customs officer in the port of Bristol, a man called Richard Amerike, who may well have financed

---

[19] Jonathan Cohen, "The Naming of America: Fragments We've Shored against Ourselves," www.uhmc.sunysb.edu/surgery/america.html.
[20] Ibid.

Cabot's voyage, and who seems to have backed numerous cod-fishing missions that may have ventured as far west as Labrador.

Another possibility is that America was named for the mythic land of the Western Star, "La Merica" which Essenes and other cultures believed was a land across the ocean inhabited by good souls. Not incidentally, some of the early (pre-Constantine) strands of Christianity held that Jesus Christ—along with John the Baptist—was an exponent of Nazorean (little fish) teaching. There is also a possible echo of this concept cited by Waldseemüller, repeating an account of the poet, Virgil:

> Many have regarded as an invention the words of a famous poet [Virgil] that "beyond the stars lies a land, beyond the path of the year and the sun, where Atlas, who supports the heavens, revolves on his shoulders the axis of the world, set with gleaming stars" but now finally it proves clearly to be true. For there is a land, discovered by Columbus, a captain of the King of Castile, and by Americus Vespucius, both men of very great ability, which, though in great part lies beneath "the path of the year and of the sun" and between the tropics, nevertheless extends about 19 degrees beyond the Tropic of Capricorn toward the Antarctic Pole, "beyond the path of the year and the sun."[21]

The Mythic Brazil

The alternative history perspective that "America" may have been a mythic "land across the sea" long before it was associated with a specific landmass has a curious parallel in respect to Brazil. The name "Brazil" also has legendary origins, not Near Eastern, but Celtic. The Celts also believed in a mythic land across the sea, called "Bresil," known in a legend dating back 3,000 years "as the Isle of the Living, the Isle of Truth, of Joy, of Fair Women, and of Apples." I don't quite see why apples got equal billing with "truth, joy, and fair women," but equally, apples also featured in the story of the fall of man in the Garden of Eden. The relative price of apples has evidently plunged in the last few millennia.

---

[21] Inscription from the Waldseemüller Map, 1507.

Seán Mac Mathúna argues that "Brazil was certainly well known during medieval times when explorers from Europe were setting out to discover what they called the "New World."[22]

As Russell-Wood elaborates: "Since the early fourteenth century, there had been references to an island called Brasil not far west of Ireland. Both name and island moved westwards, being transformed into a landmass and recognized as such by Duarte Pacheco Pereira in his *Esmeraldo de situ orbis*." Further, "Brazil" was popularized in its current spelling by Italian cartographer Angelinus Alorto's 1325 map "L'Isola Brazil."[23]

Brazil appeared out in the Atlantic in the famous Catalan Atlas from 1375. It was also shown on Toscanelli's chart, circa 1475, said to have been used by Columbus. In short, as the Age of Exploration was being launched, there was widespread agreement that the "blessed land" of Brazil lay somewhere to the west. Some early charts depicted Brazil as an island west of Ireland. Others showed it far out in the ocean halfway to Zipangu (Japan). Indeed, some cartographers have argued that part of the reason that the new continent was not named "Brazil" was to avoid confusion with the imaginary Brazil. "The term used by some of the map-makers, *Land of Brasil*, was confusing, for *Brasil* was the name of an imaginary island located somewhere in the Atlantic, according to popular belief."[24]

The footnotes of the history of early European efforts to reach the "New World" suggest that North America rather than current-day Brazil might well have been chosen for designation as the legendary land of "Brazil" had English navigation in the open seas been the equal of Portuguese methods in the late fifteenth century.

When word of a "new land to the west" reached Bristol in the late 1470s this stimulated an English merchant, John Jay, to outfit at great

---

[22] Seán Mac Mathúna, "Is the Name Brazil of Celtic Origin?" www.fantompowa. org/brazil.htm.

[23] A. J. R. Russell-Wood, "European Conceptions and Misconceptions of America: Sixteenth to Eighteenth Centuries," www.univ-ab.pt/investigacao/ceaa /actas/russell-wood.htm.

[24] "Universalis Cosmographia Secundum Ptholomei Traditionem e Et Americi Vespucci Aliorum Lustrationes," CartographicImages.net, http://cartographic-images .net/Cartographic_Images/310_1507_Walds.html.

expense an 80-ton ship to sail for "Brazil," described as "a name often given in medieval European tales to a land far to the west of Ireland." Setting sail in July, 1480, from Bristol, a dozen years before Columbus' first voyage, Jay's ship sailed west, intending to "traverse the seas" to Brazil. But the journey ended in failure. English crews had not mastered the new methods of astronomical navigation devised in Portugal and Spain: open, oceanic voyaging—as opposed to island hopping by way of Iceland and Greenland.

At a time of skimpy geographic knowledge, intrepid explorers set sail in search of faraway locales of no certain coordinates. Columbus set out to reach China, a real destination. John Jay set sail in search of Brazil, a legendary name attached to an imagined paradise over the sea.

Twenty years later, in 1500, Pedro Álvares Cabral (1460–1526), whose family hailed from Celtic Galicia, swung his fleet far to the west on a voyage around Africa to India. In the process, he bumped into present-day Brazil, which he duly claimed for Portugal.

A Difficult Dream to Realize

It is fitting, in light of current developments that both "America" and "Brazil" may have been legendary lands of no fixed address for thousands of years before either was identified with a specific locale you could visit today. Strangely, "America" and "Brazil" were two names first given to present-day Brazil.

This is ironic in light of the universal appeal the idea of "America" came to have in the terms suggested by John Locke, as a land of opportunity unimpeded by government—a concept reflected in modern times in the American Dream. If anything, the American Dream has grown more popular over the past eight decades, even as it has become more difficult to realize in the United States.

In 1931 when James Truslow Adams introduced the phrase into the language, he was a bit reticent in asserting it. He wrote,

> The American Dream is the dream of a land in which life should
> be better and richer and fuller for everyone, with opportunity
> for each according to ability or achievement. It is a difficult
> dream for the European upper classes to interpret adequately,

and too many of us ourselves have grown weary and mistrustful of it. It is not a dream of motor cars at high wages merely, but the dream of social order in which each man and each woman shall be able to attain to the fullest stature of which they are innately capable, and be recognized by others for what they are, regardless of the fortuitous circumstances of birth or position.[25]

Until recently, I would've supposed that nowhere on earth could match the United States of America as a setting for realizing the American Dream. The United States has seemed to be the ultimate beacon of economic opportunity.

But life is a candle in the wind. As I write, 48 percent of all Americans are either considered to be low income or living in poverty.[26] I argue in coming chapters that the decline in living standards in the United States is destined to become worse. This is not simply because approximately 57 percent of all children in the United States are living in homes that are either considered to be low income or impoverished. An astonishing 37 percent of all U.S. households are led by someone under the age of 35 with a net worth of zero or less than zero.[27]

Not all people can realize what they wish for. The contest of ambitions and resentments makes politics volatile. At its best, politics is an exercise in self-restraint that involves cultivating freedom rather than seeking something for nothing at your neighbor's expense. As H.L. Mencken quipped, an election is "an advanced auction of stolen goods." When everyone is bidding for favors from the Treasury, governments go broke and living standards suffer.

It is a truism that countries cannot easily retain either their prosperity or their freedom. Since the invention of gunpowder, the prospects for both have tended to depend upon the doubtful art of controlling a

---

[25] James Truslow Adams, *The Epic of America* (Boston: Little Brown & Company, 1931).
[26] "'Dismal' prospects: 1 in 2 Americans are now poor or low income," *U.S. News*, December 15, 2011, http://usnews.msnbc.msn.com/_news/2011/12/15/9461848-dismal-prospects-1-in-2-americans-are-now-poor-or-low-income.
[27] Richard Fry, D'Vera Cohn, Gretchen Livingston, and Paul Taylor, "The Rising Age Gap in Economic Well-Being," Pew Social & Demographic Trends, November 7, 2011, www.pewsocialtrends.org/2011/11/07/the-rising-age-gap-in-economic-well-being.

government strong enough to enforce property rights, but not too corrupt and overbearing to take away what is rightfully yours.

This was evident in Brazil in the last quarter of the twentieth century. Over a 15-year period preceding 1980, Brazil enjoyed startling real economic growth—averaging 9 percent per annum. Not surprisingly, foreign investment flooded in to capitalize on growth two to three times faster than that enjoyed by the North Atlantic economies.

By 1980, Brazilians had begun to demand far more of the government than it could afford. As a consequence, government spending skyrocketed beyond the available revenues. Deficit spending as high as 5.4 percent of GDP resulted in hyperinflation. Note that the actual and projected deficits in the United States over the past three years are two to three times worse than those that brought on hyperinflation in Brazil a generation ago.

By 1988, foreign direct investment in Brazil plunged by 75 percent below the average inflow during the "miracle" growth period. The root of Brazilian inflation was the monetization of the public sector's fiscal deficits. These deficits were not financed by borrowing from abroad or domestically, and they far exceeded available tax revenues.

The Brazilian government began to rely on "quantitative easing" or money conjured out of the clear blue sky to finance its deficits. Tax revenues fell sharply after 1983 as the government's annual profit on inflation jumped up to 3 percent to 4 percent of GDP. The result was a one trillion-fold increase in the price level from 1980 through 1997. As you would expect under the circumstances, economic growth came to a screeching halt. From 1981 through 1998, average annual real GDP growth in Brazil dwindled to 1.5 percent.

To make matters worse, Brazil faced recurring crises of contagion where economic trouble almost anywhere on the globe washed back with severe impacts in Brazil.

Can America's Destiny Be Fulfilled in Brazil?

During the first two and half centuries after Columbus, Latin America was more economically important than North America. Brazil, in particular, became significant after gold and diamonds were discovered in

Minas Gerais in the seventeenth century. Prior to the gold discovery, Brazil's economic importance rested with the exploitation of plantation crops such as sugar.

The General Brazil Company monopolized the Portuguese sugar fleets in competition with the Dutch West India Company until 1654. In that year, the Dutch West India Company surrendered its naval forces and soon thereafter abandoned its foothold at Pernambuco in north-eastern Brazil.

Even when Brazil enjoyed success in the backward seventeenth- and eighteenth-century economy, its forward progress was limited by a restrictive imperial mercantile policy, inadequate property rights, excessive taxation, and religious animosities, embodied in struggles between "New Christians" (Portuguese Jews) among the merchant class, and Old Christians. There was also more than a little official persecution. (In 1650, the king of Portugal issued a royal order obliging all New Christians in the realm to invest in the General Brazil Company or face the Inquisition.)

During the past 250 years, from the mid-eighteenth century forward, North America, and particularly, the United States, became more economically vital than South America, enjoying a surge in economic growth based on secure property rights, low taxes, economic freedom, a larger yeoman population, and an early advantage in exploiting energy-dense coal and then oil. In due course, the United States became the world's foremost economy, a role that it continued to enjoy as the twenty-first century began.

However, early in the twenty-first century, the economic hegemony of the United States appears to have been broken in the credit crisis that precipitated a depression (or if you prefer, "balance sheet recession"). Contrary to generally optimistic accounts that forecast a blossoming of green shoots into an early and robust recovery, I expect a protracted downturn, more traumatic and possibly longer-lasting than the Great Depression of the 1930s. In particular, the widespread expectation among economists that the loss of output during the first four years of the crisis will not prove permanent could be overly optimistic. After the Great Depression, growth exceeded its long-run average during a recovery phase before reverting to trend. As a consequence, the depression had little impact on income levels in the long run. But with the resource constraints arising from peak oil, it is by no means obvious that a surge of above-trend growth lies in store for the United States and other advanced temperate zone economies.

There is already some rough statistical evidence that Brazil has begun to eclipse the United States in terms of upward mobility. As a result of rapid economic growth, almost 40 million Brazilians rose out of poverty in the first decade of the twenty-first century. Meanwhile, 5.4 million Americans sank into poverty according to official statistics during the first year of the Obama presidency. When economies are vibrant, jobs are plentiful, and poverty shrinks. Unfortunately, the recent history of job growth in the United States does not encourage optimism about successful realization of the American Dream going forward. According to the Bureau of Labor Statistics, the United States lost 115,000 jobs during the past decade while Brazil gained 15,023,633. On a population-adjusted basis, the United States would have needed to create 25 million jobs to keep pace with Brazil.

Notwithstanding all the trillions that have been mobilized by the Bush and Obama administrations for stimulus programs and bailouts, the collapse of the greatest credit expansion in world history implies a serious depression. Most politicians and many economists seem not yet ready to face the fact that attempts at intervention to prevent liquidation after past credit cycle collapses have been singularly unsuccessful.

Trillions of dollars have been created and spent since the bankruptcy of Lehman Brothers ignited a global solvency crisis, but little of it has landed in the hands of consumers. The shape of the bailouts has been determined by the imperative in a debtist system[28] to rescue the banks in order to keep credit expanding.

Contrary to the naive assumption that leaders today are far more clever than those who presided over the Great Depression after 1929, statistical measures of the downturn, from unemployment to industrial production to world trade, are either tracking to the trajectories after 1929, or are worse. Far from assuring recovery, I believe that the massive

---

[28] In this book, a debtist system (sometimes referred to herein as debtism) is defined as a corrupt version of "capitalism" based upon fiat money and political favoritism in which the greater part of the purchasing power is funneled into the hands of a well connected few, led by bankers and their best customers.

interventions organized first by George Bush, and now by Barack Obama, virtually assure a catastrophic climax to the balance sheet recession now underway.

Much as the Great Depression of the 1930s marked the end of British hegemony, the current depression will mark the end of American economic dominance, leading to a much-rumored new world order. The United States emerged triumphant from the economic upheavals that marked the eclipse of the British Empire. The United States has dominated the world's economy and reigned supreme as the leading military power ever since.

After replacing the pound sterling as the world's dominant currency, the U.S. dollar has enjoyed uncommon advantages as the reserve currency and unit of account for international trade. The dollar's special position has permitted U.S. consumers to enjoy a standard of living 7 to 8 percent higher than they earned, as trade surplus countries have been trapped into recycling their dollars back into the United States.

Or, to put the matter another way, in a world of competitive devaluation, surplus countries have been tempted to buy ever-larger quantities of dollars in order to forestall the appreciation of their currencies.

In my view, there is a high likelihood that living standards that were inflated by decades of easy money will be deflated in the years to come as the North Atlantic economies are deleveraged. This is not easy to accept. For four decades after 1965 the economies of the G 7 countries accounted for an average of 65 percent of global GDP at market exchange rates. This remarkably stable performance, never varying by more than 3 percentage points, fostered an illusion that the prosperity of the developed, temperate zone nations was a permanent feature of the global economy. But this began to change in the first decade of the twenty-first century.

The prevailing world order is coming to an end, although not all at once. The question is what comes next? Many bets today would be that China will emerge as the new dominant power, and so it may, but unless you are ethnic Chinese, the rise of China is unlikely to afford you many opportunities. My argument focuses on another of the rapidly growing BRIC economies, Brazil, as likely to become the new venue for economic opportunity in a changed world.

All the BRIC economies are better situated to compete than the conventional wisdom would have imagined before the credit collapse. Even the Goldman Sachs forecast of 2001, which first projected Brazil, Russia, India, and China to become dominant by the year 2050, failed to anticipate many of the current strengths that have been brought into focus in the wake of the Lehman Brothers collapse and the severe crisis in the United States, the UK, Europe, and Japan.

The levels of debt raised by the developed nations to bail out their insolvent banking systems are crippling compared to the emerging BRIC nations. According to International Monetary Fund forecasts, by 2014 the average national debt of economies in the developed world is expected to be more than 114 percent of GDP (up from 78 percent in 2006).

The forecast for the emerging BRIC economies including China is just 35 percent, down from 38 percent in 2006. Note, however, that China's banking system has been weighed down by aggressive lending since 2008; much of it to backward, state-run enterprises at sums that approach 60 percent of GDP.

In addition to everything else they have going for them, two of the BRIC countries, Brazil and India, have much more favorable demographics than the United States, much less Europe and Japan. Over the long term, the three drivers of economic growth are free markets, access to energy, and population demographics.

Brazil's energy profile is arguably the most favorable to growth of any of the leading emerging economies. As we explore more thoroughly in coming chapters, Brazil is not only energy independent; it also has vast reserve capacity for energy production. This includes a reserve of up to 120 billion barrels of oil as well as the world's largest untapped hydro-electric potential. Brazil also takes more advantage of solar power than any of the other BRIC countries. Brazil, alone of the major emerging powers, is a tropical country. The average American uses more energy to heat his home than the average Brazilian uses for all purposes.

Franco Modigliani won the 1985 Nobel Prize in Economics partly for his life cycle hypothesis, which states that spending and savings patterns are predictable functions of age demographics. In other words, Modigliani's hypothesis is basically that the age distribution of the population largely determines the health and robustness of an economy. To the extent that Modigliani was correct, a major driver of the health of any country's economy is the number of its citizens who are in their peak earning and spending years. In that case, Brazil is at a competitive advantage to the United States and all the hitherto advanced economies for demographic reasons in addition to the other reasons that people write about.

Claus Vogt, editor of *Sicheres Geld* and author of *The Global Debt Trap*, agrees, saying that—other things being equal—the country with the youngest population will experience the biggest growth in the future, as it will have the highest percentage of productive people in the days ahead.[29] Unlike the United States, Brazil did not have a Baby Boom age bulge after World War II. Consequently, Brazil is not now facing the prospect that younger generations will have to support a disproportionately large number of retirees. The younger cohorts of Brazil's population are proportionately much larger than their counterparts in the United States.

This is another important reason why America's potential is destined to be fulfilled in Brazil in this century. As Richard Jackson, director and senior fellow at the Global Aging Initiative, told the White House Conference on Aging in 2005, "Countries with slowly growing workforces may have slowly growing economies. . . ."[30] Indeed, Daniel Arnold, demographer and author of *The Great Bust Ahead*, says that the aging of America points to a major depression. Arnold claims that the stock market (DJIA) has closely tracked the 45-to-54-year-old cohort of Americans for over a century. As this 45 to 54 demographic is easily projected for years in advance, Arnold's crystal ball has given him a frightening message. He sees the Greatest Depression in history looming ahead for the United States. He declares that 2008 was,

> a self-inflicted sub-prime financial crisis. This has nothing to do with the demographics based massive depression that is yet to come. . . . The sub-prime consequences are however very similar

---

[29] "Transcript: Weiss Global Forum, Part 1," Money and Markets, August 24, 2009, www.moneyandmarkets.com/transcript-the-weiss-global-forum-part-1-35161.
[30] "Richard Jackson at the UNITAR/UNFPA Workshop," CSIS, March 31, 2005, http://csis.org/press/csis-in-the-news/richard-jackson-unitarunfpa-workshop.

though mild so far compared to what is coming our way. The book clearly spelled out that along the way unpredictable short-term (1 to 3 years) disruptive events could happen. The sub-prime crisis is just that. It should be regarded as the "warmer upper" or "hors d'oeuvre" for the big one that is now rapidly closing in on us all.[31]

It almost goes without saying that the transition away from American predominance is likely to be more fraught than the transition between British and American hegemony. For one thing, Great Britain and the United States spoke the same language. America's elite consisted of anglophiles, who supported the British Empire with finance, troops, and military hardware. After World War II, when the United States more or less formally emerged as the leading global power, Great Britain became its closest and most dependable ally.

Today's circumstances are different. Among the BRIC countries, Brazil is closest ethnically and culturally to the United States. Brazil alone is an "American" economy. Indeed, it is the original "America" as christened in the Baptismal Certificate of the New World.

As you will learn in forthcoming chapters, Brazil has these and many other advantages facilitating its emergence as a haven for opportunity in a troubled world.

---

[31]Daniel A. Arnold, *The Great Bust Ahead: The Greatest Depression in American and UK History is Just Several Short Years Away* (Vorago–US, 2002).

Chapter 3

How Brazil Became Endowed for Prosperity in a Collapsing World

We are from America and we want to be Americans.
—from the "Manifesto of the Republican Party of Brazil," 1871

Among the family of nations, Brazil is not a sibling of the United States. Canada would be. Brazil is more like a first cousin with a strong family resemblance. Or, if you prefer, you could see Brazil as a half sibling, with a Portuguese rather than an English father. Both the United States and Brazil are the modern incarnations of New World economies. They are gigantic countries; among the top five on a world scale, richly endowed with natural resources and peopled by a diverse array of immigrants from across the globe.

Like only the United States and China, Brazil is a geographically large country that also is among the top five in population with roughly 203,000,000 inhabitants as of July 2011.

Brazil has more inhabitants of African descent than any country but Nigeria; more persons of Italian ancestry than any country other than

Italy; more Japanese than anywhere but Japan. Brazil also is home to 10 million persons of Arab descent, more than any country outside the Middle East. And Brazil hosts the second-largest population of German ancestry outside of Germany. These ethnic groups are so thoroughly mixed together that in most cases it is impossible to discern a clear line where one stops and another begins.

The original name of the Brazilian Republic (until 1967) was "The Republic of the United States of Brazil," a designation that reflects the long-standing ambition of Brazilians to emulate the success of the United States in South America. Indeed, the first Republican flag of Brazil was an obvious design knockoff of the Stars and Stripes with 21 white stars in a blue field, cut out against a striped background, but with 13 green and yellow rather than red and white stripes. Five of the states of Brazil have flags with stars in a square or rectangular field, with horizontal stripes. Piani's flag has 13 green and yellow stripes; that of São Paulo, 13 black and white stripes.

Even though Brazil was discovered in 1500 and Portuguese settlement began in the century before the first English colonists set out for Jamestown in 1607, Brazil seems somehow a younger country than the United States. I would argue that it is because even a casual observer of Brazil can see that only a bare fraction of its potential has yet been realized. By contrast, the United States seems to have been fully developed and is now distinctly arcing on the downside of its life trajectory. As hedge fund superstar Ray Dalio puts it, "the U.S. is trading more like a country in decline."[1] If Brazil were a half sibling of the United States it would be a junior or younger member of the family. Brazil is certainly much less developed than the United States and, at this point in history, more promising.

The Impact of Topography

To grasp Brazil's potential for the future, it is important to understand why its development was stunted while the United States rapidly

---

[1] Richard Teitelbaum, "Dalio Returns 25% This Year on Diversified Bets Even as Markets Convulse," *Bloomberg Market Magazine*, September 7, 2011.

became the world's richest country. In exploring this issue, I turn to some of the analytical tools that I developed in three earlier books in collaboration with Lord William Rees-Mogg.

In *Blood in the Streets*, *The Great Reckoning: Protect Yourself in the Coming Depression*, and *The Sovereign Individual*, Lord Rees-Mogg and I looked to what we called megapolitics or the specific characteristics of the state of nature that determine the boundary conditions of human action. Among the principal factors we examined that have played an informing role in determining the political and economic destiny of countries is topography.

In this perspective, one of the more misleading metaphors for understanding the world in the twenty-first century is to think of it as flat. To the contrary, it is textured and contoured. And the economic potential of every country going forward is informed by its past, by its debt levels, its legacy energy systems, and natural endowments. While the world may be less differentiated, with fewer nooks and crannies where information technology is concerned, it is still dominated by its physical contours. The metatruth is revealed by the very choice of "flat" as descriptive of information technology. It hints at the importance of topography in the very attempt to discount its continued predominance.

The lay of the land played a much bigger role in the history of nations before technology reached its current state. And it seems likely to play a bigger role again now that the preconditions for robust growth have eroded. We're not accustomed to thinking in these terms, but for most of history the advantages and disadvantages conveyed by topography helped determine the economic destiny of peoples and even the prevailing form of government.

Among the developments Lord Rees-Mogg and I sought to explain was the impact of topography in facilitating the profitable farming of the hinterlands of Greek city-states. A complex topography of undulating inlets facilitated the prosperity of yeoman farmers by enabling a great many of them to locate within 20 miles of the sea where they could prosper. Yeoman farmers made high profits growing olives for oil and grapes for wine and then shipping them by sea to a wide market throughout the Mediterranean. At a time when transportation costs for moving goods 75 miles overland exceeded the costs for shipping cargoes by sea across the full expanse of the Mediterranean, a complex shoreline that permitted more small holders to farm close to the sea had far-reaching implications. Greek farmers, more than other people who enjoyed the climatic conditions suitable to growing grapes and olives, were able to afford the weapons needed to become militarily, and thus politically formidable.

Equally, we sought an answer in topography to the puzzle noted by Thomas Malthus about the failure of governance in Africa's native kingdoms. Malthus noted that when Europeans first penetrated deep into sub-Saharan Africa they found "many extensive and beautiful districts entirely destitute of inhabitants." Malthus ascribed much of this population puzzle to "the insecurity of property arising from this constant exposure to plunder . . . in a country divided into a thousand petty states."[2]

Why was Africa "divided into a thousand petty states"? We pointed to details of the local state of nature. The lack of economic progress in Africa's interior for thousands of years was largely due to the lay of the land and quirks of climate. In most regions, they offered few advantages to any party seeking to organize on a large scale. Each of thousands of petty states could temporarily hold its own plot of ground, but with few natural boundaries or other topographical features that conveyed an advantage in trying to monopolize force over a large scale. None of the local warlords could suppress the constant skirmishes and plundering or even halt the marauders who beset the no man's lands. No one could build much of value where his property or his life might be forfeited at any moment. The effect of the incessant wars and violence was to keep most of Africa and most Africans in destitution. In the period before Europeans arrived, as many as three out of four black African males were slaves.[3]

Another element that helps explain the general lack of development throughout much of sub-Saharan Africa was the endemic infestation of sleeping sickness (human African trypanosomiasis). As Dorothy H. Crawford, Professor of Medical Microbiology and assistant principal for

---

[2] Thomas Robert Malthus, *An Essay on the Principle of Population*, 6th ed. (London: John Murray, 1826), I. VII.3.

[3] James Dale Davidson and Lord William Rees-Mogg, *The Great Reckoning: Protect Yourself in the Coming Depression* (New York: Simon & Schuster, 1993), 63.

the Public Understanding of Medicine at the University of Edinburgh, wrote,

> Sleeping sickness is always fatal without treatment. Most experts think that hunter-gatherers could not have survived long term in the tsetse fly belt of Central Africa, and that the problems caused by sleeping sickness may have been the impetus for the human migration out of Africa which preceded the colonization of Europe and Asia some 50,000–100,000 years ago.[4]

No doubt, the prevalence of endemic infestation by deadly pathogens also goes some distance toward explaining the "many extensive and beautiful districts entirely destitute of inhabitants."

By contrast, civilization evolved rapidly in another part of Africa—Egypt. There, as in the river valleys of Mesopotamia, topography combined with climate to create favorable conditions for organizing political structures on a large scale. Rainfall in the deserts surrounding the Nile floodplain was insufficient to permit crops to grow. Under such megapolitical conditions, individual farmers faced an unacceptably high cost for failing to cooperate in maintaining the political structure. Without irrigation, which could only be provided on a large scale, crops could not grow. That mattered because as Malthus noted, no one has yet figured out how humans can live without food. Since farmers could not move away and grow food independently, they tended to hang around to be oppressed by despotic governments that formed along the Nile.

Thus we found informing features of topography underlying developments as varied as the emergence of democracy in Greek city-states, the Hobbesian war of all against all in premodern, sub-Saharan Africa, and the Oriental despotism characteristic of hydraulic societies in the ancient Near East. A similar line of analysis helps explain the very different pace of development of two richly endowed "American" countries: the United States and Brazil.

Of the two, the United States developed far faster, rapidly becoming the richest country in the world, by the mid-twentieth century, while

---

[4] Dorothy H. Crawford, *Deadly Companions: How Microbes Shaped Our History* (Oxford, UK: Oxford University Press, 2009), 48.

Brazil, a country of similar size (Brazil is larger than the contiguous 48 states of the United States mainland), has remained famously the country of the future.

Was Brazil stunted because it began life as a Portuguese rather than an English colony? Economic historian Douglass North is among many who have "attributed the relative success of the United States and Canada to British institutions being more conducive for growth."[5] As something of an Anglophile myself, I am inclined to believe that the British settlement colonies did enjoy at least a marginal head start in importing institutions that tended to promote economic growth by protecting property rights. I confess that my feeling in this respect may turn on a romantic pride in being a descendent of Saer de Quincy, the Earl of Winchester, one of the authors of the Magna Carta. I would like to imagine that my forbearer made the world a better place by revolting against King John. Yet a closer look at the history of economic growth in the New World shows that a heritage of British institutions does not provide an encompassing explanation for differences in economic growth. For one thing, "the leadership of the United States and Canada over their hemispheric neighbors"[6] did not emerge until the early nineteenth century when these North American societies begin to participate in the Industrial Revolution, realizing sustained economic growth by incorporating high BTU energy into economic processes. It is telling that when George Washington was inaugurated as the first president of the United States that Haiti was likely the richest society in the world on a per capita basis. In the preindustrial, colonial era, the most successful economies were the Caribbean sugar islands. It made little difference which colonial power presided.

Equally, looking over a longer period, the case for the superiority of British institutions is undermined by the fact that the majority of New World economies established by the British were not notably successful in realizing sustained economic growth after the Industrial Revolution. For example, Guyana, the only former British colony on the South

---

[5] Kenneth L. Sokoloff and Stanley L. Engerman, "Institutions, Factor Endowments and Paths of Development in the New World," *Journal of Economic Perspectives* 14, no. 3 (Summer 2000): 2.
[6] Ibid.

American continent, and a neighbor sharing a long border with Brazil, enjoyed a GDP per capita of only 27 percent of the Brazilian level in 2010, according to the International Monetary Fund.[7] Having been a part of the British Empire was hardly a guarantee of growth.

Was Brazil slower to develop because Brazilians are indolent or mentally inferior to residents of the United States? I think not. No less than residents of the United States, Brazilians were keen to exploit the opportunities nature had given them. But in effect, nature's gifts, known as factor endowments in economist speak, were more complicated and more difficult to exploit in Brazil than in the United States.

Economists tend to think of factor endowments as a catchall abstraction that can be represented by a single algebraic notation in econometric models rather than seeking to analyze why and when comparative factor endowments become relatively more valuable. In many cases, economists have sought to model comparative advantage in a stylized, two-country world without pressing resource constraints. The standard Heckscher-Ohlin model (for which Bertil Ohlin won the Nobel Prize) assumes the same production function for all countries, which also implies that all firms are identical. Not so. The real world is more complicated.

Without wading too deeply into the thickets of economic theory, I think it is more useful to try to understand why natural resources are more valuable at some times than at others. My argument in this book is that the factor endowments of the United States peaked in value in the past century while those of Brazil are rapidly gaining value in the post-peak oil world. Or to put it another way, Brazil may well have been endowed with more natural resources than the present-day United States for tens of millions of years. But when Europeans arrived, they found the natural resources in what became the United States far more accessible for building an early-modern economy.

Think of a simple children's toy, like a ball, that anyone could use without elaborate instruction. Once the early English settlers, who were mainly subsistence farmers, struck a truce with the Indians and learned to survive the winter, they never turned back. The colonists and

---

[7] International Monetary Fund, World Economic Outlook Database, September 2011.

immigrants who followed all had access to more or less free land, which they cultivated as yeoman farmers. At a time when Europeans were suffering with wood shortages, English settlers found an area densely covered with hardwood forests that could be readily exploited for building materials and fuel. While economic growth during the colonial period in North America was slow by later standards, progress was cumulative.

Other features of the North American mainland as encountered by the early settlers of Canada as well as what became the United States contributed to the evolution of middle-class societies. For one thing, colonies located on the northern part of the North American mainland were not stocked with "substantial populations of natives able to provide labor, nor with climates and soils that gave them a comparative advantage in the production of crops characterized by major economies of using slave labor."[8] Most of the settlers of European descent had similarly high levels of human capital. And their principal labor was invested in the production of grains and hay, crops that provided negligible scale economies to large producers in the colonial period. Consequently, as economic historian Kenneth L. Sokoloff observes, "the great majority of adult men were able to operate as independent proprietors."[9]

By contrast, Brazil was complicated from the very beginning, more a Rubik's Cube than a simple tool. When the Portuguese first arrived, they found the native inhabitants of Brazil living naked in a Stone Age paradise. Unlike the native Inca, Maya, and Aztec empires that had flourished elsewhere in what became Latin America, the native tribes in Brazil had not developed complex societies. They built no cities and they left behind no storerooms of gold; nor had they established any systems of tribute and taxation that the Portuguese could take over in the way the Spanish viceroys took over the Inca Empire. The first European settlers in Brazil were starting from scratch.

Among other things, they found soils and climates well-suited to growing sugar, the most valuable crop of the early-modern period. Unlike the hay and grain produced by the yeoman farmers in North America, sugar was a crop that could not be grown in Europe. It was

---

[8] Sokoloff and Engerman, "Institutions," 5.
[9] Ibid.

a highly valued commodity that justified the large and previously unprecedented intercontinental flows of labor and capital required to produce and bring it to market. Like all the New World economies, Brazil evidenced a high marginal product of labor, hence the great numbers of migrants who crossed the Atlantic from Europe and Africa. Prior to the harnessing of high BTU hydrocarbon fuels, the somatic energy provided by slaves seemed essential to the exploitation of the land and natural resources found in such abundance relative to labor.

In addition to this, sugar production entailed great economies of scale for those who could afford to acquire multitudes of slaves to farm large plantations. Under these conditions, it is not surprising that sugar became big in colonial Brazil. By 1650, sugar comprised 95 percent of Brazil's exports. At that time, northeastern Brazil was richer than the New England colonies. But within a few decades, that prosperity petered out, in part because of Portuguese policies that are interesting in light of the Douglass North thesis that an English legal tradition improved prospects for growth. While that may not have proven true over the long run, Portuguese law was evidently counterproductive during the seventeenth century.

The rapid proliferation of competition to Brazil in the seventeenth century sugar trade owed much to dysfunctional, repressive policies. Consider the victory of the General Brazil Company in the Sugar War over the Dutch West India Company in 1654. Other things being equal, the military defeat of the Dutch should have secured Brazil's position as the dominant supplier of sugar to Europe. But other things were not equal. The advantage for Brazil proved to be fleeting precisely because of Portuguese policies that contributed directly to the proliferation of competitive sugar plantations in the Caribbean, thus eclipsing the Brazilian sugar industry for centuries to come.

How did this happen?

Many of the early Brazilian sugar plantations were owned by Marranos, so-called New Christians who had formally converted to Christianity, but many of whom continued to practice Judaism in private. When the Dutch captured parts of the northeast Brazilian coast in 1630, they were unconcerned about enforcing religious orthodoxy. Consequently many New Christians returned to living openly as Jews. After the Dutch surrendered in 1654, the relapsed converts found themselves in a perilous position. Under Portuguese law, converts who returned to their old religions could be punished by death. Consequently, many Marrano planters fled, lest they be captured and turned over to the Inquisition.

Note that the Marranos in Pernambuco had good reason to fear being denounced to the Inquisition. One of the principal grievances cited by the Portuguese settlers who led the revolt against Dutch rule was a complaint that the Dutch authorities had been lax in suppressing the New Christians.

As a consequence, experienced Brazilian sugar planters migrated to the Caribbean, where they introduced sugar cultivation to practically every island with even a patch of arable land. As a result, the Caribbean, which was closer to Europe, soon eclipsed Brazil in supplying the sugar trade. That was certainly not the only example of Brazil's economic progress being derailed by heavy-handed government.

Just as the yeoman tradition of farming by independent proprietors helped inform the legal institutions of what became the United States and Canada, so the highly unequal land tenure associated with the sugar plantations in colonial Brazil gave rise to institutions, laws, and policies that tended to reinforce the advantages of the elite. As Sokoloff suggests, "government policies and other institutions tend generally to reproduce the sorts of conditions that gave rise to them. Specifically, in those societies that began with extreme inequality, elites were likely better able to establish a basic legal framework that ensured them disproportionate shares of political power."[10] Recent research in Brazil has confirmed that "municipalities originally related to the sugarcane cycle present higher land concentrations today."[11] So while the prosperity generated by the successful cultivation of sugar in Brazil in the seventeenth century may have been fleeting, the institutional impact of the extreme inequality that necessarily accompanied sugar plantation under

---

[10] Sokoloff and Engerman, "Institutions," 6.

[11] Fernando Zanella and Christopher Westley, "The Western Expansion as a Common Pool Problem: The Contrasting Histories of the Brazilian and North American Pioneers," *American Journal of Economics and Sociology* 68, no. 3 (July 2009).

colonial conditions was not. Today's institutions reflect the heritage of past institutions.

In my view, you could almost consider the riches of Brazil as having been sealed in a time capsule, where to a large extent they remained locked out of reach until the value of those assets escalated to be very great indeed. That time has come, or is coming, as the conditions for economic growth recede in the United States and most of the advanced temperate zone economies.

Yesterday's Limitations as Today's Strengths

The slower pace of Brazilian development was dictated by megapolitical conditions, in particular by peculiarities of topography that long hampered growth in Brazil, but that ironically have endowed Brazil to become an economic superpower in the post-peak-oil world. Not only was Brazil held back by topography, its progress was also retarded by a largely tropical climate that for centuries seemed to limit the productivity of Brazil's farms. In Chapter 9, we will explore Brazil's role as an emerging superpower in world agriculture in more detail and why experts formerly believed that productive farming was limited to temperate climates (or, more specifically, why experts formerly believed that modern civilization depended upon farming formerly glaciated land "centering essentially about the North Atlantic basin").[12] Little wonder that the Cerrado (translated in English as "closed") that comprises 21 percent of Brazil was long thought to be worthless for agriculture.

It has long been known, as the old Frank Sinatra song contended, "There is an awful lot of coffee in Brazil," but only recently has it become obvious that Brazil's warm climate is actually an advantage in the production of cereals and seeds that originally evolved in temperate climates. Now that Brazilian scientists have developed varieties of grains and seeds that thrive in warm weather, and learned how to enhance the soils of the vast Brazilian savanna, the Cerrado previously thought to be unproductive, is emerging as the new breadbasket of the world. Brazil's

---

[12] O. D. Von Engeln, "Effects of Continental Glaciation on Agriculture. Part I," *Bulletin of the American Geographical Society* 46, no. 4 (1914): 242.

farm exports are growing 670 percent faster than those from the United States.[13]

The issues associated with the introduction of temperate crops into warm weather climates aside, the crux of Brazil's longstanding growth challenge is highlighted by an hypothesis spelled out by Nicolas Rashevsky in *Looking at History through Mathematics*.[14] In seeking to explain the more rapid development of the European West, Rashevsky looked to an important characteristic of topography—the ratio of shoreline to landmass—the very feature that helped precipitate the growth of democracy in ancient Greece. He argued that prosperity first developed in Europe because Europe has a specific shoreline almost a magnitude longer than that in China, for example. The implication of an extensive specific shoreline, as illustrated by the prosperity of small-holding farmers in ancient Greece, was that it permitted more extensive and profitable trade.

In the case of Brazil, Rashevsky's hypothesis requires amendment. His unspoken assumption is that the rivers and waters are navigable. Brazil's development was hampered not by a low ratio of specific shoreline, per se, but by a concatenation of geographic features that rendered much of the shoreline of Brazil inaccessible or ill-suited to navigation. Brazil is endowed with the world's most dense and vast river system. Other things being equal, that should have made Brazil the world's richest country. But other things were not equal. A higher proportion of Brazil's hydrological system than elsewhere is useless for transport. Due to the terrain through which Brazil's rivers flow, many areas containing ruptures and deep valleys, they have greater potential for the generation of electric energy than for navigation. As of 2008, hydroelectric power plants accounted for 85 percent Brazil's electricity, with 282 GWh of power generation.[15] Of course, for the first four

---

[13] Lael Brainard and Leonardo Martinez-Diaz, eds., *Brazil as an Economic Superpower? Understanding Brazil's Changing Role of the Global Economy* (Washington, DC: Brookings Institution Press, 2000), 64.

[14] Nicolas Rashevsky, *Looking at History through Mathematics* (Cambridge, MA: MIT Press, 1968).

[15] "Global Hydropower Scenario," www.erg.com.np/hydropower_global.php.

centuries of Brazil's existence generating electric power was beyond the technological horizon.

Chapter 10 spells out the many ways that Brazil is endowed to enjoy a competitive advantage in energy in the twenty-first century as sky-rocketing demand for a diminishing supply of cheap oil undercuts the basis of prosperity in the formerly advanced economies. Brazil is one country where city lights are unlikely to fizzle and flicker out due to electricity shortages. In 1950, Brazil's electric generating capacity was only 1.9 million kilowatts, mostly based upon burning petroleum, which in those days was imported. After the first oil shock, Brazil embarked on heavy investments in hydroelectricity that by 2008 had created 81,955 MW of generating capacity, second globally, behind only China.

In addition to hydropower, Brazil also enjoys advantages in other forms of renewable energy, including biomass and ethanol production from sugar cane. Brazil is self-sufficient in oil and is poised to become a major exporter of high-priced oil as production from newly discovered fields comes online. Also important is the fact that Brazil enjoys greater benefits of solar energy than most other large economies. Brazilians employ less energy relative to GDP than the world at large. One statistical measure underscores this fact: residents of the United States spend more energy heating their homes than Brazilians do for all purposes.

While Brazil has more fresh water than any other country—itself a major advantage going forward—the waterways are not situated to facilitate transport. Among Brazil's major rivers, only the Amazon and the São Francisco flow to the sea. But the area drained by the Amazon is mostly tropical jungle—a region of low productivity. The São Francisco has its origins in Minas Gerais, an area of high productivity. But only the last 172 miles of the lower river are navigable. Brazil's most productive regions, in the southeast of the country do not have easy access to the sea through waterways.

Unlike coastal regions of the United States that are open to the sea, a high wall known as the Grand Escarpment defines most of Brazil's Atlantic Coast. (Think of the mountains looming over Rio.) This is the exposed face of another difficult topographical feature, the so-called Brazilian or Amazonian Shield, an area of one million square miles where most of the rivers flow away from the sea; either north as tributaries of the Amazon, or to the west where they eventually feed into the Paraná River system, which winds for more than 3,000 miles through the center of South America, merging first with the Paraguay River, then farther downstream with the Uruguay River (which also drains Brazil's two most southerly states Santa Catarina and Rio Grande do Sul) to form the Río de la Plata. This river, the widest in the world, reaches a maximum width of 140 miles as it flows past Buenos Aires and Montevideo into the Atlantic Ocean.

The easy navigability afforded by the Río de la Plata and the rivers that feed into it helps explain why Argentina became one of the world's wealthiest countries late in the nineteenth and early twentieth centuries, while Brazil languished. Like the United States, Argentina (and to a lesser extent Uruguay) rapidly achieved prosperity by exploiting its favored natural transportation system. Meanwhile, no such system facilitated the early export of Brazil's products.

Put simply, the engineering required to provide infrastructure for transport of Brazilian products has been much more complicated and costly than the equivalent infrastructure in the United States. Although Brazil may be potentially the world's richest country, many of its riches have been effectively locked out of circulation by difficult and complicated topography. Remember, it is 10 to 30 times more cost-efficient to haul goods via water transport than doing so overland.

The geography of the United States was well understood after Thomas Jefferson commissioned the Lewis and Clark expedition early in the nineteenth century. Not so with Brazil. It is no exaggeration to say that much of Brazil was terra incognita (or, "unknown land") until the twentieth century. Consider that the U.S. President Theodore Roosevelt authored *Through the Brazilian Wilderness*, a travel memoir of his long expedition through Brazil begun after his defeat in the election of 1912. Just the titles of some of his chapters convey a sense of how unmapped and inaccessible Brazil was in the twentieth century:

"Up the River of Tapirs"
"Through the Highland Wilderness of Western Brazil"
"With a Mule-Train Across Nhambiquara Land"
"The River of Doubt" (so named because its full length was said to be unexplored at the time of Roosevelt's expedition)
"Down an Unknown River into the Equatorial Forest"

As a traveler to Brazil on the eve of the First World War, the former president was in a far different frame of mind from the one that brought him to advocate expanding the National Park System in order to preserve "scenery" for future generations. In 1913 Brazil, he was literally making his way through uncharted territory. Roosevelt explains how he was invited by the Brazilian foreign minister to "undertake the leadership of a serious expedition into the unexplored portion of western Matto Grosso," to explore and to attempt the descent of a "very big river, utterly unknown to geographers."

Later, he recounts,

We were within the southern boundary of this great equatorial forest, on a river which was not merely unknown but unguessed at, no geographer having ever suspected its existence. This river flowed northward toward the equator, but whither it would go, whether it would turn one way or another, the length of its course, where it would come out, the character of the stream itself, and the character of the dwellers along its banks—all these things were yet to be discovered.[16]

Another prominent foreigner who took a hand in exploring Brazil in the twentieth century was the eccentric English geographer, Colonel Percy Fawcett. He famously disappeared somewhere in Mato Grosso or Goiás state in 1925, on an expedition to find a "Lost City of Z." It is telling that, as late as 1925, the jungles where Colonel Fawcett sought his lost city were home to Indian tribes that had never before encountered white men. That is an unmistakable indication of how remote and unsettled the Center/West region of Brazil was within living memory. Peter Fleming, later travel editor of the *Times* of London, and brother of James Bond originator, Ian Fleming, joined an expedition in 1933 into the little-explored reaches of Brazil to search for Colonel Fawcett. Fleming tells of his journey on which he discovered "one new tributary to a tributary to a tributary of the Amazon" in the comic masterpiece, *Brazilian Adventure*. Reading it makes clear that even in

---

[16] Theodore Roosevelt, *Through the Brazilian Wilderness* (New York: Charles Scribner's Sons, 1914).

living memory travel through central Brazil could be so difficult that it made the Lewis and Clark Expedition seem like a stroll in the park. And accurate knowledge of the land was so sketchy that mountain ranges that did not exist figured in the coordinates of the search for Colonel Fawcett. Only three decades later, a corner was cut out of Goiás to form the Federal District where Brasilia, the new capital of Brazil, was located.

Another comparative marker of the difficulty of the Brazilian environment as compared to the United States is the relative frequency and success of slave revolts in the past. There were no successful slave revolts in the United States, partly because there were no unmapped and inaccessible regions where runaway slaves could escape and live beyond the reach of authority. But there were runaway slave communities in the wilds of Brazil, called *quilombos*.[17] These were not always located in the vast interior of Brazil. In fact, the most famous of the *quilombos* was the fortified settlement of Palmares, in the coastal state of Alagoas, which survived for 60 years and fought off six failed efforts to subdue it, reaching a population of 20,000 runaway slaves at its height. There was no equivalent to Palmares in the United States, mainly because there were no wilds equivalent to those found in many parts of Brazil in the past.

The United States, in contrast to Brazil, began life relatively devoid of wilds with an extensive installed transportation system provided by nature, an elaborate network of navigable rivers, and a relatively flat coastline, dotted with many excellent harbors. Think of Boston, where the Charles River meets the Atlantic; New York, where the Hudson empties; Philadelphia, located at the confluence of the Delaware and Schuylkill rivers on the eastern border of Pennsylvania; Baltimore in the Chesapeake Bay, fed by more than 150 rivers and streams; and Charleston at the confluence of the Ashley and Cooper rivers, which flow together into the Atlantic Ocean.

Imagine how it would have affected the development of the United States if the Appalachian Mountains had extended to the Atlantic shore. And if the great eastern rivers, like the Hudson, the Susquehanna, and the Potomac, instead of emptying into the sea or tidewater bays, had taken different turns—either tumbling down rapids and waterfalls to the

---

[17] Thomas E. Skidmore, *Brazil: Five Centuries of Change*, 2nd ed. (New York: Oxford University Press, 2010), 36.

east, or flowing on meandering tracks that eventually emptied into the ocean thousands of miles away through a great port in Mexico or Canada. The story of U.S. economic development would have been very different. The United States would not have developed as rapidly. And it would not now be facing collapse because of a severe and irremediable decline in production of crude oil and the debt crisis it has engendered. As I spell out later in this book, U.S. oil output peaked in the early 1970s and global oil output appears to have peaked around 2005, with far-reaching consequences.

As it was, the United States happened to be well endowed for success under nineteenth- and twentieth-century conditions. Historian of water, Stephen Solomon, comments,

the global ascendance of the United States closely paralleled its mastery of its 3 disparate hydrological environments: its rainy, temperate, river-rich eastern half, dominated by the continent's arterial Mississippi River; its predominantly arid, drought-prone, Far West descending to the Pacific ocean from the 100th meridian of the high Great Plains; and its frontage on the sea lanes between the world's two largest oceans. By fusing these diverse water frontiers into a coherent national political and economic realm, America leveraged its favorable geographical location and the abundant natural resources of its vast island continent to become civilization's world superpower in the twentieth century.[18]

From its early days, the United States was able to grow, building capital by cheaply exporting goods through a number of excellent eastern harbors formed where rivers flow into the sea. Later, when settlement extended into the Midwest, the United States continued to bootstrap its way to wealth, utilizing the Mississippi River and its feeder waterways, including the Ohio and Missouri rivers, to provide low-cost transportation of products for export. The plains areas surrounding the Mississippi were relatively flat, simplifying the engineering challenge and

---

[18] Steven Solomon, *Water: The Epic Struggle for Wealth, Power, and Civilization* (New York: Harper Perennial, 2010), 266.

the cost of constructing roads and railroads. For example, Minneapolis is 1,299 miles upstream from New Orleans, but it has an elevation of only 298 meters. By comparison, Brazil's most favorably situated city, São Paulo, is only 70 kilometers (43 miles) inland from the port city of Santos, but São Paulo's elevation is 760 meters.

This helps explain why São Paulo was relatively slow to develop compared to New York. In 1870, New York City had a population of 942,292. By contrast, in 1870 just 23,000 people lived in São Paulo, making it about 10,000 inhabitants smaller than Reading, Pennsylvania. Since then, according to the Fernand Braudel Institute of World Economics, São Paulo has topped world growth charts enjoying "the fastest long-term rate of big-city growth in human experience."[19] Today, according to the CIA, greater São Paulo has a population of 19.96 million, making it larger than the New York–Newark metropolitan area, which has a combined population of 19.3 million.[20] Meanwhile, Reading's population has expanded to 88,082 (with the highest urban poverty rate in the United States). An early lead in industrialization doesn't always foretell a bright future.

The topographical advantage the United States enjoyed opened a gateway for building capital and rapidly exploiting plentiful energy resources, running from wood to coal to oil. Crucially, this precipitated a growth spurt employing the great energy-consuming innovations of the nineteenth and twentieth centuries—tractors, assembly lines, steam- and diesel-powered ships and locomotives, then cars, and airplanes. These technologies, along with electricity and modern communications, introduced more than a century ago, were the building blocks of the modern economy, powered by cheap oil.

In contrast to the United States, Brazil developed slowly because of its daunting topography. In effect, Brazil was obliged by nature to conserve its prosperity for a future time, almost as if a forward-looking decision had been taken in terms similar to those that economic theorist Harold Hotelling spelled out in his seminal 1931 article, "The

---

[19] Cited by Larry Rohter in *Brazil on the Rise: The Story of a Country Transformed* (New York: Palgrave Macmillan, 2010), 150.
[20] CIA, "The World Factbook," www.cia.gov/library/publications/the-world -factbook.

Economics of Exhaustible Resources."[21] Hotelling suggested that owners of such resources as oil should only produce to optimize cash flow if the returns on the proceeds of the sales placed in bonds or cash deposits in the bank exceeded the rate of appreciation of the asset in the ground. In other words, don't trade appreciating oil for depreciating money if the oil is gaining value faster than interest on the funds compounds.

Of course, the actual situation with the early U.S. oil industry was more complicated than Hotelling's simple trade-off implies. The United States pioneered the world oil industry before there was any real understanding of how far-reaching the effect of adopting oil would be in raising growth and reconfiguring the economy. The consequences of introducing oil were so far-reaching that they were not only unimaginable in advance; they are still barely understood a century and a half later.

Three Radical Changes

The amount of energy, per capita, powering the U.S. economy compounded by more than 4,000,000 percent from 1850, the decade when Edwin Drake launched the oil business, through 1990. Energy use rose from a baseline contribution of one-tenth of one horsepower per capita, per annum, mostly unaided human and animal muscle power, in 1850, to an astonishing 140,000 horsepower per capita, per annum in 1990. This not only permitted an escalating rise in living standards, it also precipitated radical changes in the nature of the economy itself.

Three of the more far-reaching changes involved:

1. The explosion in the size of government
2. A shift in the nature of money and thus the proliferation of debt
3. Spatial reconfiguration of the U.S. economy

---

[21] Harold Hotelling, "The Economics of Exhaustible Resources," *Journal of Political Economy* 39, no. 2 (1931).

Predatory Government

Notwithstanding the myth of limited government that figures so prominently in the political narrative of the United States, the surge in energy use made the U.S. government the largest, richest, most powerful government in the history of the world.

Prior to the harnessing of hydrocarbon energy, the standard for the predatory diversion of human energy by rulers was set by the pharaohs of ancient Egypt who famously conscripted labor four millennia ago to build gigantic mausoleums for themselves. The Great Pyramid of Giza, built for Pharaoh Khufu circa 2540 B.C., was the largest building on earth until early in the twentieth century. The Greek historian Herodotus reported 2,000 years after the pyramids were built that the pharaoh "made all Egyptians work for him. . . . One hundred thousand men at a time worked for three months. Ten years of this forced labor were consumed merely in making the causeway along which the stones were hauled."[22]

Harvard Egyptologist Mark Lehner disputes the image transmitted from Herodotus through Cecil B. DeMille's *The Ten Commandments* of legions of slaves toiling "in the scorching sun beneath the whips of pharaoh's overseers."[23] Lehner suggests that just a few thousands skilled workers at a time held down the ancient equivalents of cushy government jobs, in which they were fed "tremendous quantities of cattle, sheep and goat." Lehner also argues that the pyramid builders were not slaves, but that all Egyptians owed obligatory labor, called *bak*, to their overlords.[24]

Although Lehner is silent on the question of whether Egyptian peasants were healthy enough to toil in the scorching sun, there is good reason to suppose that they were not. Papyrus scrolls authored by Egyptian physicians, at about the time the Sphinx and the pyramids of Giza were built, detail an annual epidemic that struck Egypt each year as the Nile flooded. Professor Dorothy H. Crawford suggests in *Deadly Companions* that the annual epidemic was malaria. But that wasn't the

---

[22] Herodotus, *Histories*.

[23] Jonathan Shaw, "Who Built the Pyramids?" *Harvard Magazine* (July–August 2003).

[24] Ibid.

worst of it. According to Crawford "the most problematic infection at the time was schistosomiasis, a fatal disease caused by waterborne microbes that exploited irrigation farming to aid its spread."[25] It was this infection that was so common as to account for Herodotus' reference to Egypt as "the land where men menstruate."[26] If the population of Egyptian farmers was weakened by exposure to dangerous microbes transmitted through the irrigation channels, that argues in favor of Lehner's thesis that the pyramids were built by a smaller, professionalized force, perhaps drawn from Egypt's growing urban population rather than from the infected and therefore weakened mass of peasant farmers.

Obligatory labor or simple slavery, it was a rare government in the pre-industrial era that was able to harness human muscle-power on a scale approaching that enjoyed by the pharaohs. Only the rulers of hydraulic societies who had a monopoly on food had sufficient leverage over the general population to be able to extract enough energy to undertake a project like building the pyramids. But even the success of the pharaohs in aggrandizing themselves was predicated on weather conditions conducive to inundations.

When bad weather dried up the source of the Nile for many years after 1250 B.C., the ability of the pharaohs to command allegiance (hak) dried up as well. Around 1182–1151 B.C., during the reign of Rameses III, low inundations and crop shortfalls led to surging food prices. Craftsmen and workers for the royal tombs near the Valley of the Kings went on strike after their food rations went unissued.[27]

Governments could not easily extract large amounts of energy from human muscle power when the entire annual energy output of society was limited to about one-twentieth of a horsepower per capita. The margin above subsistence available for capture was simply too meager. Economic historian Richard Steckel points out that even within the context of real GDP growth in a favored environment like the early United States one of the faster-growing economies of that time apart from the UK, that growth from the nineteenth into the twentieth

---

[25] Crawford, *Deadly Companions*, 68.

[26] Ibid.

[27] Brian Fagan, The *Long Summer: How Climate Changed Civilization* (New York: Basic Books, 2004), 187.

centuries "must have been many times higher than experienced during the colonial period."[28] How does he know? He writes,

> This conclusion is justified by considering the implications of extrapolating the level observed in 1820 ($1,257) backward in time at the growth rate measured since 1820 (1.73 percent). Under this supposition, real per capita GDP would have doubled every forty years (halved every forty years going backward in time) and so by the mid 1700s there would have been insufficient income to support life. Because the cheapest diet able to sustain good health would have cost nearly $500 per year, the tentative assumption of modern economic growth contradicts what actually happened. Moreover, historical evidence suggests that important ingredients of modern economic growth, such as technological change and human and physical capital, accumulated relatively slowly during the colonial period.[29]

The advent of hydrocarbon energy changed that multiplying energy in the U.S. economy by more than 4,000,000 percent from 1850 to 1990. By raising income dramatically above the threshold of subsistence, the surge in available energy in the United States permitted the U.S. government to far surpass even the pharaohs of ancient Egypt in extracting resources from the population. Government spending skyrocketed from 1.8 percent of GDP in 1850 to 36 percent in 1990, further escalating to 41 percent by 2011.[30]

Based on Steckel's analysis, it would have been impossible for government to engross 35 or 40 percent of income before hydrocarbons lifted the energy quotient in the economy above a margin that was barely sufficient to support life. An expression of the prosperity that resulted from the staggering increase in horsepower per capita was a

---

[28] Richard H. Steckel, "A History of the Standard of Living in the United States," EH .net, February 1, 2010, http://eh.net/encyclopedia/article/steckel.standard.living.us.
[29] Ibid.
[30] "Time Series Chart of US Government Spending," www.usgovernment spending.com/spending_chart_1990_2010USb_12s1li011mcn_F0t.

surge in life expectancy, which doubled in the United States from 36.3 years at birth in 1850 to 75.4 years by 1990.[31]

This and other aspects of material living standards that reached higher levels in the United States than in Brazil can be seen as flowing from the earlier and more far-reaching adoption of hydrocarbon energy in the United States. In large measure, that was a function of the topographical features of the two countries and their natural endowments. In the first instance, Brazil, like most tropical countries, had little anthracite coal. Secondly, Brazil's oil deposits were more difficult to find and exploit than those in the United States.

Growth Imperatives Lead to Fiat Money and Runaway Debt

As ever more energy was incorporated into the U.S. economy it had far-reaching consequences. Skyrocketing per capita energy use not only dramatically raised U.S. living standards (and life expectancy); it also precipitated a major shift in the nature of money as well.

During the long centuries when living standards grew only erratically, or not at all, it would have been impossible to adopt a monetary system that could only function under conditions of rapid growth. The reason is simple. When money is borrowed into existence as it is today in "modern," fractional reserve banking systems, the loans must be repaid with interest. If the economy grows, the repayment of principal plus interest is facilitated. Borrowers, if they are lucky and well placed, can make their payments from the growth increment. They need not resort to austerity and curtail their budget in order to service their debt. But if growth falters, the impact of debt-based money changes dramatically. Rather than amplifying growth through the ready availability of credit, the need to repay debt amplifies the contraction of the economy. Fiat money is problematic in a slow-growth or no-growth environment.

Commodity-based money was the option of choice in a preindustrial world without growth. Throughout the globe, there was a strong tendency to base money upon gold and silver, two precious metals with the notable characteristic of being assets that are not someone else's liabilities.

---

[31] Steckel, "Standard of Living."

Inevitably, however, the economy is informed by the physical resources that underlie it. When the introduction of hydrocarbon energy dramatically lifted growth rates, it also introduced an almost hydraulic pressure to restructure money. An apparent drawback of commodity-based money in a high-growth environment is the fact that supplies of gold and silver are inelastic. Therefore, credit cannot be expanded as readily as is possible under a fiat regime. Gradually, as growth rates accelerated, authorities in one economy after another moved to replace commodity-based money that incorporated limitations on the contracting of debt (and thus also tended to limit the nominal GDP growth) in favor of a pure fiat money borrowed into existence through fractional reserve banking. It was no drawback that fiat money facilitated the enrichment of governments, enabling them to garner more resources, fight more wars, and create the illusion of democratic consensus through deficit spending, as they could not do when hampered by the restrictions of a gold standard.

The introduction of hydrocarbon energy began a process that changed money and banking. The availability of an elastic supply of credit permitted at least a temporary acceleration of growth. Part of this linkage derives from the fact that fiat money is largely borrowed into existence. A growing economy allows room for interest payments without necessarily constraining other outlays. But the fatal flaw of debtism, sporadically evidenced during cyclical downturns and now chronically in view with peak oil, is that without growth the requirement to pay interest on money borrowed into existence obliges debtors to curtail outlays with the threat of deflationary contraction lying in the shadows of widespread debt default.

Just as fiat money can be created out of thin air through credit expansion, so it can also vanish into thin air through debt default. With fiat money in an environment of rising energy inputs, businesses and consumers could make outlays that spurred growth in the current period without first restraining their budgets to accumulate savings. (And not incidentally, just as economic growth spurred the hypertrophy of predatory government, so it opened an opportunity for bankers to appropriate a hefty increment of the growth.)

In other words, the spur to growth provided by the oil-powered economy created an almost irresistible inducement to revamp the monetary system. This resulted, almost inevitably, in a debt-ridden economy. Just as no one could have anticipated the impact that dense, portable BTUs from oil would have in goosing economic growth, so there is as yet little general appreciation of the impact that the slowdown in energy growth has had in depressing the progress of advanced economies. As a consequence, they are all overly indebted and increasingly crisis prone.

It is not unlikely that the slowdown in growth coincident with peak oil will eventually precipitate a move away from fiat money and back to a commodity-based system, but those are issues for another book.

Energy Surges Alter Spatial Configurations of Economies

Another important consequence of the fact that the United States pioneered the world oil industry, gaining rivers of oil at minimal cost, was to radically alter the spatial configuration of the U.S. economy. As Douglas W. Rae, Richard S. Ely Professor of Management and Professor of Political Science at the Yale School of Management, points out, a century ago,

> the United States was organized primarily around what now seem relatively limited powers of movement. . . . One could move with speed between fixed points such as rail stations, but one then entered a world of shoe leather, trolleys, and slow travel within local society. This made for a combination of good long-distance transportation over a fixed-path grid of terminals and weak local transport over variable paths to specific destinations.[32]

Although Rae's principal focus is on inequality in American life, like Sir Isaac Newton inventing calculus to solve a problem, Rae compiled an important history of energy in the American economy to advance his argument. His *A Short History of American Horsepower* highlights the dramatic surge of energy production in the United States from 8,495,000 hp in 1850 to 34.958 billion hp in 1990. Not only did total

---

[32] Douglas W. Rae, "Viacratic America: *Plessy* on Foot v. *Brown* on Wheels," *Annual Review of Political Science* 4 (June 2001): 417–438.

energy use expand by more than 4,000,000 percent but the huge increase also precipitated a revolution in the spatial configuration of the U.S. economy. Rae points out that "a very high fraction" (84 .4 percent) of total energy in the U.S. economy of 1850 was provided by totally stationary sources (mines, factories) or slow-moving sources (work animals).

Furthermore all of the "faster-paced power plants—aboard rail and steamship—were designed for fixed-path movement."[33] In other words, they operated only along pre-established routes with infrequent stops. A passenger in 1850 could not board a train or a steamship and expect it to take him wherever he wished to go. By 1890, total available energy had expanded fivefold to more than 44,000,000 hp. But a much greater percentage (47 percent) involved vehicular transport. Almost 17 million horsepower (16,980,000 hp) were devoted to powering railroads while another 1,124,000 hp were powering steamships. For each horsepower of rail service "available in 1850, 29 hp were available 40 years later." The total fast track rail network jumped from 9,021 miles in 1850 to 166,703 in 1890.[34]

Between 1890 and 1950, total horsepower in the U.S. economy expanded by more than a hundredfold—from 44,086,002 horsepower to 4,754,038,000. Rae describes this as "almost certainly the greatest run of energy expansion in the history of any society, industrial or otherwise (the full century following 1890 produced a 792:1 change).[35] Not only did economic growth in the United States during the century after 1890 consume unprecedented amounts of energy, the power that was generated was increasingly devoted to motion. In 1850, almost 85 percent of all horsepower was stationary. By 1890, power was still mostly stationary although 45 percent was devoted to motion. By 1950, 95.9 percent of horsepower was devoted to vehicular use. And 96.6 percent of vehicular horsepower was automotive. By 1990, vehicles still accounted for about 96 percent of total horsepower, with automobiles comprising 99 percent of that category. By 1993, cars in the United States traveled 1.624 trillion miles annually.

---

[33] Rae, "Viacratic America."
[34] Ibid.
[35] Ibid.

In a little more than a century, cars went from being nonexistent to accounting for 95 percent of the horsepower in the economy. In Rae's words,

> still more important is the fact that cars and other motor vehicles provide high-speed, variable-path transportation to every habitable nook and cranny of the 3.5 million miles^2 of land that constitute the United States. Except for arid wasteland, some mountains, and the most remote corners of our park system, you can go anywhere you like in a private automobile as long as you can afford the operating cost. This is a revolutionary fact, unparalleled in any previous era and unmatched in scale by any other national system. Running on nearly 4,000,000 miles of paved roads, automobile travel offers those who can afford it an utterly unprecedented form of power. . . .[36]

Compare that to what happened in Brazil. Brazil is 40,000 square miles larger than the 48 contiguous states of the U.S. mainland, and is said to have the world's fourth-largest road system. Brazil has only about 1,250,000 miles of roads, of which a little over 125,000 miles are paved but according to the Alaska Department of Transportation, there are about 4,900 miles of paved roads in Alaska.[37] That equates to about 1 mile of paved road per 119.67 square miles in Alaska. For the United States as a whole, including Alaska, there are 1.0759 miles of paved road per square mile of U.S. territory.

By contrast, Brazil has about 1 mile of paved road for every 26.4 square miles of territory. The overall Brazilian road network is only about one twenty-fifth as dense as that in the United States as a whole, while being 4.5 times as dense as that in Alaska. But for the purposes of comparison, allowance needs to be made for the fact that 1,930,510 square miles of Brazil is comprised of the Amazon wilderness, an area that has fewer paved roads per square mile than Alaska. The conclusions to be drawn are that all of the higher density of the U.S. road network is

---

[36] Rae, "Viacratic America."

[37] Answers.com, "How Many Miles of Paved Roads Are There in Alaska," http://wiki.answers.com/Q/How_many_miles_of_paved_roads_are_there_in_Alaska#ixzz1bbutZXTL.

attributable to the built-out of roads in the 48 mainland states, and the density of paved road in the portion of Brazil outside the Amazon is probably no lower than 1 mile per 12.5 miles. Given the comparative density of the road networks, and the larger U.S. population (at this writing, the U.S. population of 312 million is more than 50 percent larger than Brazil's population of 203 million), it is perhaps not surprising that total driving on U.S. roads, which peaked at 3.03 trillion miles in 2007, vastly exceeds miles driven in Brazil. The median Brazilian motorist, as of 2009 drove 12,983 kilometers annually (about 8,000 miles), or roughly half as much as the median driver in the United States.[38]

The much higher density of roads relative to surface area in the United States finds expression in an extraordinarily high number of motor vehicles per person in the United States—828 per 1,000 people as of 2009—compared to 249 per 1,000 people in Brazil in 2011. That is after the total number of Brazilian vehicles rose by 114 percent in a decade. A further expression of the U.S. legacy commitment to dispersion and mobility is the much higher U.S. oil consumption than that in Brazil—68,699 BBL/day per 1,000 people in the United States in 2007, as compared to 12,484 BBL/day per 1,000 people in Brazil in 2007. Brazilian per capita petroleum consumption, at just 18 percent of the U.S., reflects more than just parsimonious driving habits.

Part of Brazil's energy advantage is a greater endowment of solar power. As mentioned, Americans use more energy to heat their homes than Brazilians do for all purposes. But Brazil's advantages in energy use for mobility are also substantial. This is another crucial reason why Brazil is destined to prosper more than the United States during the coming decades. By and large, the warmer weather that prevails in most of Brazil precludes the need to devote energy to heating.

As a late developer, Brazil's transportation system relies much more than the United States on fixed-path movement over public

---

[38] "Média de veículos quebrados aumentou 26,8% nos últimos anos na cidade de São Paulo e a falta de manutenção é a principal causa do problema," www.carro100.com.br/site/imprensa/release_25.php.

transportation systems. This is exactly what you would expect from a system designed to reflect a higher cost of fuel. Indeed, the Brazilian model city of Curitiba, a metropolis of about 2.5 million people, has attracted worldwide attention for the remarkable efficiency and popularity of its transit system.

The Curitiba system was designed by the famous Brazilian architect, Jaime Lerner, who served as mayor of Curitiba three times and was twice elected governor of the state of Paraná. His Directo (Speedybus) service has earned worldwide acclaim. The Chinese, who are building new urban areas to house a population larger than the United States, have consulted Lerner for help in designing effective public transportation systems that enable riders to get where they want to go as rapidly as possible in an energy-efficient way.

In the words of public transportation expert Leroy W. Demery, Jr., "in the U.S., Curitiba has become the veritable poster child for 'bus rapid transit.'"[39] Demery reports of Curitiba's system: "The total number of passengers per work day was stated at 2,140,000."[40] Even though the area had 562,000 "registered motor vehicles," residents were inclined to use the well-organized and efficient Directo (Speedybus) service rather than drive their own cars. In 1991, Curitiba had an astonishing 230 revenue passengers annually per capita. In other words, the average person in Curitiba paid to use the bus 230 days a year rather than drive his car.

Demery attributes a good part of the success of Curitiba's public transit to the different spatial organization of the Brazilian economy: "In Brazil, the 'well-off' (high-income residents) have historically sought to live as close to the city center as possible, in order to be near the cathedral and other amenities. Employment and retailing have not been dispersed to suburban locations as in the U.S."[41] The Curitiba system would not work in the United States because we have already invested so much in dispersion that riders of public transit cannot be as efficiently

---

[39] Leroy W. Demery Jr., "Bus Rapid Transit in Curitiba, Brazil—An Information Summary," publictransit.us, Special Report No. 1, December 11, 2004, www.publictransit.us/ptlibrary/specialreports/sr1.curitibaBRT.pdf.

[40] Ibid.

[41] Ibid.

collected from hither and yon and rapidly delivered to their equally scattered destinations.

The spatial reconfiguration of the U.S. economy, precipitated by cheap energy that Rae documents, creates a challenging obstacle to future economic growth. Because Americans put early access to cheap oil to the service of mobility, we create a hostage to fortune when energy prices rise. The dispersal of the U.S. population into suburbs and satellite communities that made economic sense when gasoline cost $0.30 a gallon suggests that a costly and wrenching transition must accompany any attempt to refit the American economy to run on more expensive alternative energy.

Suburban home values were already reeling after 2008 in the wake of the subprime crisis. As suburban real estate values represent a substantial portion of the highly leveraged collateral of the U.S. banking system, they cannot be easily written off. Note, as reported in the *New York Times*, poverty in U.S. suburbs has surged by 53 percent. The Great Contraction accelerated this process as "two thirds of the new suburban poor were added from 2007 to 2010." As Edward Hill, dean of the Levin College of Urban Affairs at Cleveland State University, says in the article, "The whole political class is just getting the memo that Ozzie and Harriet don't live here anymore."[42]

In this respect, it is not a coincidence that total vehicle miles traveled in the United States peaked at 3.03 trillion miles in 2007, along with gasoline usage, just before the Great Correction began. You can expect growing numbers of suburban drivers to be priced off the roads as oil prices rise.

It is not easy for an economy as dispersed as that of the United States, over 3.5 million square miles to adjust when mobility is curtailed by high energy prices. For reasons spelled out previously and addressed elsewhere in this book, a country like Brazil can continue to prosper in the face of energy prices that will prove ruinous to the U.S. economy.

Seen in a longer-term perspective, the changes precipitated by the surge in energy from cheap oil made for an impermanent, crisis-prone prosperity in the United States and other so-called advanced economies.

---

[42] Sabrina Tavernise, "Outside Cleveland, Snapshots of Poverty's Surge in the Suburbs," *New York Times*, October 25, 2011, A1.

You are now living through the endgame of the rapid growth phase based on cheap oil. Coming chapters spell out reasons to believe that Brazil can continue to prosper in the face of steeply higher energy prices that will prove ruinous to the United States and other advanced economies.

As we look forward into the twenty-first century, the world is divided into important economies of two types:

1. *Heavily indebted advanced economies dependent on cheap oil that will grow slowly or not at all.* These countries, the United States foremost among them, face dim prospects. For generations, U.S. leaders have compounded shortsightedness with extravagance. The United States and other leading economies have run down their sovereign balance sheets because they were rich enough to get away with it for prolonged periods. You can expect that political leaders in the United States, Europe, and Japan will continue to spend trillions out of empty pockets, while creating more trillions out of thin air in a vain attempt to circumvent the fact that declining oil availability, reflected in higher oil prices, tends to lead to economic stagnation or contraction.

   In other words, the legacy systems because of their very large amounts of built infrastructure will show declining marginal returns. The slowdown of growth will inevitably precipitate sporadic debt crises.

2. *Developing economies with growing energy inputs that have the potential to grow further.* In the case of a country like Brazil, among the great advantages it enjoys is a surplus of energy combined with a low level of debt, partly because for most of the past century Brazil was a little-respected underdeveloped country whose leaders commanded such scant confidence that they long ago ceased being able to get away with chronic, runaway deficits.

As we will continue to dissect, the reason that Brazil has a low debt today is that it received its natural blessings in an encrypted package that could not easily be opened and squandered. They couldn't even be easily hypothecated as collateral. During the whole of the twentieth century, the price level in Brazil increased by at least a quadrillionfold. By contrast, the U.S. dollar has only lost 96 percent of its value over the past century. Brazilians long ago learned the lessons that loom painfully ahead for the United States of America.

The United States has been on a multidecade binge of borrowing from China, Japan, OPEC, Brazil, and others so that it could fund one of the worst malinvestments ever—pouring more and more billions into housing. The typical American's home has doubled in size since 1970. But a big house doesn't mean that Americans are any wealthier. The new McMansion has now plunged in value, causing Americans to lose an aggregate of $7 trillion. Our assets have shriveled, but net liabilities have grown. And large numbers of homes sit empty. According to the U.S. Census Bureau, nearly one home in five in Florida sits vacant.[43]

Our modern financial system is dependent on perpetual growth. As long as the economy grows at a threshold rate, servicing the debt isn't a problem. But if the growth of the economy slows below the threshold rate (which rises as indebtedness rises), much less goes negative, debts go into default, and prosperity recedes.

The problem is that perpetual growth requires perpetually expanding energy and the current "Great Contraction" reflects the financial strains accompanying a peaking of oil output on a global basis circa 2005. The result to be expected is the end to prosperity in the United States and other advanced economies and a new phase of economic history where previously underdeveloped countries, Brazil being a prominent example, will enjoy greater prosperity because of their greater potential to expand energy use, and for other reasons we explore in coming chapters.

While some would claim that it is desirable and possible to decouple the compounding of living standards from energy growth, the evidence suggests otherwise. It appears that a decline in energy supply causes a slowdown or actual decline in economic growth, along with a deflationary contraction in credit. Chapter 4 details this symbiotic relationship of energy density to economic prosperity.

---

[43] "Nearly 20% of Florida Homes Are Vacant," CNNMoney, March 18, 2011, http://money.cnn.com/2011/03/18/real_estate/florida_vacant_homes/index.htm.

Chapter 4

Prosperity and Energy Density

The Hidden Role of BTUs in the Rise and Fall of Economies

The hope is that the discoveries will provide a nation already rich in renewable energy with an embarrassment of resources with which to pursue the goal of becoming a U.S. of the South.

— Joe Leahy in the *Financial Times,* March 16, 2011,
commenting on the growth of oil in Brazil

O ne of the fond fantasies of alternative energy advocates is the conceit that oil is unnecessary to prosperity. The economy could be fueled entirely by renewable sources, they say. This conceit found its most extreme expression to date in a cover story in the November 2009 issue of *Scientific American*. Mark Z. Jacobson, professor of civil and environmental engineering at Stanford, and Mark A. Delucchi, laid out a scheme to supply all the world's energy needs entirely from solar, wind, and water.

Their plan would require the installation of 3.8 million giant wind turbines of 5 MW capacity each, plus plastering at least 500,000 square kilometers (an area larger than California) with billions of photovoltaic cells. Note the complicating footnotes. To build 3.8 million giant wind turbines means completing 520 every day for 20 years. (When we are talking "Giant wind turbines," that is "Giant" with a capital "G," as the turbines would have blades 100 meters across—roughly the length of a football field.) Jacobson and Delucchi acknowledge that their plan would cost at least $100 trillion. Critics contend that it would cost twice that amount.[1] This would mean a cost of $333,000 per American or $1.333 million per family of four. Even spread over 20 years that figures out to $66,000 per year per family to replace our current energy system. With prosperity already collapsing, it is hard to conceive how Americans, whose median household income in 2010 was $46,326, would be able to afford an additional $66,000 per year for energy. Not since Jonathan Swift's imagined account of research at the Grand Academy of Lagado, has anyone proposed so ambitious a plan for extracting "sunbeams from cucumbers."

The difficulties with Jacobson and Delucchi's plans to secure each American citizen's future energy needs with renewable sources are many. Chief among them is the minor detail that they ignore the importance of energy density to prosperity. The likely consequence of a great decline in the density of BTU sources is economic collapse.

Denser Energy Equals a Rise in Prosperity

The history of economic progress is synonymous with the employment of denser energy sources. It is a little appreciated fact that there was scarcely any economic growth through most of human experience. If you think about it, the energy sources employed in the ancient economy and throughout history prior to the Industrial Revolution were mostly of the kind proposed by Professor Jacobson. A sailing ship was a

---

[1] See Kevin Trenberth, "Comparing the Interstate Highway System to *Scientific American's* 'A Path to Sustainable Energy by 2030,' " ClimateSanity, November 14, 2009, http://climatesanity.wordpress.com/2009/11/14/comparing-the-interstate -highway-system-to-scientific-americans-a-path-to-sustainable-energy-by-2030/.

device for leveraging the energy of wind and water to move people and goods. From the Roman period forward, windmills and water wheels powered machinery to crush grain, pump water, tan leather, work iron, saw wood, and carry out a variety of other early industrial processes. As productivity increased, dependence on human and animal muscle power gradually declined, and locations with good waterpower resources became centers of economic and industrial activity.

Green energy advocates like Jacobson and Delucchi gloss over a fact that is unfortunately too well supported by the historic record. Whatever prosperity was ever attained with such low density, renewable energies proved virtually impossible to compound. Then as now, wind and water power were too variable, site-specific, and unpredictable to be adopted everywhere and leveraged into broadly higher living standards.

Yes, water wheels in the right locations provided the energy to mill grain and thus improve local productivity. Windmills were used to power pumps and sometimes adapted for other mechanical applications. Still, these applications were limited. Prosperity was mostly determined by the weather. The extra bounty that came with good weather and bumper crops enabled people to live better lives. Good weather meant more food. Poor weather meant hard times and hunger. People lived from hand to mouth with minimal savings and almost no margin for error. Economic growth from year to year and generation to generation was negligible. The Pilgrims who led the settlement of America lived less well than the Romans had during the heyday of their Empire, because the weather was better in the first century A.D. than it was in the seventeenth century.

The first and crucial departure from the record of stagnation from generation to generation occurred with the advent of the Industrial Revolution in Great Britain in the second half of the eighteenth century. What happened to make this possible? Put simply, it was more intense use of a higher density fuel—coal.

Coal and Adam Smith

Historians sometimes analyze the intellectual antecedents of Adam Smith whose *Wealth of Nations* became the masterpiece of economic growth. Their speculations sometimes run far afield. For example, Leslie Young argued that "Adam Smith's famous doctrine of the Invisible Hand . . . was anticipated by the great Han Dynasty historian Sima Qian," further claiming that "[Smith's] concept of 'natural order' was imported from China."[2] Mohammad Siddiqi claims that "Ibn Khaldun anticipated Adam Smith on several points."[3]

Adam Smith's role a prophet of abundance may indeed mirror or rediscover the views of ancient scholars like Sima Qian or Ibn Khaldun. But I suspect that one of Adam Smith's most important antecedents was not an analyst, but a man of action, Sir George Bruce of Carnock, Culross, Scotland. It was he who opened the first industrial coal mine in the UK under the sea on the Firth of Forth. Sir George's innovative mining techniques were later exploited to fuel the Industrial Revolution. By the mid-eighteenth century, just as Adam Smith was coming of age, significant amounts of coal were being mined in England and Scotland. By the time that Smith published *The Wealth of Nations*, in 1776, annual output of coal in Britain was approximately 6.25 million long tons, or about as much as was produced in Britain every eight days in the time of peak coal there before World War I. "[England's] output of coal grew roughly six-fold between 1750 and 1830," according to Dr. Michael Flinn, one-time president of the Economic History Society of Great Britain.[4]

Before the surge of coal production combined with James Watt's steam engine to power the Industrial Revolution, there was little prosperity or economic growth to analyze. Adam Smith became the prophet of abundance in describing the free market only because the higher BTU density of coal permitted the growth of prosperity. Note that the BTU content of seasoned wood (dried for two years) is 6,050 per pound. That assumes 25 percent water content. Newly cut wood has water content of 50 percent reducing its number of available

[2] Leslie Young, "The Tao of Markets: Sima Qian and the Invisible Hand," *Pacific Economic Review* 1, 137–145.

[3] Mohammad Nejatullah Siddiqi, *Muslim Economic Thinking: A Survey of Contemporary Literature* (Leicester: The Islamic Foundation, 1981),

[4] Gerald Turnbull, "Canals, Coal and Regional Growth during the Industrial Revolution," *Economic History Review*, n.s., 40, no. 4 (November 1987): 537–560.

BTUs to 3,230 per pound. By contrast, anthracite coal has 12,000 BTU per pound. The energy density of coal is up to 400 percent higher than that of wood.

Yes, free markets are beneficial for eking out as much prosperity as possible in a world of scarcity. But the advantages of free markets and free trade over the old-fashioned mercantilist system would have been much less evident in the absence of a high-density fuel to power the Industrial Revolution.

Peak wood helped to precipitate the Industrial Revolution by doubling the price of a million BTUs from 6 grams of silver to 12 grams of silver. Peak wood was partly caused by a slowdown in forest growth due to the Little Ice Age conditions during the Maunder Minimum of low solar output in the late seventeenth and early eighteenth centuries. As wood supplies dwindled, manufacturers could not find enough wood to produce wrought iron. Wood historian John Perlin wrote in "Peak Wood Forges an Industrial Revolution,"

> The problem had nothing to do with a deficiency of ore. "In that respect," an anonymous pamphleteer of the period observed, "nature has been very liberal." But, he added, "for lack of wood and charcoal they are not being worked."[5]

In 1750, English ironworks produced 19,000 tons of metal annually. By 1850 that production had skyrocketed to 250,000 tons. In comparison, coal production rose from 5,000,000 tons in 1750 to 10,000,000 tons just 50 years later.

Another factor facilitating the growth of prosperity in eighteenth-century Britain was the improvement of transportation—an integral factor in improving the energy return on energy invested. A big step forward was the development of canals by the Duke of Bridgewater, who owned coal mines in Lancashire and built a canal to move his coal to the large market town of Manchester six miles away. Investing the then considerable sum of more than 25,000 pounds, the duke built the canal over two years. It was completed in 1761 with a series of tunnels

---

[5] John Perlin, "Peak Wood Forges an Industrial Revolution," Miller-McCune, April 19, 2010, www.miller-mccune.com/science-environment/peak-wood -forges-an-industrial-revolution-14608/.

linked directly to the coal mines. The canal greatly reduced the cost of transporting coal to Manchester, precipitating a plunge in the price of coal. As the price of coal fell, more coal was employed, lowering the cost per BTU of energy. The Duke's canal to Manchester set off a canal boom in England. By 1830, England had 3,875 miles of navigable waterways.

Economic historians such as Kenneth Pomeranz and Robert Allen say you can credit coal as the main impetus for the transformation of the English economy in the Industrial Revolution. The results were far-reaching. In the words of Nobel Prize winner Robert E. Lucas Jr., "For the first time in history, the living standards of the masses of ordinary people have begun to undergo sustained growth. . . . Nothing remotely like this economic behavior has happened before."[6]

Going Forward or Backward?

Jacobson and Delucchi are trying to answer the wrong question. The right question is not whether the total energy throughput of the current system could be mimicked with renewable sources without respect to cost. The right question is how can the energy density so crucial to prosperity be maintained at an affordable cost per BTU?

If you triple or quadruple the cost per BTU of energy consumed, you would soon reverse much of the progress in living standards achieved since the eighteenth century. Before you knew it, horses would reappear in the streets. And, of course, the situation would not have to regress that far to have ruinous consequences. A collapse in the return in BTUs per energy dollar expended would be the coup de grace to the teetering prosperity of the United States.

I am afraid that Americans are ill-suited to rebuild prosperity from the bottom up without the benefit of a free ride from a bountiful nature. Residents of the United States have had it easy for so long that we have become a little too soft to meet the rigors of an energy-light life.

Yes, there are other energy sources than cheap oil (upon which American prosperity has been largely based over the past century).

---

[6] Robert E. Lucas Jr., *Lectures on Economic Growth* (Cambridge, MA: Harvard University Press, 2002), 109–110.

Yes, of course, in an extreme circumstance, you could burn your furniture for fuel as many European families did in World War II. But where would you sit down to sup after you broke up the dining room table for kindling?

It should go without saying that you would rather employ affordable, dense energy that permits you to enjoy a high standard of living.

The importance of oil has been that it provides energy dense BTUs in a cheap, easily portable form. The prosperity of societies is not a matter of total energy throughput used, but a function of the energy return on energy invested. Put another way, prosperity emerged as the return on investment in energy rose.

The Phases of Extracting Energy

More than we commonly realize, the rise of the United States to the forefront of the world economy is a multiphase tale based on the exploitation of advantages in extraction of readily available cheap energy.

Phase One: An Abundance of Wood

In the first phase, English settlers in North America exploited the thick woods that stretched from the Atlantic seaboard far inland. Areas like Ohio and Indiana, that today are largely open farmland, were almost impenetrable forest when settlers first arrived. Ohio was said to have presented "the grandest unbroken forest of 41,000 square miles that was ever beheld."[7]

Much of the surge in prosperity that we tend to credit to the intelligence and hard work of America's intrepid pioneers was really a gift of nature.

Through the eighteenth and early nineteenth centuries Americans enjoyed an advantage relative to Europeans because we could employ plentiful, cheap wood in building our economy. John Perlin explains,

---

[7] John Perlin, "Peak Wood: Nature Does Impose Limits," Miller-McCune, June 1, 2010, www.miller-mccune.com/environment/peak-wood-nature-does-impose-limits-16596/.

Cheap lumber and cheap fuel extracted from these forests made possible America's development from the Revolution to the Civil War into a powerful and prosperous nation. Such growth, though, took a terrible toll on the woodlands. By 1877, one observer reported in *The Popular Science Monthly* that "the states of Ohio and Indiana . . . so recently a part of the great East-American forest, have even now a greater percentage of treeless area" than portions of Europe settled and cultivated for thousands of years.[8]

Phase Two: An Abundance of Coal

The United States was doubly blessed with a large endowment of readily exploitable coal that became seamlessly available to fuel further and more rapid economic growth when the East-American forests had mostly been chopped to the ground. The smooth transition from wood to coal was another blessing from nature. The United States not only had a large endowment of virgin forest, it also sported large coal deposits that were rapidly exploited. U.S. coal production grew logarithmically at a steady 6.6 percent per year from 1850 to 1910. Then the growth leveled off.

The famous oil geologist M. King Hubbert, originator of the peak oil hypothesis, actually formulated his oil forecast by studying coal output in the United States. Believing that no finite resource could support long-term exponential growth, he projected that the production rate plotted versus time would result in a bell-shaped curve that would drop as sharply as it had risen. Production would eventually have to peak, and then decline, until the resource had been exhausted. Hubbert based this peak oil prediction on his observations of U.S. coal production. More on that later.

Before oil production could peak, it first had to begin.

Phase Three: The Original Petroleum Industry

The third phase of the extraordinary natural blessing the United States enjoyed where energy is concerned began in 1859 when Colonel

---

[8] Perlin, "Peak Wood: Nature Does Impose Limits."

Edwin Drake discovered light sweet crude oil in a small northwestern Pennsylvania lumber town, Titusville. There were 16 lumber mills operating in Titusville when Colonel Drake arrived. They were soon eclipsed as the stars of the Titusville economy.

Drake's first well pumped only 45 barrels a day, but it was the beginning of the petroleum industry in the world. Titusville experienced a tremendous surge of prosperity as its population multiplied 40 times over. More oil was soon discovered. Within a few years, Titusville boasted the greatest density of millionaires per capita of any incorporated town on earth.

From that day in the summer of 1859 when Colonel Drake's first well began to pump until 1971, U.S. production of light sweet crude continued to increase. So did U.S. prosperity. As the first nation to exploit petroleum, the United States soon became the leader of the world economy. Great Britain, the country that had led the Industrial Revolution lost its leading role in the carnage of World War I that began just one year after British coal production peaked in 1913.

Of course, if you recall your high school history, you may suppose that the proximate cause of World War I was the assassination of the Archduke Franz Ferdinand in Sarajevo by Gavrilo Princip on June 28, 1914. Dig more closely into history's footnotes, and you will find references to the role played by Serbian Military Intelligence, particularly Dragutin Dimitrijević. The assassination was undoubtedly an aggressive act of state terrorism, as the Austrian authorities suspected.

Still, I have a hard time crediting the thesis that a war that practically destroyed European civilization and killed 16 million people while wounding 21 million others was really fought over nothing other than the murder of one prominent man. I believe something deeper was involved in setting the conditions for a conflagration.

The Shift from Coal to Oil and World War I

The advent of peak coal in Great Britain, along with the ensuing desperate scramble for oil fields between Britain and Germany, was a more fundamental cause of World War I than the assassination of the Archduke Ferdinand. Political assassinations have occurred at other times and places without triggering global war. But rarely do dominant global powers find themselves in a major transition of energy sources.

The transition by the Royal Navy from coal to oil, instituted by First Lord of the Admiralty Winston Churchill and Admiral Sir John (Jacky) Fisher, was informed primarily by technical rather than geopolitical considerations. There were practical, military advantages of powering ships of the Royal Navy with oil that mirrored its advantages in the civilian realm. As Churchill put it, "The ordeal of coaling [a] ship exhausted the whole ship's company. In wartime it robbed them of their brief period of rest; it subjected everyone to extreme discomfort."

Admiral Fisher was an early, vocal advocate of converting the British navy to oil power. Consider this from 1902: "It is a gospel fact . . . that a fleet with oil fuel will have an overwhelming strategic advantage over a coal fleet."[9]

Fisher saw the advantages of oil's energy density, which drove the conversion from coal to oil. Even if the technology had been available, there would have been no question of covering super-dreadnaughts with photovoltaic cells, or harnessing thousands of watts of wind power by deploying sails to propel the Royal Navy.), Upon seeing a new Russian ship that only burned oil, Fisher exclaimed, "at one stroke, oil fuel settles half our manning difficulties! We should require 50 percent less stokers."[10] This not only meant lighter ships, but also critical personnel savings, as oil-powered ships could operate with fewer trained sailors. As naval warfare analyst Erik J. Dahl wrote:

> Oil offered many benefits. It had double the thermal content of coal so that boilers could be smaller and ships could travel twice as far. . . . Oil burned with less smoke, so the fleet would not reveal its presence as quickly. Oil could be stored in tanks anywhere allowing more efficient design of ships, and it could be transferred through pipes without reliance on stokers,

---

[9] Erik J. Dahl, "Naval Innovation: From Coal to Oil," *Joint Force Quarterly* (Winter 2000–2001): 50. Available at www.dtic.mil/doctrine/jel/jfq_pubs/1327.pdf/.
[10] Ibid.

reducing manning. Refueling at sea was feasible, which provided greater flexibility.[11]

A pound of bunker oil contained 23,000 BTUs as compared to 12,000 BTUs in a pound of anthracite coal. Because the fuel aboard weighed less, greater speed was possible. Again, quoting Dahl,

> In 1912, Fisher wrote to Churchill, "What you do want is the super-swift—all oil—and don't fiddle about armour; it really is so very silly! There is only one defence and that is speed!"
>
> The war college was asked how much speed a fast division would need to outmaneuver the German fleet. The answer was 25 knots, or at least four knots faster than possible at the time. Churchill concluded, "We could not get the power required to drive these ships at 25 knots except by the use of oil fuel." This was enough for him.
>
> Queen Elizabeth-class Super Dreadnought battleships were built to burn oil only. Once this decision was made, Churchill wrote, "it followed that the rest of the Royal Navy would turn to oil."[12]

In other words, the decision to convert to oil propulsion had a sound technological and military rationale, especially when oil was cheap. There was just one fateful drawback. Even after peak coal production was reached, Great Britain still had ample coal supplies, but on the eve of World War I, virtually no domestic oil was known in the UK. BP did not discover the first commercial quantities of oil in Britain until 1939 at Eakring, Nottinghamshire.

A crucial reason why Britain faded as a world power is that it lacked oil. When the evolution of technology created unequivocal military advantages in shifting to a more energy-dense fuel, the UK could ante up the money for oil-powered capital ships. But unlike the United States in the early twentieth century, Britain had no oil of its own. Britain then was dependent on foreign oil, as the United States is today. The lack of ready access to cheap oil in the United Kingdom inevitably

---

[11] Dahl, "Naval Innovation: From Coal to Oil," 50.
[12] Ibid., 50.

informed geopolitical maneuvering to secure oil fields elsewhere. Hence, World War I.

The British deficit in oil also retarded economic growth. As World War I was ruinously expensive, it cost Great Britain the greater part of its gold reserves and its overseas foreign assets. Thereafter, the British economy operated within the straitjacket of its export earnings. Unlike the recent situation in which the United States has borrowed trillions to fund imports of foreign oil, there was no group of creditors standing by to fund a yawning British deficit in petroleum trade. Consequently, the British economy employed oil more sparingly than did the United States.

In particular, the UK failed to share in the rapid development of suburbs that resulted from motorization. The early adoption of automobiles and trucks powered the U.S. economy to an average annual growth of 4.2 percent in the 1920s.[13] Greater use of automobiles in the United States was also linked to the adoption of assembly lines and higher incomes for blue-collar workers, as well as to greater vitality of ancillary industries like home appliances and furniture, where sales were stimulated by the growth of the new housing in the suburbs and satellite communities. Suburban building booms, of course, were second-order effects of the growth of auto traffic over paved roads.

Notwithstanding the steep plunge in U.S. economic activity during the Great Depression, auto ownership was more than 400 percent higher in the United States in 1939 than in the UK. Almost 23 percent of Americans owned cars while only 5.4 percent of the British population drove.

A graph of rising U.S. per capita income directly traces the graph of rising U.S. domestic oil output. By 1950, petroleum had become the primary source of energy consumed in the United States. At that time, the United States accounted for 52 percent of world oil production. But the first shadows appeared on the energy-dense prosperity of the United States in 1956. In that year, M. King Hubbert, then working for Shell Oil, interpolated a frightening conclusion from coal production data.

---

[13] United States Census, *Historical Statistics of the United States: Colonial Times to 1970*, 1976.

Hubbert accurately predicted that U.S. oil production would peak about 15 years later.

This logistics model now known as the Hubbert Theory described with fair accuracy the progression to the peak and then decline of production from individual oil wells, oil fields, regions, and countries (and now, the entire planet). Hubbert foresaw the inflexion and tailing off of cheap domestic oil in the early 1970s. He was right.

Peak Oil and Declining Money

It is no coincidence that 1971, the year of peak domestic U.S. oil production was also the year when the United States started its descent into the thrall of debtism. In 1971, the old America went broke. Richard Nixon repudiated the gold reserve system, and put the United States on the road to becoming the greatest debtor nation in the history of the world.

Capitalism in the United States, as defined by the accumulation of capital in an economy based upon savings, came to an end when cheap domestic oil production tailed off. Our current debtist system is one that substitutes debt for capital at the center of its economy. The current depression is a direct consequence of the failed attempt to substitute global debt for cheap domestic BTUs as a recipe for sustaining prosperity. Put simply, it didn't work. Governments can print money. But no one can print BTUs.

The United States did manage to continue increasing its aggregate consumption of energy-dense oil, as population increased, with total domestic demand peaking at 21 million barrels a day—at the time the subprime housing boom peaked. But strangely enough, the per capita consumption of BTUs in the United States stabilized at 1970s levels, and has remained remarkably consistent since then, even as real per capita income has stagnated.

As long as light sweet crude was available somewhere for purchase with easily manufactured dollars, we could forestall a collapse in energy density and continue to pretend that the United States was prospering. Note, however, that the money we created out of thin air was not just cranked off a printing press; it was borrowed into existence through a fractional reserve banking system that created liabilities to be repaid, along with the credits on the ledger. The accumulated bills for years of living beyond our means in energy terms are still to be paid.

Declining Energy and Systemic Collapse

In his groundbreaking study, *The Collapse of Complex Societies*, Joseph A. Tainter argues that

> The best key to continued socioeconomic growth, and to avoiding or circumventing (or at least financing) declines in marginal productivity, is to obtain a new energy subsidy when it becomes apparent that marginal productivity is beginning to drop.[14]

Europeans reacted to the stress of falling, passive solar energy during the Little Ice Age to obtain new sources of energy in two ways:

1. They followed the traditional path for economic systems "activated largely by agriculture, livestock, and human labor (and ultimately by solar energy), this was accomplished by territorial expansion."[15] Europeans acquired energy subsidies through colonies in the Americas, Africa, and Asia.
2. The novel path the Europeans, and particularly the British, pioneered in the wake of the Little Ice Age was the adoption of energy-dense coal to power the Industrial Revolution. As Leslie White observed, the increased energy harvested in an industrial system permitted a huge margin above a system activated primarily by human energy. White estimated that a system powered by human energy alone could generate only about one-twentieth hp per capita annually. By contrast, industrial systems powered by hydrocarbon energy could generate horsepower per capita per year many magnitudes higher.[16]

---

[14] Joseph A. Tainter, *The Collapse of Complex Societies* (Cambridge, UK: Cambridge University Press, 1988), 124.

[15] Ibid., 214.

[16] Leslie A. White, *The Science of Culture* (New York: Farrar, Straus and Giroux, 1949).

Indeed, hydrocarbon energy put tens of thousands of times more annual energy per capita into the economy. That surge of incremental energy in the European system after the introduction of coal explains the previously unprecedented growth in living standards after 1750.

As higher-density energy came into use, economic growth accelerated. The Industrial Revolution raised living standards for average people as never before. peak coal at the eve of World War I precipitated a scramble for a still-higher-density energy source: oil. This broke the peace and shattered the nineteenth-century free trade system.

Now we face another crisis associated with an energy peak—peak oil. Unfortunately, there is no obvious, higher-density fuel in reserve to be exploited to forestall a collapse of complex societies already suffering from declining marginal returns in many areas. As Tainter concludes,

> a new energy subsidy is necessary if a declining standard of living in a future global collapse are to be averted. A more abundant form of energy might not reverse the declining marginal return on investment in complexity, but it would make it more possible to finance that investment.[17]

Unfortunately, the result to be expected is the collapse of the advanced economies, the United States included.

Notwithstanding a drastic 469 percent increase in the real price of BTUs, since 1945 (calculated in terms of the annual average inflation-adjusted price of oil), so-called alternative energy continues to provide no more than a trivial contribution to meeting the world's need for power. For example, as of July 2011, solar power produced only 661,339 billion BTUs, or 0.002 percent of total world production of 267,757, 600 billion BTUs. Wind power produced 0.012 percent while geothermal accounted for just 0.0007 percent.

This implies that a Malthusian resource panic lies ahead as countries scramble to reserve as much precious hydrocarbon fuels, especially as much petroleum for themselves as they can secure. Therefore, a reasonable basis for forecasting the future prosperity of different economies

---

[17] Tainter, *Collapse of Complex Societies*, 215.

is their relative capacity to sustain or even expand their current energy use. For reasons I spell out in greater detail in Chapter 10, Brazil has more capacity than most other economies to increase energy inputs per capita in a way that increases the return on energy invested.

Equally, the United States is ill-suited to effect a seamless transition to alternative sources of energy. For one thing, the United States lacks many of Brazil's natural advantages. For another, the spatial organization of the U.S. economy is dependent upon cheap oil. In addition to other risks, the United States faces strategic vulnerability as well as economic vulnerability. Among the many systems facing declining marginal returns for the United States is its military establishment, which costs as much as all the rest of the world's armies combined. It is not immaterial that the U.S. military alone consumes 300,000 barrels of oil daily—more oil on a daily basis than three-quarters of the world's countries.[18] Brazil has one of the world's largest standing militaries, with 2.5 million men under arms. But annual security outlays at $28 billion in 2010 comprised only three percent of U.S. annual security spending of $929 billion.

The Real Symptoms of Peak Oil

I am persuaded that a not insignificant cause of the decline in the fortunes of the British economy after the advent of peak coal on the eve of World War I was the lack of access to higher energy-density oil in the United Kingdom. Similarly, as we look forward to growing global supply constriction associated with peak oil it is obvious that the U.S. economy will be especially challenged. Gail Tverberg, an editor of *The Oil Drum*, points out that slow growth or no growth in the availability of BTUs to the U.S. economy will be manifested as debt distress and recession. She writes,

> Let me tell you what I think the symptoms of the arrival of peak oil are:
>
> **1.** Higher default rates on loans
> **2.** Recession

---

[18] Phyllis Cuttino, "Military Going Green to Save Lives, Money," CNN.com, September 22, 2011, www.cnn.com/2011/09/22/opinion/cuttino-military-green/index.html.

Furthermore, I expect that as the supply of oil declines over time, these symptoms will get worse and worse—even though people may call the cause of the decline in oil use "Peak Demand" rather than "Peak Supply."[19]

Tverberg shrewdly points out that many aspects of dysfunction in the current economy are disguised symptoms of more expensive energy. She writes,

Cheap energy keeps our cars and factories running. It leaves homeowners with money to repay their mortgages, and permits the long-distance transfer of goods needed for globalization. . . . When economies of countries are able to grow rapidly, they can repay their debt with interest. But as growth wanes, it becomes much more difficult to repay debt, and many more defaults occur. Our debt-based financial system needs growth to continue. It is not a Ponzi scheme, but it has the same problem with not being sustainable without growth.[20]

Tverberg argues persuasively that the collapse in the U.S. housing bubble and the subsequent recession were disguised indicators of peak oil. Equally, you can expect this to be reflected in geopolitical terms in maneuvering between the world's two largest energy consumers, China and the United States.

I think it is entirely credible that the Chinese may choose, at some not-too-distant moment, to strategically deploy their financial clout to deflate the U.S. government debt bubble that Bernanke, Obama, and other U.S. authorities have labored so assiduously to inflate.

Quantitative easing or counterfeiting of trillions of dollars out of thin air is a recipe for forcing quantitative tightening in rapidly growing emerging economies like China's. You should not be surprised if it turns out that Bernanke and Obama have outsmarted themselves with monetary inflation. By lighting the fuse that set the world on fire, at a time when

---

[19] Gail Tverberg, "Peak Oil: Looking for the Wrong Symptoms?" Next Generation O&G, Editor's Blog, February 16, 2010, www.ngoilgas.com/editors-blog/peak-oil -symptoms.
[20] Gail Tverberg, "Where we are headed: Peak oil and the financial crisis," The Oil Drum, March 25, 2009, www.theoildrum.com/node/5230.

we had already traded far up the scale of vulnerability, they may have brought nearer the day when we will feel a blast of cold water in the face.

The United States has made itself hostage to fortune by becoming the most deeply indebted nation in history. You cannot indenture yourself to someone else and expect your creditor to always act with your convenience in mind. With your and my financial well-being closely tied to the prosperity of the United States, we probably are prejudiced to suppose "what is good for the United States is good for the world economy."

The Competition for Prosperity

As we went on our merry way using as much of the world's available cheap oil as we could borrow the money to buy, something else happened. Emerging economies like China, India, Brazil, Turkey, South Korea, and Mexico began to develop. People in those previously retarded economies started making money. As they did, they found something unsurprising. They preferred driving automobiles rather than riding bicycles and burros or just walking. Today, China has replaced the United States as the world's largest auto market. Brazil has replaced Germany as the world's fourth-largest auto market.

The growth of auto use in emerging economies implies skyrocketing oil use and skyrocketing prices. "From now to 2020, world oil consumption will rise by about 60 percent. Transportation will be the fastest growing oil-consuming sector. By 2025, the number of cars will increase to well over 1.25 billion from approximately 700 million today."[21] Not only does this imply a lot of traffic jams and time lost looking for a parking space, it also prefigures runaway oil prices and thus multiplying solvency stresses.

You're looking down the road toward gasoline prices of $8.00 to $10.00 per gallon. Global consumption of gasoline could double while yours may fall dramatically.

The two countries with the highest rate of growth in oil use are China and India, whose combined populations account for a third of

---

[21] "The Future of Oil," Institute for the Analysis of Global Security, February 25, 2002, www.iags.org/futureofoil.html.

humanity. In the next two decades, China's oil consumption is expected to grow at a rate of 7.5 percent per year and India's at 5.5 percent. (Compare to a 1 percent growth for the industrialized countries, or more probably, declining consumption.)

Dramatically augmented demand in developing economies against a backdrop of dwindling production from the world's heritage oil fields spells higher prices. As Hubbert explained half a century ago, the first oil that was found was the cheapest and easiest to produce. As of 2010 the annual depletion rate of those cheap oil fields was about 4 million barrels per day of production. That implies that by 2014, there would be 20 million fewer barrels of oil production per day to satisfy the surging world demand.

Expensive Oil Remains

Many quibbles have been advanced to challenge the theory of peak oil. Mostly, these relate to the question of whether the world is truly running out of oil. Almost certainly those who argue that oil will not run out are correct. But this is a misleading truth.

What is happening is that the world is running out of the type of oil that fueled the prosperity of North America at a price that people could afford. Light sweet crude, by far the most desirable form of oil as it flows easily and can be readily refined into gasoline, appears to be rapidly depleting. The most famous varieties of light sweet crude including West Texas intermediate, Brent oil from the North Sea, and Saudi Light Crude are being used up.

According to OPEC figures, annual output of light sweet crude dropped by 2.6 million barrels per day from 2000 to 2004. While the OPEC figures are somewhat suspect because they don't completely integrate across the total production curve, it is incontrovertible that lighter, more desirable varieties of crude oil have been replaced with heavier, more sulfurous oil: hence, Saudi Arabia's persistent suggestion that the world's problem with oil was not a lack of oil per se, but a lack of refining capacity for heavy oil.

So at the very least we see the depletion of light sweet crude and its replacement with heavy sour crude or synthetic oil such as that from the Alberta tar sands, which is extremely expensive to produce.

The original Saudi Light oil discovered at Dhahran in 1938 was wildly profitable to pump, with oil at three dollars a barrel. The Saudi production cost was just $0.19 a barrel, plus $0.21 royalty, as late as 1947.[22] When oil was discovered in Texas at Spindle Top, it sold for just three cents a barrel early in the past century. Today, the synthetic oil from tar sands costs $70 a barrel to produce. Perhaps more. At higher prices, it will be profitable to extract increasing volumes of synthetic oil from various tar sands and from deposits deep beneath the sea.

A hint of things to come was registered in 2005, when Saudi Arabia entered into three-year contracts with Rowan for five jack-up rigs for offshore wells, all of which were bid away from work in the Gulf of Mexico. Given that offshore drilling is both one of the most costly and slowest ways to develop oil, the fact that the Saudis were ready five years ago to pay premium prices to secure jack-up rigs strongly implies that they have run out of cheap sources of oil to drill out on land.

There are 300 billion barrels of difficult-to-extract oil in Athabasca tar sands in Alberta and untold more billions of barrels in shale deposits in the American West. There are many more billions of barrels under the ocean off the coast of Brazil.

It is true that there is oil in the world. The problem is that much of the oil that remains will be priced so high that you can't afford to use it.

When oil costs $200 a barrel, as it will soon, whether Saudi Arabia, Kuwait, and Venezuela follow Libya and Egypt into chaos, gasoline will cost at least $7.00 per gallon. How much driving will you be doing under those conditions? You may not choose to completely scrap your car at those prices, but others will. They will have no choice. The average American drives about 15,000 miles a year. You have to assume that this is not merely joyriding. When gasoline costs $7.00, much less $10.00 per gallon, the part-time jobs to which many Americans commute will no longer pay the tariff entailed in traveling to and fro. Whole suburbs and neighborhoods will go off-line.

---

[22] Richard Cowen, "Chapter 13: OPEC and Crude Oil," http://mygeologypage .ucdavis.edu/cowen/~gel115/115ch13oil.html.

A 665,000 Percent Increase in the Price of a BTU?

When the oil from the Lucas Gusher in Texas sold at three cents a barrel, BTUs were priced at 193 million per dollar. True, the dollar was worth more then. But oil at $200 a barrel gets you only 29,000 BTU to the dollar. Nominally, that is a 665,000 percent increase in the price of a BTU. While this is exaggerated because not much oil changed hands at three cents a barrel, the direction of the change is not in doubt. The radical falloff in the energy density of BTUs per dollar implies a continuing and perhaps precipitous drop in American living standards.

Prosperity will fall away as the return on energy investment falls. This is a development pregnant with implications. I review some of them next, before introducing some topics for analysis in more detail in later chapters.

The SS *Great Britain* Sails Again

I would guess that American living standards are set for at least a 25 percent decline over the next couple of decades. As we regress to lower-density energy, you can expect to see a closure of the economy. Economic freedom will be curtailed. Globalization will be rolled back. The high price of bunker oil will effectively serve as a stiff tariff to refocus the production of heavy, relatively low-value products like steel domestically. Already, the *Wall Street Journal* has reported how the world's longest containership, the *Eugen Maersk*, has cut its cruising speed to 10 knots from its usual 26 knots. This cuts fuel consumption by 100 to 150 tons of fuel daily from 350 tons, saving up to $5,000 an hour.

I expect to see the reintroduction of sailing ships for long-haul transport. The web site www.treehugger.com has already begun to extol the promise of long-haul ocean freight under sail. If expensive oil requires container ships to poke along at 10 knots, they enjoy only an equivocal advantage over sail-powered freight.

International steel companies that do not serve large domestic markets will suffer. So will shipping companies. There will be fewer Chinese goods at Wal-Mart. Hence, Wal-Mart will lose some of its competitive advantage. We will move backwards toward a more local, closed economy.

You can see where this leads. When oil gets to $200 to $300 a barrel, many suburbs and satellite communities will become uneconomic. Housing values that capitalize on low energy prices will plunge. As real estate values are primary collateral to the banking system, you can expect a deeper systemic solvency crisis to come. This deflationary pressure will probably lead to a hyperinflationary response by the authorities. You will want to own physical gold and silver.

"Yes! We Have No Bananas"

Agriculture is highly energy intensive. Oil at $200 will lever up the cost of groceries and make your choice of food simpler and less exciting. Restaurants will find their margins squeezed as food costs in general will jump. With fewer internationally grown vegetables, fruits, meats, and fish on your grocery shelves and in restaurants, the quality of your diet will suffer. You may have to go without fresh fish, avocados, and out-of-season blueberries from halfway around the world.

If you want to get a view of the kind of food you will be eating take a look at an old restaurant menu from the 1940s. Instead of Dover sole or fresh Alaska cod flown in overnight, an exciting meal may once again consist of steak with mashed potatoes and gravy.

As economic closure reduces productive efficiency, and energy density falls, you can expect the economy to retrace aspects of its evolution. In many respects, the future may look like the past. Increasing transportation costs will negate much of the cost advantage of low-wage labor in China, Vietnam, and other remote locales. An increasing share of the products consumed will be produced locally and probably to a lower standard of quality. Most things that you will consume in the future will cost you more. As your standard of living falls, you'll have less spare cash to lavish on services. The prominent, financial services sector will probably be cut down to four percent of GDP or lower.

The tertiary sector (services and the government) will necessarily shrink as a percentage of the economy, as more people are employed in goods making and farming. As the United States grows poorer, our trading partners will have less reason to finance our deficits, so they will stop doing it. Government spending will be forced back within the straitjacket of what a poorer public can actually afford. That means dramatically fewer government services and fewer entitlements, but within the context of higher taxes and more financial repression.

Another important implication: the United States will no longer have the wherewithal to police the world. I expect U.S. military spending to be slashed, but perhaps not until after the United States becomes embroiled in another major war.

For reasons explored previously in this book, I am persuaded that our civic myths exaggerate the role of popular choice in informing the determination of such issues as the size of government, and the nature of money and debt. I see the high government percentage of GDP as having been informed more by the changing calculus of cost and reward rather than through a process of deliberative choice. As we have seen, the introduction of hydrocarbon energy has made the U.S. government large, rich, and powerful—more so than any other government in the history of the world. Government spending as a percentage of the economy surged from 1.8 percent of GDP in 1850 to 41 percent by 2011. But now, with energy growth receding, living standards are falling, and big government has become an unaffordable burden rather than a blessing.

The challenge that this poses during the coming transition crisis as the economy grows slowly or not at all is complicated by the anachronistic views of the public. Many or most Americans of the former middle-class have naturally grown to consider government as an agency for achieving miracles of wish fulfillment. During the past century and a half, politicians have encouraged voters to believe that they, the politicians, could answer the life problems of their con-stituents and shower them with benefits worth more than they cost. The rapid economic growth that seemed to give substance to this illusion is winding down with consequences that will disappoint millions.

Forthcoming chapters explore the deficits, the debts, and the ulti-mate insolvency crisis that are epiphenomena of declining energy inputs. Throughout, I argue that the crisis arising from the collapse of growth will probably entail the grand collapse forecast by Joseph Tainter: "Once a complex society enters the stage of declining marginal returns, collapse becomes a mathematical likelihood, requiring little more than sufficient passage of time to make probable an insurmountable calamity."[23]

In contrast to the large array of U.S. sectors evidencing sharply declining marginal returns, Brazil is enjoying rising returns in enough areas to permit it to grow, and even thrive. As the future of the American economy seems to get bleaker by the day, it is tempting to look abroad for business opportunities. Europe, in particular does not provide much hope, but what about somewhere that is both closer to home and sunny year-round?

Brazil is a haven for those looking to make money in a world in turmoil. With just 62 percent of the population of the United States, Brazil added 15,023,633 jobs over the eight years through January 2011, while the United States lost jobs over the same period.

In a world burdened by bankrupt governments and aging populations, Brazil is solvent, with two people of working age to every dependent.

In a world of peak oil, Brazil is energy independent, having increased its oil production since 1980 by 876 percent. With at least 70 billion barrels of oil in reserve, 60 percent of the world's unused arable land, and 25 percent of its fresh water (more freshwater than all of Asia combined), Brazil is a haven of opportunity in a collapsing world.

---

[23] Tainter, *Collapse of Complex Societies*, 195.

Chapter 5

Malthus Again

*Population Pressures, Global Cooling,
and the Coming Dark Age*

*[A] look at the interaction of climate and history over the past 15,000
years reveals another process at work more or less continuously over that
span. In our efforts to cushion ourselves against smaller, more frequent
climate stresses, we have consistently made ourselves more vulnerable to
rarer but larger catastrophes. The whole course of civilization (while it is
many other things, too, of course) may be seen as a process of trading up
on the scale of vulnerability.*

—Brian Fagan, The Long Summer: *How
Climate Changed Civilization,* xv

*[F]or 55 out of the last 57 centuries Malthus was right. What I mean is
that for almost all of the history of civilization improvements in technology did not lead to sustained increases in living standards; instead,
the gains were dissipated by rising population, with pressure on resources
eventually driving the condition of the masses back to roughly its
previous level. . . . It was Malthus's great misfortune that the power of
his theory to explain what happened in most of human history has
been obscured by the fact that the only two centuries of that history for*

*which it does not work happen to be the two centuries that followed
its publication.*

—Paul Krugman, "Seeking the Rule of the Waves"

C lassical economists had little or nothing to say about bad weather. In this respect, economics has regressed since the days of the pioneering economist and student of Socrates, Xenophon, who lived four centuries before Christ. In his *Oeconomicus*, Xenophon writes, "It is impossible for men to foresee the results of most agricultural operations, for sometimes hail-storms and frost and droughts, unseasonable rain, and mildew and other things spoil what has been well planned and well done."[1]

In more modern economic textbooks, as in *Brave New World*, there is always fair weather. The main exception is found with the Reverend Thomas Malthus, who devoted rapt attention to the "but too frequent" bouts of bad weather that afflicted China where "millions of people" perished of hunger in "times of famine."

In the process, it is sometimes imagined that Malthus single-handedly inspired the historian Thomas Carlyle to describe economics as "the dismal science." Carlyle said, "Not a 'gay science,' I should say, like some we have heard of; no, a dreary, desolate and, indeed, quite abject and distressing one; what we might call, by way of eminence, the dismal science."[2] In fact, however, Carlyle's insult to economists was not aimed solely at what came to be known as "Malthus' Dismal Theorem."

Carlyle's taunt first appeared in an 1849 polemic in support of slavery, his "Occasional Discourse on the Negro Question." It was a purely racist complaint that economists treated all people as equals, a

---

[1] Xenophon, *Oeconomicus*, translated by Aubrey Stewart (Cambridge: J. Hall & Son, 1886).
[2] Thomas Carlyle, "Occasional Discourse on the Negro Question," originally published in *Fraser's Magazine for Town and Country*, 1849.

point underscored when Carlyle reissued, his broadside in 1853 as "An Occasional Discourse on the Nigger Question." In Carlyle's terms, Malthus may have been a bad guy, like Adam Smith and John Stuart Mill, but not because of his "Malthusian" views on diminishing returns. From Carlyle's perspective, Malthus was too liberal and optimistic, too willing to accord all individuals, regardless of race, the same status in his population economics.[3] Yet in spite of the narrow-minded bias of some of his critics, Malthus appeared to have forfeited the love of optimists by advancing what came to be known as "Malthus' Dismal Theorem."

One does not have to swallow the bitter version of Malthus' Dismal Theorem to appreciate the window it opens on reality. As Paul Krugman notes, ". . . for 55 out of the last 57 centuries Malthus was right."[4] And he may be again.

The Dynamics of Weather

In his theories, Malthus points attention away from the economists' conceit of a static world in equilibrium toward a more realistic recognition of a dynamic environment where (among other things) the weather can indeed be bad; and crops can fail, terribly afflicting millions of people.

Even if that does not doom us all, and especially if it does, it is important to understand and bring more carefully into focus the contingencies upon which prosperity rests. One of these most assuredly is the weather.

There has recently been a growing attention to the relationship between economics and the climate, particularly among those concerned about "global warming." In this respect there has been lavish criticism directed at economists such as Larry Summers, "who spent Clinton's term pushing back against [Carol] Browner on climate policy

---

[3] See David Colander et al., eds., *Race, Liberalism and Economics* (Ann Arbor: University of Michigan Press, 2004).
[4] Paul Krugman, "Seeking the Rule of Waves," *Foreign Affairs*, July/August 1997, www.foreignaffairs.com/articles/53234/paul-krugman/seeking-the-rule-of-the-waves?page=show.

and who has popped up on green radars thus far mainly as the guy who had a hand in cutting back transit funding in the stimulus package."[5]

In this chapter, I explore a contrarian perspective on one of the more overhyped propositions in the history of civilization, namely the idea of anthropomorphic global warming. For reasons I spell out, prosperity is more at risk from a turn toward colder, rather than warmer, weather. Unhappily, there is credible evidence that the world is turning toward another Little Ice Age. As was reported at the annual American Astronomical Society (AAS) meeting of solar physicists:

> All the findings indicate a decrease in solar activity. . . . Several scientists at the venue strongly believe that we are near the start of a Maunder Minimum, a period of solar activity that lasts for decades also known as prolonged sunspot minimum. . . .
>
> In 1645 to 1715, experts believed the last Maunder Minimum triggered the Little Ice Age that hit Europe and North America.[6]

The Maunder Minimum is named after E.F. Maunder, an English astronomer who died in 1928. By comparing temperature records from the depths of the Little Ice Age with contemporary seventeenth-century observations of sunspots, Maunder noticed that the coldest period coincided with an almost total 70-year cessation of sunspot activity. In fact, the total number of sunspots observed over the whole 70-year period was less than occurred in a single year during the heyday of Al Gore's global warming party in the 1990s.

This was more than just an astrophysical curiosity. Sunspots are a visual proxy for solar activity. When there were lots of sunspots, as there were in the 1990s, it gets warmer. When sunspots trail off to the vanishing point, as they did in the Maunder Minimum, the earth can get

---

[5] David Roberts, "Some Thoughts on Economists and Climate and So Forth," Grist, February 22, 2009, www.grist.org/article/Rhetorical-diseconomies-of-scale.

[6] "Solar Physicists Believe Last Ice Age May Happen Again," MyTechVoice.com, www.mytechvoice.com/solar-physicists-believe-last-ice-age-may-happen-again -719.html. Accessed June 2011. Also see "Solar event that may have caused last ice age happening again?" IB Times Los Angeles, June 14, 2011, http://losangeles.ibtimes .com/articles/162919/20110614/solar-flare-ice-age-global-warming-sun.htm.

much colder. People suffer from famine, disease, and mass insanity as the plunging marginal returns on maintaining complex systems like ancient empires or modern industrial governments precipitate their collapse. The famine is easy to understand. With colder weather, crops are more difficult to grow. Or if they grow, they barely ripen. Wheat, in particular, is vulnerable to cold. Recurring crop failures lead to starvation. People weakened by malnutrition were easy prey to disease and often reluctant taxpayers. More than once, famine caused by suddenly colder weather has led to collapse, followed by Dark Ages.

The Bronze Age prosperity in antiquity coincided with an exceptionally warm period. This was followed by an era of extended cold, between 1300 and 500 B.C., now known to historians as the Dark Centuries.

Equally, the growth and prosperity of the Roman Empire coincided with much warmer climate, known as the Roman Warming, when it was so much warmer than today that wine grapes and citrus trees grew in England as far north as Hadrian's Wall. Temperatures during the heyday of the Roman Empire were 2 degrees Celsius to 6 degrees Celsius warmer than today's allegedly unprecedented Global Warming.

The collapse of the Roman Empire reflected fiscal exhaustion and a lot of bad policy—such as punitive taxes that forced abandonment of up to 50 percent of farmland in some provinces. Remember, 90 percent of the economy of the Roman Empire was based upon agriculture. Rather than seeking to cushion or offset the impact of cold weather in suppressing their economy, the Roman state adopted counterproductive policies that amplified the damage done by colder weather.

As Joseph Tainter observed in *The Collapse of Complex Societies*,

> The collection of taxes and rents was so unvarying that, however poor [the] crop, the amount due was seized even if the cultivators were left without enough. People couldn't meet taxes and so were jailed, sold their children into slavery, or abandoned their homes and fields.[7]

---

[7] Joseph A. Tainter, *The Collapse of Complex Societies* (Cambridge, UK: Cambridge University Press, 1988), 146.

The predatory policy of the state was aggravated by a sharp drop in global temperatures that led to a long, bitterly cold spell now remembered as the Dark Ages.

It was so cold in the Dark Ages that the Nile River froze. Food production plunged along with temperatures. Plagues and pandemics joined with malnutrition to sharply reduce human population. These became major contributing factors to the Muslim conquest of the Levant in the seventh century, as the Byzantine Empire was weakened by crop failures and disease before the Muslims invaded.

Not Wrong, but Early

Footnotes from the history of economics provide us with the storied work of the Reverend Thomas Malthus, one of the pioneers of population studies. Malthus was not the first to recognize that humanity was at risk of multiplying itself more rapidly than the means of supporting itself. Most of the Malthusian perspective on population was set out in the sixteenth century by Giovanni Botero, a Jesuit scholar. Writing in *On the Cause of the Greatness of Cities* (1588), Botero anticipated Malthus's dismal theorem of two centuries later, arguing that because *virtus generativa* was stronger than *virtus nutritiva*, there was a danger of subsistence crises.[8] He argued that the ultimate cause limiting population is provision of the means of subsistence.

Malthus came at this another way, through a dispute with William Godwin over the latter's contention that a more egalitarian economy could end poverty. Malthus argued otherwise. He thought that a more egalitarian society might lead to greater misery if it nullified the signals that lead people to keep population under control. Malthus thought checks on population growth arising from insecurity over sustenance were crucial to preventing overpopulation. He built his argument on two postulates,

First, that food is necessary to the existence of man.
Secondly, that the passion between the sexes is necessary, and will remain nearly in its present state.

---

[8] Charles Emil Strangeland, *Pre-Malthusian Doctrines of Population: A Study in the History of Economic Theory* (New York: Columbia University Press, 1904), 106.

What Malthus meant has often been misconstrued. Consider these passages from *The Concise Encyclopedia of Economics*:

Noting that while food production tends to increase arithmetically, population tends to increase naturally at a (faster) geometric rate, Malthus argued that it is no surprise that people thus choose to reduce (or "check") population growth. . . . Malthus was fascinated not with the inevitability of human demise, but with why humans do not die off in the face of such overwhelming odds. As an economist, he studied responses to incentives. . . .

. . . Malthus is arguably the most misunderstood and misrepresented economist of all time. The adjective "Malthusian" is used today to describe a pessimistic prediction of the lock step demise of humanity doomed to starvation via overpopulation. When his hypothesis was first stated in his best-selling *An Essay on the Principle of Population* (1798), the uproar it caused among non-economists overshadowed the instant respect it inspired among his fellow economists. So irrefutable and simple was his illustrative side-by-side comparison of an arithmetic and a geometric series—food increases more slowly than population— that it was often taken out of context and highlighted as his main observation. The observation is, indeed, so stark that it is still easy to lose sight of Malthus's actual conclusion: that because humans have not all starved, economic choices must be at work, and it is the job of an economist to study those choices."[9]

While Malthus' argument may have been often taken out of context, there is no doubt that his name is linked in modern political economy with almost any pessimistic projection about the adequacy of resources in the future.

As Walter Russell Mead observes, Malthusian panics are sometimes incongruous. He quips that most of the Chicken Little's earnest followers

---

[9] "Thomas Robert Malthus," *The Concise Encyclopedia of Economics*, www.econlib .org/library/Enc/bios/Malthus.html.

. . . are simultaneously running two Malthusian horror movies in their heads that have incompatible plots. One is the Peak Oil horror film, predicting havoc as our doomed and destructive dependence on hydrocarbons exhausts the natural supply, despoiling the environment and driving the prices to ruinous levels. The other is the Mass Burning horror movie, in which non-renewable hydrocarbons remain so cheap and abundant that we burn them in such accelerating, vast quantities that the CO_2 they release dooms the planet. A graceless old reptile like me can't help reflecting that one of these two ideas might be right, but they can't possibly both be. If we run out of fossil fuels, we will stop emitting as much CO_2. If we keep emitting ghastly quantities of CO_2, then fossil fuel must be pretty damn abundant, given the projected increase in developing world industrial activity.[10]

Not only is the global warming panic apparently incoherent with the concept of peak oil, but opponents of industrial society often get it tangled in another profound confusion. You have certainly heard the well-worn cliché that the United States and other advanced economies need to wean themselves from their addiction to oil. This is fantasy on the same level as the millennial hope from Isaiah that "the lion will eat straw like the ox." It won't happen, because short of a holy miracle, it can't happen.

Oil is the lifeblood of advanced economies. Expecting them to overcome this "addiction" is equivalent to expecting humans or animals to wean themselves from reliance on blood flow. BTU-dense energy is not a recreational drug, but the lifeblood of a modern economy. The attempt to simply dispense with oil, natural gas, and coal in favor of "alternative" noncarbon forms of energy would rapidly lead to economic collapse.

This is implicit, or even explicit, in the works of some stalwarts of the Malthusian perspective, such as Richard Heinberg, author of *Peak Everything: Waking Up to the Century of Declines*. He essentially argues that modern economies are the equivalent of a house of cards, and that

---

[10] Walter Russell Mead, "Doing What Comes Naturally," *American Interest*, April 7, 2010.

peak oil will precipitate calamitous declines in the output and consumption of practically every measure of living standards. He recommends "transitioning gracefully from the 'Age of Excess' to the 'Era of Modesty.'"

If you think closely about the obvious contradiction between apprehensions about peak oil and the global warming scare blamed on the burning of hydrocarbon fuels, the real reason for this ill-grounded, cynical campaign may come into focus. It involves the difficulty of using price alone to ration what is bound to be diminishing access to world petroleum supplies. The basic problem, faced most acutely by economies that consume the greatest amount of energy per capita is that the marginal value of oil use is highest in emerging economies that do not have imbedded demand for oil in systems designed when oil was cheap. If the United States, and Western Europe, for example, through heroic effort, were able to reduce their annual oil consumption by five billion barrels, roughly the annual exhaustion of legacy supplies of cheap oil, there is no guarantee that energy-dense hydrocarbons saved thereby would be available at a later time to the North American and European users. To the contrary, it is more likely that new users in China, India, and other emerging economies would bid this oil away.

Hence the appeal of the global warming scare, as a rationalization for imposing limits on hydrocarbon use enforced through mechanisms of global governance. Such limits have the appeal from the perspective of the advanced economies, of promising to stifle growth in emerging economies, and help prevent them from increasing their downstream consumption of ever-diminishing supplies of cheap oil. Global warming remedies are not about protecting the climate, but about forestalling growth in emerging economies, and thereby preserving as far as possible the current proportions in the consumption of hydrocarbons between economies. As we explore next, the use of emission limits and carbon trading would effectively cap use at current levels and even drive it down. In other words, global warming remedies and policies meant to enforce a shift to the Era of Modesty can best be understood as cynical rationalizations for permitting the so-called advanced economies to continue consuming a disproportionately large share of global hydrocarbons, even after they could otherwise no longer afford to do so.

Waiting for Our Malthusian Moment

In this sense, Malthusian perspectives on resource limitation are not solely limited to food supply and population. In a broader sense, they encompass other concerns about outstripping available resources and the economic consequences that follow.

When Malthus first published his *Essay on Population* in 1798, the total population of the world was about 900 million. Today, it is about 7 billion. We have succeeded in feeding a population more than seven times larger than that in Malthus's day. While that is impressive progress, and seems to discount the dynamic that Malthus set out, it does not. If, on one level, Malthus can be supposed to have been proven wrong because humanity has not been devastated by mass starvation, on another, more basic level, his underlying proposition is indisputable, as when he says: "I do not know that any writer has supposed that on this earth man will ultimately be able to live without food."

The danger of Malthus' Dismal Theorem coming true does not arise from the prospect that billions of couples will suddenly reverse the trend of the past two centuries and arbitrarily decide to have 17 children apiece. That is logically possible, but it isn't going to happen. The danger of a subsistence crisis arises almost entirely from the prospect of a discontinuity that abruptly reduces food supplies.

The relatively successful matching of population growth with the growth of the means of sustenance that produced a sevenfold multiplication of human population since 1798 shows successful economic choices at work. It also helps explain the impatience of economists such as Joseph Schumpeter with Malthus. Schumpeter wrote, "There is of course no point whatever in trying to formulate independent 'laws' for the behavior of two interdependent quantities."[11] Essentially, Schumpeter was complaining that Malthus' Dismal Theorem was redundant and unnecessary because population growth and food production do not operate independently of one another—at least under what we have come to view as "normal" climate conditions.

---

[11] Joseph A. Schumpeter, *History of Economic Analysis* (New York: Oxford University Press, 1954), 579, n. 1.

Yet climate historian Brian Fagan suggests an important amendment to Socrates' view that the whole history of civilization is "a story of gradually increasing human control over contingency."[12] This may indeed be true in one sense. Humans have gained greater control over likely and frequent contingencies but at the expense of making ourselves more vulnerable to the rarer and larger ones. As Fagan put it, the "course of civilization" over the past two centuries may indeed "be seen as a process of trading up on the scale of vulnerability."[13] A larger population than ever awaits its Malthusian moment.

A foretaste of this was provided in early 2008 and again in 2011 as food prices soared and riots swept North Africa and the Middle East. Even with temperatures plunging at a record pace, the shift toward a colder climate has barely begun, and food prices have already started to skyrocket. Food prices hit an all-time high in February 2011 according to the UN's Food and Agricultural Organization (FAO). Note, too, that prices exceeded the previously record levels of 2008 that sparked food riots in more than 30 countries. Famine-style prices for food and energy that prevailed early in 2008 may also have helped precipitate the credit crisis that Federal Reserve Chairman Ben Bernanke described in closed-door testimony "as the worst in financial history, even exceeding the Great Depression."[14]

This time around, the turmoil surrounding commodity inflation took center stage with more serious riots and even revolutions across the globe. Popular discontent was not just confined to basket case countries like Haiti and Bangladesh as in 2008. High food prices roiled Arab kleptocracies with young populations and U.S.-backed dictatorships such as Tunisia, Egypt, Bahrain, and Yemen. Even dynamic economies were affected. Indeed, all of the BRIC countries, except Brazil, witnessed food rioting.

---

[12] Martha C. Nussbaum, *The Fragility of Goodness: Luck and Ethics in Greek Tragedy* (Cambridge, UK: Cambridge University Press, 2001).

[13] Brian Fagan, *The Long Summer: How Climate Changed Civilization* (New York: Basic Books, 2004), xv.

[14] "Bernanke: All but One Major Firm at Risk in 2008," Reuters, January 27, 2011, www.reuters.com/article/2011/01/27/financial-regulation-fcic-idUSN271 3264020110127.

The most overt unrest among the BRICs occurred in India, where food costs absorbed more than 25 percent of the typical Indian's budget before India's Food Price Index jumped by 15.57 percent on January 27, 2011. Indians were particularly incensed by a surge in the price of onions, a major ingredient in the food consumed by poor families. A government report at the end of 2010 confirmed that the price of onions had risen to 85 rupees ($1.87) per kilogram from 35 rupees only a week earlier. Dismay over soaring onion prices incited major demonstrations against alleged government corruption.

A big part of the problem with food supply is that attempts to expand production have been plagued by diminishing marginal returns for the past half-century. Even without an adverse change in the climate, expanding existing food reserves would be difficult. Donella H. Meadows and colleagues documented this in their 1972 volume, *The Limits to Growth*. They showed that in order to increase world food production by 34 percent between 1951 and 1966 required increases in outlays on tractors of 63 percent, a 146 percent jump in nitrate fertilizers, and a 300 percent increase in expenditures on pesticides. Typically, this type of cost curve leads to an even greater escalation of costs to achieve an equivalent growth in future production.[15] Declining marginal returns in good weather augur ill for outcomes under adverse growing conditions.

While Indian protests mushroomed without grabbing attention on CNBC, an unassuming 26-year-old fruit vendor named Mohamed Bouazizi launched a revolution in Tunisia when he set himself on fire to protest the confiscation of his fruit cart and apples. His efforts to improvise a living had run afoul of stifling bureaucracy. Bouazizi became so furious and frustrated that he adopted the extreme protest technique pioneered among Buddhist monks in Vietnam by Thích Quáng Đúc almost half a century ago. Thích Quáng Đúc burned himself to death on June 11, 1963, to protest oppression of Buddhists by the despotic Diem regime.

Mohamed Bouazizi was enraged that corrupt officials had stolen his fruit wagon, along with his prized, new electronic scale. He became a

---

[15] Donella H. Meadows et al., *The Limits to Growth* (New York: Universe Books, 1972), 53.

martyr of the revolution that toppled the 23-year dictatorship of Zine el-Abidine Ben Ali. He also inspired desperate advocates of regime change in Egypt, the world's biggest wheat importer, where three people set themselves ablaze igniting protests against the government. In Algeria, tied with Indonesia as the world's third-largest wheat buyer, three people were killed in clashes with police during rallies against high food prices. The government responded by purchasing as much 800,000 metric tons of wheat a day in an effort to placate a public squeezed by rising prices.

Less than a month after the fall of Ben Ali, a similar popular uprising in Egypt toppled the 30-year authoritarian regime of Hosni Mubarak. A dictatorship that U.S. taxpayers had spent some $70 billion dollars to prop up was swept away.

In addition to the fact that the Arab homelands are generally arid, with little land suited to food production, also underlying their particular vulnerability are population growth rates among the highest on the planet. The population of the Arab world was 73 million in 1950. Now it has more than quadrupled to 350 million.[16] The World Bank expects that to double again by 2050—a suggestion that augurs ill for future oil exports from the Middle East given peak oil concerns.

On current trends, even Saudi Arabia's export capacity will be pinched by surging domestic consumption—a consideration of capital importance to anyone who takes a long-term Malthusian view of access to resources.

Saudi domestic oil and gas use has been rising at an annual average of 5.9 percent since 2005, far faster than population or GDP. A big part of the reason for the rapid growth in domestic consumption is that the Saudis, and, indeed, most Middle East oil producers, sell oil and gas to domestic consumers at "giveaway" prices. In spite of its small population Saudi Arabia is the world's 15th-ranked energy consumer, with 56 percent of its electric power generated by direct burning of petroleum.

This all becomes more important in the context of bad weather around the globe that has adversely affected crop yields and multiplied the mischief done by aggressive (some might think "belligerent") U.S.

---

[16] IRIN Global, "FOOD: Is There a Crisis?" IRIN, January 21, 2011, www .irinnews.org/Report.aspx?ReportID=91683.

monetary policy in raising commodity prices. The conventional view of weather disturbances is that they are down to manmade global warming. I think otherwise.

The Next Little Ice Age

Contrary to what you have been told repeatedly by the mass media, weather disturbances, including the 2010 summer's drought in Russia, various floods, and the shrinking of growing seasons in North America are caused not by warming, but by potentially catastrophic cooling of temperatures.[17]

Piers Corbyn is a disheveled astrophysicist who forecast Russia's drought and the floods in Pakistan and whose brother Jeremy is a left-wing member of the British Parliament. Piers works in a drab office in Borough High Street, without a telescope or supercomputer: "Armed only with a laptop, huge quantities of publicly available data and a first-class degree in astrophysics, he gets it right again and again."[18] In November 2009, when the Met Office (Britain's official weather forecasting service) was still nattering on about a "mild winter" coming due to "Global Warming," Corbyn said it would be the coldest for 100 years.

Interestingly, Corbyn finances his weather forecasting by placing bets on future weather outcomes through William Hill and other legal gambling sites. He looks at radiation from the sun and how it interacts with the upper atmosphere, especially air currents such as the jet stream. Corbyn also considers the moon to be an important mediating influence on weather. As Wesley Smith says in an article, Corbyn "takes a snap-shot of what the Sun is doing at any given moment, and then he looks back at the record to see when it last did something similar. Then he

---

[17] For more on the connection between droughts and floods and waning solar output, see "Never Mind the Heat, Climate Change Is Hoax by Gravy-Train Scientists," YouTube, August 9, 2010, www.youtube.com/watch?v=eEmUS7PAWFw &feature=related (an English language interview originally broadcast on *Russia Today*).
[18] Wesley J. Smith, "Global Warming Hysteria: Mini Ice Age on the Way?" Secondhand Smoke (blog), December 21, 2010. www.firstthings.com/blogs /secondhandsmoke/2010/12/21/global-warming-hysteria-m.

checks what the weather was like on Earth at the time—and he makes a prophecy."[19]

Corbyn has made a lot of money by being right. Rather than worry about changes in CO_2 levels from motor exhaust and popping champagne bottles, which have no predictive value, Corbyn focuses on issues that more directly impact weather. He says, "CO_2 has never driven, does not drive, and never will drive weather or climate. Global warming is over and it never was anything to do with CO_2."[20]

There are many reasons to suggest that the anthropomorphic global warming hysteria is ill-founded. Start with the fact that CO_2 is a highly diffused trace element in the atmosphere. CO_2 from all sources makes up only 3.618 percent of the atmosphere, and manmade CO_2 is even more miniscule, at only 0.117 percent. Some 31,000 U.S. scientists have signed a petition urging the U.S. government not to adopt expensive measures to curtail carbon emissions, as they are not the driving force in climate change. Dr. Willie Soon, astrophysicist and geoscientist at the Solar and Stellar Physics Division of the Harvard- Smithsonian Center for Astrophysics, puts it this way:

> It's close to being insane to try to keep insisting these changes in carbon dioxide are going to create all of the disasters that the politicians and doomsayers are trying to tell us. Saying the climate system is completely dominated by how much carbon dioxide we have in the system is crazy—completely wrong. Carbon dioxide is not the major driver for the earth/climate system.[21]

Obviously, the sun is. If nothing else were known, the historic record also calls into doubt the proposition that higher atmospheric concentrations of CO_2 necessarily lead to a warmer Earth.

Note that the Ordovician-Silurian glaciation that occurred between 420 and 450 million years ago, as well as the Jurassic-Cretaceous

[19] Smith, "Global Warming Hysteria."

[20] Piers Corbyn, "The Role of the Spotless Sun," www.weatheraction.com /displayarticle.asp?a=6&c=1.

[21] Willie Soon, "We Are Being Brainwashed" (interview), http://itsrainmakingtime .com/2009/climate-part2/.

glaciation of 132 to 151 million years ago, both happened when atmospheric CO_2 content was many times higher than at present.

Al Gore and company have never explained how the earth could become an uninhabitable inferno if their program to slash atmospheric CO_2 below 350 parts per million is not adopted when evidence shows that the earth sank into an Ice Age for 30 million years with atmospheric CO_2 at 4,000 parts per million. Still, you have to give Gore credit for an incredible job of salesmanship. Not that the idea of concocting a ban on useful substances out of fear of farfetched harm to the atmosphere is entirely original with Gore. As David S. Van Dyke observed in "The CFC Ban: Global Warming's Pilot Episode," Gore copied a lot of his scare tactics from the campaign to ban chlorofluorocarbons (CFCs):

> The CFC ban was a perfect pilot for the anthropogenic global warming fraud. It established all the characters: the eco-left NGOs, the environmental "scientists" (both real and self-proclaimed), and big industry poised to make huge profits and political control over human choices and behavior. It had buy-ins by governments all over the planet. It was based on an unproven (and probably unprovable) hypothesis. Many industries stood to gain at the expense of consumers. To this day, research continues to be funded to study CFCs in the atmosphere. Most significantly, the "ozone hole" hasn't changed appreciably. It remains stable . . . as if we ever really knew what "stable" was.[22]

Gore may have copied the techniques of the project to ban CFCs, but his is a more audacious and far-reaching scam orchestrating one of the most effective campaigns of intellectual hysteria in history. In the process, he has succeeded where the Inquisition failed, in countering the work of Galileo, who put the sun, rather than the earth at the center of the solar system.

---

[22] David S. Van Dyke, "The CFC Ban: Global Warming's Pilot Episode," American Thinker, February 4, 2010, www.americanthinker.com/2010/02 /the_cfc_ban_global_warmings_pi.html.

I don't think Gore's science marks much of an improvement over that of the Inquisition. Evidence still strongly supports the view that global warming originates with the sun.

Russian solar physicists Galina Mashnich and Vladimir Bashkirtsev have bet $10,000 with British climate activist James Annan that the world will be colder in a decade. Based at the Institute of Solar-Terrestrial Physics in Irkutsk, Mashnich and Bashkirtsev believe "that global temperatures are driven more by changes in the sun's activity than by the emission of greenhouse gases. They say the Earth warms and cools in response to changes in the number and size of sunspots. Most mainstream scientists dismiss the idea, but as the sun is expected to enter a less active phase over the next few decades the Russian duo are confident they will see a drop in global temperatures."[23] And make money in the process.

Mashnich and Bashkirtsev, like Piers Corbyn, forecast another Little Ice Age, possibly matching that of the Maunder Minimum that lasted from the 1640s into the early eighteenth century. The following story is by Lewis Page for *The Register*, datelined June 14, 2011:

Physicists Say Sunspot Cycle Is "Going into Hibernation"

What may be the science story of the century is breaking this evening, as heavyweight U.S. solar physicists announce that the Sun appears to be headed into a lengthy spell of low activity, which could mean that the Earth—far from facing a global warming problem—is actually headed into a mini Ice Age.

The announcement made on 14 June 18:00 UK time comes from scientists at the U.S. National Solar Observatory (NSO) and U.S. Air Force Research Laboratory. Three different analyses of the Sun's recent behaviour all indicate that a period of unusually low solar activity may be about to begin.

The Sun normally follows an 11-year cycle of activity. The current cycle, Cycle 24, is now supposed to be ramping up towards maximum strength. Increased numbers of sunspots and

---

[23] For more information about solar output and sunspot cycles, see Timo Niroma, "One Possible Explanation for the Cyclicity in the Sun," http://personal.inet.fi /tiede/tilmari/sunspots.html.

other indications ought to be happening: but in fact results so far are most disappointing. Scientists at the NSO now suspect, based on data showing decades-long trends leading to this point, that Cycle 25 may not happen at all.

This could have major implications for the earth's climate. According to a statement issued by the NSO, announcing the research,

> "An immediate question is whether this slowdown presages a second Maunder Minimum, a 70-year period with virtually no sunspots [which occurred] during 1645–1715." As NASA notes,

> Early records of sunspots indicate that the Sun went through a period of inactivity in the late seventeenth century. Very few sunspots were seen on the Sun from about 1645 to 1715. Although the observations were not as extensive as in later years, the Sun was in fact well observed during this time and this lack of sunspots is well documented. This period of solar inactivity also corresponds to a climatic period called the "Little Ice Age" when rivers that are normally ice-free froze and snow fields remained year-round at lower altitudes. There is evidence that the Sun has had similar periods of inactivity in the more distant past.

> During the Maunder Minimum and for periods either side of it, many European rivers which are ice-free today—including the Thames—routinely froze over, allowing ice skating and even for armies to march across them in some cases. "This is highly unusual and unexpected," says Dr. Frank Hill of the NSO. "But the fact that three completely different views of the Sun point in the same direction is a powerful indicator that the sunspot cycle may be going into hibernation."[24]

The scary part of this forecast is that it incorporates a projection of a "solar hibernation" not seen for centuries. Interestingly, the hibernation hypothesis was supported by NASA's Long Range Solar Forecast through

---

[24] Lewis Page, "Earth May Be Headed into a Mini Ice Age within a Decade," *The Register*, June 14, 2011, www.theregister.co.uk/2011/06/14/ice_age/.

2022, published in 2006, "The Sun's Great Conveyor Belt has slowed to a record-low crawl," said NASA solar physicist David Hathaway on May 10, 2006. "It's off the bottom of the charts. Solar Cycle 25, peaking around the year 2022, could be one of the weakest in centuries."[25]

In the unlikely event that Al Gore is right, the economic impact of climate change would largely be felt in the form of falling prices for food as warmer weather extends growing seasons. But if the astrophysicists are right, we could experience the greatest crisis in history as protracted crop failures multiply food prices at a time when there are billions more mouths to feed than ever before. This could write down living standards in the way that colder weather seems to have toppled the prosperity of the Roman Empire.

The evidence of colder weather is not merely theoretical, as you know if you follow the news. The first decade of the twenty-first century witnessed the single fastest temperature change ever recorded. Contrary to predictions by global warming alarmists, however, temperatures fell rather than rose. In December 2010, Fort Lauderdale broke a 162-year low temperature record, and snow fell in Jacksonville, Florida. Meanwhile, I-5, one of Southern California's iconic freeways, was closed at the beginning of 2011 for almost two days by heavy snows. The early months of 2011 saw Europe submerged in a deep freeze, with heavy snow blanketing the continent, causing transportation delays and raising heating costs. And no review of colder weather would be complete without reference to the informing irony that marked the UN's Cozumel Conference on Global Warming—three successive days with all-time record low temperatures for that part of Mexico. You can't make this up.

Equally, it would be hard to exaggerate the food deficit that would likely accompany a return to Little Ice Age conditions, such as those that characterized the seventeenth century. In the cold climate countries, field crops would either suffer persistently low yields or not grow at all. Farming would become a more industrial activity, undertaken at greater expense in heated greenhouses. Even where outdoor agriculture could be pursued in what are currently temperate climates, it would become

---

[25] "Long Range Solar Forecast," NASA Science News, May 10, 2006, http://science.nasa.gov/science-news/science-at-nasa/2006/10may_longrange.

more expensive and energy intensive. Consequently, meat consumption would necessarily recede as livestock feed costs soared.

Food prices would skyrocket, much as they did in 1816, now remembered for "the last great subsistence crisis in the Western world." For further background, consider this passage from Willie Soon and Steven Yaskell's "Year Without a Summer," which recounts how "a weak solar maximum, a major volcanic eruption, and possibly even the wobbling of the Sun conspired to make the summer of 1816 one of the most miserable ever recorded."[26] They write: "The year 1816 is still known to scientists and historians as 'eighteen hundred and froze to death' or the 'year without a summer.' It was the locus of a period of natural ecological destruction not soon to be forgotten. During that year, the Northern Hemisphere was slammed with the effects of at least two abnormal but natural phenomena" including the Dalton Minimum, one of the sun's extended periods of low magnetic activity resembling the Maunder Minimum and sandwiched within the Little Ice Age that lasted from the fourteenth through nineteenth centuries, and the eruption of Tambora on the island of Sumbawa (located in modern-day Indonesia). In addition, Soon and Yaskell write about a third factor called inertial solar motion (characterized by the sun shifting its place in the solar system), which also might have played a role in the climate's change.

In a repeat of the Maunder Minimum today, residents of most of the advanced cold climate economies would be faced with a food price shock more pronounced than that which provoked the Arab Spring revolutions of 2011. Ultimately, they would face the unpalatable choice of consuming costly domestic foods, partially produced in industrial greenhouses or importing high-priced conventional foodstuffs from Brazil, and perhaps a few other warm weather countries, where there is a reserve capacity for additional food production. Obviously, a deep freeze in the global climate would sharply reduce the apparent productivity advantage of farming in temperate zones and increase the attractiveness of farming in tropical and subtropical savannahs.

It is not overheating, but record-setting colder temperatures that accounted for the destruction of up to 40 percent of Mexico's winter

---

[26] Willie Soon and Steven Yaskell, "Year Without a Summer," *Mercury Magazine* 32, no. 3 (May–June 2003): 13f.

wheat crop in 2011.[27] The story from *Vanguardia* reports "catastrophic" losses to Mexican wheat due to "frost."[28]

A moment's consideration of the impact of climate upheavals on human history will convince the thinking person that the danger of a shift to colder weather vastly exceeds the supposed dangers of global warming, which is only another phrase for good weather.

I believe that Gore's views and indeed the whole global warming hysteria are based on dubious science. Gore maintains that governments have the capacity to dictate global temperatures by altering carbon emissions. This is a sweeping proposition that implies a heretofore unimagined capacity of government intervention. However, the identification of manmade carbon emissions as the crucial variable in climate change is difficult to square with solar physics, and much that history, archaeology, and geology tell us about the actual record of climate in the past.

If you listen to Gore and the global warming alarmists, you might suppose that CO_2 made up a big proportion of the total atmosphere and was put there recently by humans burning oil and coal to power a lavish, modern standard of living. This supposition is wrong.

Roughly 186 billion tons of CO_2 enter the atmosphere annually. Of that amount, only about 6 billion tons or 3.3 percent is attributable to human activity—apart from breathing.[29] Note, however that about 71 billion tons of CO_2 are exhaled by humans and animals in the course of breathing. This accounts for more than 10 times the CO_2 attributable to economic activity that Gore wants to squelch.

Based on Gore's and Obama's push for sweeping and costly climate legislation, you might think that atmospheric CO_2 had reached unprecedented levels. Wrong again. Atmospheric carbon has previously been 25 to 100 times higher than current levels—with no evidence that it caused runaway greenhouse effects, much less any of the other horrifying hypotheticals that Gore and the remorseless liars in the

---

[27] "Frost Destroys The Wheat Crop in Coahuila" [in Spanish], *Vanguardia*, February 13, 2011, www.vanguardia.com.mx/acabaheladasconeltrigodecoahuila-650012.html.
[28] Ibid.
[29] Ian Plimer, *Heaven and Earth: Global Warming: The Missing Science* (Lanham, MD: Taylor Trade Publishing, 2009), 180.

Intergovernmental Panel on Climate Change (IPCC) of the UN pretend to be alarmed about.

This is not merely the opinion of an eccentric holdout for the lost virtues of a liberal education. There are mounds of evidence compiled by reputable scientists who are not being paid large government grants to inflame alarms about anthropomorphic global warming. In 2011 alone, the U.S. government spent some $4 billion to show that "carbon dioxide from the burning of fossil fuels, will almost certainly contribute to additional widespread climate disruption."[30] As this comment shows, there is scarcely even a pretense of objective intent to study whether or to what extent CO_2 emissions actually alter the climate.[31] They are simply paying billions a year out of an empty pocket to purchase propaganda with footnotes that says what they want to hear. It is remarkable therefore that there are still independent-minded scientists who are prepared to follow their research to conclusions that the powers that be do not wish to hear.

Dr. Jan Veizer, an eminent isotope geochemist, has demonstrated from analysis of seawater that there has been no relationship between atmospheric carbon and temperatures over the past 545 million years. That's how far back he and his colleagues have measured the amounts of various chemicals found in marine shells from around the world.

These reveal major changes that took place in oxygen isotopes in seawater, a key indicator of changes in atmospheric composition and temperature. Looking over that long time scale, exceeding half a billion years, atmospheric carbon showed no correlation to temperature. None. Indeed, there was nothing about having much higher CO_2 concentrations that prevented the earth from plunging into Ice Ages. Equally, evidence suggests that global temperatures are now 7 degrees Celsius cooler than they were for most of the past 500 million years.

The long record correlating CO_2 to temperature also shows that high amounts of atmospheric CO_2 are transient phenomena. Contrary to Gore

---

[30] Paul A.T. Higgins "Climate Change in the FY 2011 Budget." In: AAAS Report XXXV, Research and Development FY 2011, (Washington, DC: The American Association for the Advancement of Science, 2010), 171-178. Available at www.aaas.org/spp/rd/rdreport2011/11pch15.pdf.

[31] AAAS Report XXXV, Research and Development FY 2011, Chapter 15, available at www.aaas.org/spp/rd/rdreport2011.

and company, there is no tendency for "runaway" CO_2 concentrations to increase and cause detrimental climate change. Past increases in CO_2 emissions due to volcanic eruptions dwarf those now attributable to human activity. Contrary to claims by the IPCC that high atmospheric CO_2 persists, carbon dioxide is naturally recycled by the earth.

This is something that any thinking environmentalist should understand. CO_2 is bioactive. It is not a pollutant. CO_2 is an essential ingredient to life. After all, you are a carbon-based life-form. There is a high probability that some of the organic carbon in your body was recycled from atmospheric CO_2. CO_2 is crucially important to plant nutrition. It is also captured in marine life. Seashells and coral reefs are composed largely of the mineral calcite (calcium carbonate: $CaCO_3$) recycled from atmospheric CO_2. What was once atmospheric CO_2 is assimilated into vegetation and soil. Eventually, it finds its way into sedimentary rocks, like limestone. From there, limestone is sometimes turned into cement and concrete and formed into everything from sidewalks to skyscrapers.

Looking into the evidence, it is far from obvious that there is currently an excess of CO_2 in the atmosphere. To the contrary, CO_2 comprises just 1/10,000th more of the atmosphere today than it did in 1750 before the Industrial Revolution. Far from being alarmingly high, atmospheric CO_2 is within a tiny margin of its lowest level ever.

The idea that there is some pressing emergency that requires drastic action to slash carbon emissions is remote from the facts. Claims to the contrary have involved hysterics over manufactured evidence and some astonishing intellectual contortions. Consider the solemn forecast proclaimed by the IPCC in 2007 that global warming due to carbon emissions would melt most of the Himalayan glaciers by 2035. Oops. They had to retract this whopper after it became known that the prediction was just an arbitrary assertion unsupported by any formal research.

This is by no means the only example of bogus evidence of a global warming crisis that has been promulgated by the IPCC. In 2001, the IPCC published its famous "hockey stick" graph that purported to show that 1998 was the warmest year in the warmest decade of the past millennium. This conclusion was drawn entirely from a paper by a recent graduate, who earned much fame and fortune by contradicting thousands of studies and innumerable historic records showing that the climate was far warmer during the centuries of the Medieval Warm Period.

Like the warning of melting Himalayan glaciers, the hockey stick temperature graph had to be withdrawn by the IPCC after two Canadian scientists, Steven McIntyre and Ross McKitrick, showed that the temperature data upon which it was based was rife with errors.[32]

In theory, the IPCC was set up to ensure that world leaders had the best possible scientific advice on climate change. The reality is that the IPCC doesn't care a fig about scientific truth. They are only interested in promoting hysteria over atmospheric carbon as a justification for one of the great power grabs in history—a power grab. (More on this to come.)

In my view, evidence is strong that human carbon emissions play no more than a trivial role in global warming—if indeed there is any such warming to explain. But suspend judgment on that. Suppose for a moment that Gore is right, and global climate can indeed be determined by political diktat.

"The Dog That Did Not Bark"

You would think that if you believed that the world's governments could dial up or down the global climate like revelers spinning the thermostat at a Super Bowl party, that the first topic for discussion would be to determine what the optimum global temperature is. And the answer is . . .

Don't hold your breath. A telling detail of the climate debate is that Gore, Obama, the IPCC, and other climate vigilantes are adamant that they have the capacity to regulate climate, and that they must do so urgently. But they have nothing to say about the ideal temperature they intend to dial in on the global thermostat.

I think their silence on this score betrays the gag. So long as the battle against global warming is a self-righteous campaign to Save the Planet, it requires no further justification.

No one need apologize for fending off the grab bag of horrors forecast by Gore and company, ranging from endless reruns of Hurricane Katrina, if not the tornado scene from the *Wizard of Oz*, to

---

[32] See "Hockey Stick Studies," www.climateaudit.org.

the inundation of coastal cities, including New York and Miami (Gore says sea levels will rise by 20 feet by the end of this century) to a global epidemic of malaria and dengue fever, "the destruction of Mt. Everest," heat stroke for polar bears and the desertification of Australia and Africa.

We can all agree that those things don't sound good. No one wants to get malaria, dengue fever, or heat stroke. And it certainly would not do much for the collateral of the banking system if Miami, lower Manhattan, Charleston, New Orleans, Tampa, Los Angeles, San Diego, New Orleans, Washington, Baltimore, and other low-lying cities were wholly or partially underwater.

But the further the global warming vigilantes stray from writing sad obituaries for future generations of polar bears into actually specifying the climate control they would like to achieve, the more they risk undermining their support. Let them specify some target temperature to which they hope to cool the planet, and the whole debate could be transformed.

Why? Because lower temperatures have ponderable consequences, most of them bad, like shorter growing seasons, food shortages, and higher prices in a hungry world. It is no exaggeration to suppose that lowering global temperatures by a few degrees Celsius could cost the lives of hundreds of millions, even billions, of poor people around the globe.

Get people thinking about this, and it could jeopardize the big power grab/money grab that Obama, Gore, and the IPCC are so keen on. That is why the manipulators who orchestrate the campaign over global warming only want to rail against far-fetched consequences of a runaway global heat wave, rather than tell us how far they intend to cool the planet.

For all the recent hysteria and fulmination, warming has historically been a positive for civilization, while cooling has meant famine, disease, depopulation, and political collapse. Even a nodding acquaintance with history suggests a lot of good reasons to question the wisdom of trying to cool the planet as Gore and company seem intent on doing. But there is a method to Gore's madness. He will make billions of dollars if he can prevail on the United States and China and other leading economies to join the European Union in adopting cap and trade legislation. His payday is getting closer as several U.S. states and six Chinese provinces have adopted cap and trade programs.

Gore owns about 10 percent of the Climate Exchange PLC, (CLE) a public company listed on the AIM section of the London Stock Exchange. The Climate Exchange PLC owns the European Climate Exchange, the Chicago Climate Exchange and the Chicago Climate Futures Exchange. According to the UK newspaper *The Guardian*, the carbon trading market could be worth $3 trillion annually—twice that of oil in the next decade—if global governments ratify the "cap and trade" proposal Gore is pushing.[33]

No wonder Gore is so keen. He'll make many billions if Obama can convince enough congress-folk to enshrine his global warming theories into law. By their say-so they can make the trading of nothing the biggest market on the globe. Yes, that is what the carbon markets trade, not carbon, per se, but something close to nothing—promises of not-carbon, known as carbon offsets.

Consider if you purchase a contract of frozen pork bellies on the Chicago Mercantile Exchange for February delivery, and you don't liquidate your contract before it settles; you'll be contacted by someone to find out where you want to take delivery of 40,000 pounds of uncut bacon.

Not so with carbon trading. Carbon traders don't actually trade carbon. If you buy a CO_2 emissions contract on the European Climate Exchange and you neglect to sell your contract before settlement, no worries. You don't have to fret about someone pumping a metric ton of CO_2 through your letter slot. It doesn't work that way. With Gore's carbon market there are no physical deliverables.

You see you are not actually trading carbon dioxide. You are trading the right to emit CO_2. Much of the time, that right is tied to an offset, or a promise from someone, somewhere not to produce CO_2. So Gore's carbon market is not actually a carbon market. It is a fun house mirror version of a carbon market—a not-carbon market that deals in promises not to produce carbon dioxide.

---

[33] Terry Macalister, "Carbon trading could be worth twice that of oil in next decade," *The Guardian*, November 29, 2009, www.guardian.co.uk/environment/2009/nov/29/carbon-trading-market-copenhagen-summit.

As Mark Schapiro reported in the February 2010 issue of *Harper's*,

> . . . unlike traditional commodities, which sometime during the course of their market exchange must be delivered to someone in physical form, the carbon market is based on the lack of delivery of an invisible substance to no one.[34]

So you have a multitrillion dollar market in promises invented by a politician who will become a multibillionaire for his pains, if the eloquent Mr. Obama can only persuade enough congress folk to join others in ratifying it.

Putting Two and Two Together

When you consider how many energy inputs are required to live a middle-class life in a developed country, the global warming remedy championed by Gore and company is really a recipe for lowering living standards worldwide. It would make the middle class poor and the poor destitute. But it would put billions in Gore's pockets.

It is really a perverse attempt to mobilize incentives in order to maximize malinvestment in the energy field. In this respect, the estimate that carbon markets could reach a volume of $3 trillion within a few years of broad enactment of cap and trade underestimates the amount of capital that would be misallocated through the system.

For one thing, the fact that the CO_2 emission offset credits could be available only on projects with certified "additionality" means that providers of not-carbon could only receive payments through the system's clean development mechanism (CDM) so long as their projects did not make economic sense. To decipher this requires close attention.

The requirement of additionality involves a complex counterfactual in which credits are permitted for projects that do not emit carbon only if the carbon they don't emit would otherwise have been emitted. Got

---

[34] Mark Schapiro, "Conning the Climate: Inside the Carbon-Trading Shell Game," *Harper's Magazine*, February 2010, www.harpers.org/archive/2010/02/0082826.

that? It means that to qualify, the project receiving the payments would otherwise have had to be unprofitable.

Consider how this might work in these two examples:

1. Suppose you own a state-of-the-art ethanol facility in Brazil. You power the facility by burning macerated, processed sugar cane to generate electricity, most of which you sell back to the grid. Your operation is clean, efficient, and profitable. You might be tempted to submit a proposal to provide a carbon offset because you are producing biofuels to displace petroleum products.

2. Suppose you have a corn/ethanol facility in Iowa powered by standby diesel generators. The generators burn dirty. They emit lots of soot (carbon); nitrogen; carbon monoxide; aldehydes; nitrogen dioxide; sulfur dioxide; and polycyclic aromatic hydrocarbons. If the owners submitted a proposal to provide 150 million tons of carbon offset over a period of years, at the carbon offset price of $13.90 they could collect millions of dollars to plant a small forest, which they would later burn down to produce charcoal for use in place of diesel to power their corn/ethanol facility.

As I understand the rules, example number two could qualify for carbon offset payments, as it would reduce CO_2 emissions by employing otherwise uneconomic techniques. Example number one seems like a much more environmentally friendly approach, but would not qualify because it is a best practice that already makes economic sense. Developers of carbon offsets must prove that their projects make no economic sense in the absence of CDM funds.

Gore's approach is designed to ratchet up the price of carbon offsets as it places a stranglehold on carbon emissions, a formula for lowering living standards, and also raises the total value of carbon trading on his climate exchanges. The requirement of additionality places pressure for an upward ratchet on the prices of offset projects by implying that as carbon emission prices rise, the price rises necessarily become self-reinforcing. Previously-uneconomic offset projects stand to be disqualified as they begin to make economic sense due to higher prices.

Another notable drawback of Gore's plan is that it requires the creation of a vast new bureaucracy of otherwise unnecessary emissions assessors. Operating under the auspices of the United Nations, the emissions assessors function through what are known in UN-speak as Designated Operational Entities (DOEs). They are best understood as climate accountants who audit promises of "not-carbon." Among the prominent firms that have signed on as DOEs is Deloitte Touche.

The emergence of climate auditors is a corollary to the lack of physical deliverables in Gore's carbon market. Presently, most of their attention is directed to first validating and later verifying emissions reductions (the promises of not-carbon) that can be used by purchasers against their emission caps.

Ultimately, however, as carbon emissions become more expensive, you can expect climate accountants to spread and conduct climate audits on practically every business and even on you. If you are fond of barbecue, you can bet that you will someday be obliged to contribute another increment to Gore's fortune by buying an offset on one of his climate exchanges if your jurisdiction joins the cap and trade scheme.

This no longer seems as inevitable as it did when Obama was elected.

At the margin, even congress folk will hesitate to slash the living standards of their constituents in order to cool the planet when it is already too cold for comfort. Another factor that will deter your august leaders from behaving like puppets in Gore's scheme is the fact that there are serious concerns about fraud on multiple levels in the European Climate Exchange.

Mark Schapiro explained in the *Harper's* February 2010 issue that, "Study after study has demonstrated that CDMs (clean development mechanism offsets) have not delivered the promised amount of emissions reductions." The anti-CO_2 fanatics are not convinced that trading "not-carbon" works to reduce emissions as much as advertised.[35]

Meanwhile, more traditional fraud appears to be rampant in CO_2 emissions trading. As Bloomberg's Matthew Carr has reported, there is a

---

[35] Schapiro, "Conning the Climate."

serious problem with theft, tax evasion, and traffic in stolen emissions certificates:

> European regulators need to take "decisive action" after a new round of fraud tainted the world's biggest emissions market, according to the head of carbon trading at Barclays Capital.
>
> Germany's Federal Environment Agency said Feb. 3 that about 250,000 CO_2 allowances with a market value of 3.2 million euros ($4.4 million) were improperly transferred after cyber attacks. The "phishing" incidents on Jan. 28, with fraudsters impersonating regulators to steal passwords, comes after Europe lost a total of 5 billion euros in revenue for the 18 months ending in December 2009 because of value-added tax fraud in the CO_2 market, according to Europol, the law enforcement agency.
>
> "Without consistent and decisive action by the European Union, the world's flagship carbon market will become mired in fraudulent activity," Louis Redshaw, managing director at the investment-bank unit of Barclays Plc, said in a phone interview.[36]

All told, there is good and bad news about the progress of Gore's project to make billions by making the world colder. The best news is that he can no more dial down the world's thermostat than King Canute could turn back the tide.

A big piece of the bad news, however, is that the quality of public discourse has sunk so low that millions of people, including many in authority, are quite prepared to accept propositions like the anthropogenic global warming fraud—the concept that manmade CO_2 emissions threaten to turn the planet into an uninhabitable inferno. The true believers are not even polite about it.

For example, Jeff Goodell, who wrote an article entitled "You Idiots: Meet the Planet's Worst Enemies" for *Rolling Stone*, is quick to castigate entrepreneurs like David Koch who dare to challenge global

---

[36] Matthew Carr, "EU Needs Quick Action on New CO2 Fraud, Barclays Says," Bloomberg, February 5, 2010, www.bloomberg.com/apps/news?pid=newsarchive&sid=avLf2LqR6Szs&pos=13.

warming myths. And he vents with hysterical hyperbole about any resistance to Gore's schemes. Witness,

> As the failure to pass the climate bill reveals, it may be easier to defeat a dictator like Hitler than to overcome internal threats to our future as powerful as Big Coal and Big Oil. Despite the near-certainty of a climate catastrophe, there are no crowds marching in the streets to demand action.[37]

But he and others have been silent about Gore's luminous conflicts of interests in advocating a cap and trade mandate that would make him a billionaire while making the world poorer.

Equally, one could infer that episodes like the banning of CFCs and now global warming misinformation somehow parallel the financial crisis. They imply an exhaustion of profit potential from conventional economic activity, as many industries seem to prefer counterproductive political campaigns as the route to raise profitability in saturated markets. (The logical flaw here is that if markets are really saturated, the scope for politicians to extract extra trillions from them is smaller than they seem to think.)

Consider the unspoken subtext of the CFC ban, as reported by David Van Dyke:

> The other significant coincidence that happened about this same time was that DuPont, a major CFC manufacturer, was poised to lose its patent on one of the most widely-used CFCs. Three Canadian investors who owned 25 percent of the company led the campaign to ban CFCs. DuPont initially fought the CFC phase out, but the company finally acquiesced when it had secured a patent on a CFC substitute. After all, billions of dollars were at stake.[38]

---

[37] Jeff Goodell, "As the World Burns," *Rolling Stone*, February 27, 2010, www.rollingstone.com/politics/news/as-the-world-burns-20100106.

[38] David S. Van Dyke, "The CFC Ban: Global Warming's Pilot Episode," *American Thinker*, February 4, 2010, www.americanthinker.com/2010/02/the_cfc_ban_global_warmings_pi.html.

In short, the CFC ban was a cynical scheme to replace cheap, effective, generic products with costly, less-effective proprietary products with high margins. The CFC ban was all about money for manufacturers of refrigerant and refrigeration equipment, and money for drug manufacturers who were able to scam consumers into acquiescing in political actions that raised costs of refrigerants and propellants by magnitudes. Van Dyke summarizes:

> The media never seemed to report the real economic impact of the CFC ban. Replacing CFCs was not at all easy. There really are no suitable, safe, and affordable replacements for Halon fire control systems. Most propellants were not too difficult to replace (although many are flammable). One notable exception is the CFC propellant used in metered dose inhalers of asthma medication. CFCs were ideal for this application because they are both chemically and biologically inert. Eventually, the pharmaceutical industry found a solution: hydrofluoroalkanes (HFA). Of course, this new delivery method meant that previously inexpensive generic drugs (e.g., albuterol) suddenly became expensive proprietary drugs. The CFC ban effectively tripled the cost of managing asthma.
>
> From the time the "Freon phase out" began, virtually hundreds of millions of refrigeration systems worldwide had to be replaced. This included automobiles, homes, businesses, and food and medical refrigerators. The systems still functioned, but they could not be economically recharged with CFCs (does this sound familiar?). This enormous cost continues to be silently passed on to consumers. It is important to recognize that the alternatives to CFCs are many orders of magnitude more expensive than CFCs themselves. This is roughly analogous to comparing the cost per kWh of electricity produced by coal versus solar or wind.[39]

The asthma inhalers incorporating new, proprietary propellants were not only up to 10 times more expensive than the old ones using

---

[39] Van Dyke, "The CFC Ban."

CFCs; they were also less effective. A number of asthmatics died as a result when they failed to reach emergency rooms after using ineffective new inhalers. In my view, this is the moral equivalent of murder over a concocted hysteria about holes in the Antarctic ozone layer.

For reasons that could be debated for ages, people who were crucial gatekeepers in public discourse seem to have lost their bearings. They were only too willing to be scammed by preposterous hysteria over chlorine in CFCs, which are four-times heavier than air, somehow finding their way from the bottom of the atmosphere in the Northern Hemisphere where most of them were used, into the upper atmosphere over Antarctica.

No one ever proposed any physical mechanism by which that could occur, nor for that matter, did anyone produce even a shred of empirical evidence that CFCs harmed the atmosphere. No one could explain how the free chlorine ions from the annual use of 7,500 tons of CFCs could be crucial to damaging the ozone when the oceans of the earth emit 600,000,000 tons of chlorine annually.

Even more amazing, it was never even established that the seasonal ozone holes near Antarctica were anything out of the ordinary. When skeptical scientists attempted to publish evidence that Antarctic ozone holes predated the introduction of CFC, they were muzzled. It was not even established that chlorine ions, of any origin, were implicated in ozone depletion, as compared to cosmic rays or astrophysical phenomena.

The global credit collapse of 2008 served notice that the world's pockets are not as deep as previously supposed. With Obama apparently ruthless in his determination to press ahead with additional spending initiatives, the passage of cap and trade, could prove to be the "straw that broke the camel's back." As Joseph Tainter argued, "a complex society that is investing heavily in many cumulative organizational features, with low marginal return, may have little or no reserve for containing stress surges."[40] This would certainly seem to describe the United States. Equally Tainter says, "once a complex society enters the stage of declining marginal returns, collapse becomes a mathematical likelihood,

---

[40] Tainter, *Collapse of Complex Societies*, 207.

requiring little more than sufficient passage of time to make probable an insurmountable calamity."[41]

A New Maunder Minimum

As argued, the evidence points to actual climate change as dictated mainly by cyclical fluctuations in solar output and other astrophysical phenomena. The expectation that the sun's output should be stable is incredible in a dynamic universe. It is also belied by evidence from studies of paleoclimate, archeology, solar physics, history, and geology.

Reality is more complicated than the idea of a steady sun that radiates exactly the same amount of energy day in and day out for billions of years.

In fact, there are innumerable sources of fluctuation. Among the simpler of them is the fact that the earth does not really revolve around the sun. It orbits around the center of mass of the solar system. This is almost, but not quite the same as revolving around the sun, as the solar system's center of mass is offset by the mass of the large planets, particularly Jupiter (318 × the mass of the earth). The Jovian year, consisting of 11.86 earth years, coincides with one of the cycles of solar output, the Schwab or sunspot cycle of 11 years (also represented as 22 years). Put simply, when Jupiter is closest to the sun, its output of radiant energy tends to fall.

Just as there are short- and long-term economic cycles, so there are short- and longer-term cycles of solar activity (in combination with other astronomical variables). There is a Suess Cycle of 210 years, also known as the DeVries Cycle. There is a Halstatt Cycle of 2,300 years. A still longer cycle of solar radiation has been identified at 6,000 years.

The main driver of climate is variation in the sun's radiant energy, as it always has been. When other astrophysical factors come into play, like the transit of the solar system through the spiral arms of the galaxy, they tend to have catastrophic consequences. At those times, when the sun's output is too weak to shield the earth from intensified bombardment by cosmic rays, the world tends to go into long-lasting Ice Ages.

---

[41] Tainter, *Collapse of Complex Societies*, 195.

While the earth is spinning around the solar system, it is also trailing the sun through the Milky Way at a speed of 250 kilometers per second. Israeli astrophysicist Nir J. Shaviv has shown that the earth's trajectory through the galaxy is probably responsible for cycling in and out of the deepest and longest Ice Ages.[42]

Whenever the sun traverses the dense spiral arms of the galaxy, the earth is bombarded by cosmic rays and stardust, including such exotic materials as helium 3 (He_3) that can only form in outer space. This increases cloud cover and reflects solar radiation back into space sending the earth into a deep freeze.

By comparison, a Little Ice Age like that endured in the seventeenth century and thereafter is a blessing. Indeed, the last Little Ice Age during the Maunder Minimum was a blessing in more ways than one. While weather turned decisively colder it remained much warmer than in a full fledged Ice Age when glaciers spread over much of the Northern Hemisphere. It is estimated that the ice cover in the area where Detroit is now located was as much as a mile thick during the deepest freeze of the last Ice Age. (And you thought that the plunge in the median price of homes in Detroit to $6,000 was drastic.)

Dearth, Insanity, and Revolution

It may seem an exaggeration to say that cold weather makes people crazy. But every climate upheaval in recorded history has come as a disorienting shock to the people who experienced it. Without exception, leaders have tended to do the wrong thing, wasting precious resources. (You might well include the Bernanke/Obama policy of consciously creating inflation at a time when the weather seems destined to curtail food supplies as one of those wrong things that leaders do in climate upheavals.) Mostly, they have wanted to make offerings to whatever false gods they were worshipping at the time, or undertake bloody campaigns to purge society of evildoers imagined to have provoked the wrath of those gods. The Mayans routinely practiced human

---

[42] Nir J. Shaviv, "The Milky Way Galaxy's Spiral Arms and Ice-Age Epochs and the Cosmic Ray Connection," ScienceBits, March 30, 2006, www.sciencebits .com/ice-ages.

sacrifice to appease the gods of climate. Europeans were somewhat less barbaric, but only marginally.

Peter Christie recounts the story of Barbara Gobel, who woke up to a hard frost one seventeenth century morning in late May in Wurzburg, Germany. Miss Gobel was a teenager, listed in the executioner's logbook as "the fairest maid in Wurzburg." When the late spring freezes killed the wheat crop and destroyed all the wine grapes around Wurzburg, Barbara Gobel, like many others, fell afoul of her cruel, superstitious neighbors. She and 900 other residents of Wurzburg were rounded up and put to death as "witches." Christie reports, "About one million people are believed to have been burned, hanged, strangled, drowned or beheaded for witchcraft."[43]

Whatever the precise number of victims of violent hysteria surrounding extraordinarily cold weather, their fate should be cautionary. Some of those who helped to kill the prettiest girl in Wurzburg and 900 others for imaginary crimes were probably not so much deluded that their victims caused the cold through witchcraft as just ruthless. They probably sought to keep for themselves a larger ration from meager, local food supplies that were suddenly inadequate for all the hungry mouths.

At that time, Germany's population was 95 percent smaller than it is now. Nine hundred persons would have comprised about 10 percent of the local population. Disposing of them not only helped to placate the superstitious, it left more food for the survivors.

Remember, in the seventeenth century, almost all food was consumed in the vicinity where it was produced. There were no railroads or 18-wheel trucks to haul grain or meat from one locale to another. Since the areas adjacent to Wurzburg had all suffered from the same savagely colder climate, there were few handy reserves upon which to draw when the grain crop failed, year-after-year.

If anything like the last Little Ice Age recurs today, you can expect bloody insanity in the world. Those with power will use it, arbitrarily, no doubt unjustly, to secure as much as possible of a diminished supply of food and other vital resources for themselves. When that moment comes, you do not want to be dependent on Food Stamps to survive.

---

[43] Peter Christie, *The Curse of Akkad: Climate Upheavals That Rocked Human History* (Richmond Hill, Ontario: Annick Press, 2008), 67.

Given the current fixation on imaginary global warming, you can expect the authorities to respond to the turn toward colder weather ineptly by further curtailing access to hydrocarbons, thus making it more difficult and costly to grow food and heat homes and other structures. But the bare chemical trace of manmade carbon dioxide (0.117 percent) in the atmosphere will be reduced by a bare chemical trace.

By the end of the seventeenth century, during the deepest cold of the Maunder Minimum, the winter of 1693–1694, the cold had catastrophic impact on local populations. In France, wine froze on Sun King's table at Versailles, and 1/10th of the population of France "perished from famine and attendant epidemics."[44]

Louis XIV was lucky to keep his throne. The French people were too enervated to revolt successfully when savage cold led to famine. The Chongzhen emperor in China did not fare so well. In fact, he lost his throne early in the Little Ice Age. When crop failures led to famine, peasants revolted under the leadership of Li Zicheng. Li mobilized avid support in mountainous Shanxi Province, where higher altitudes amplified the adverse impact of colder weather on crop yields. Famine-stricken peasants rallied behind Li's slogan of "dividing land equally and abolishing the grain taxes payment system."

After many adventures and some improbable good luck, Li's rag-tag forces defeated the home guard of the Ming army, and then sacked the capital Beijing, leading the last Ming emperor to commit suicide. Li moved to fill the power void, declaring himself emperor of the short-lived Shun Dynasty.

The story of how Li Zicheng mobilized famine-stricken peasants to overthrow the long-established Ming Dynasty during the last Little Ice Age in 1644 is a footnote to most investors. Ask your neighbors or your colleagues at work. I can assure you they know nothing about it. But I am equally confident that it is well known among the current hierarchy of China. You can count on them to act in whatever way they perceive will limit the risk that their dynasty will be turfed out by the modern equivalent of famine-stricken peasants.

---

[44] Brian Fagan, *The Little Ice Age: How Climate Made History, 1300–1850* (New York: Basic Books, 2000), 155.

As you know, the Chinese control trillions in foreign exchange reserves. Their economy is now the second-largest on the globe, and only marginally smaller than the U.S. economy on a purchasing power parity (PPP) basis.[45] This is an astonishing change, considering that as recently as 20 years ago, China's economy amounted to just 5 percent of the U.S. economy. The building spree associated with the greatest surge of economic growth the world has ever known puts the Chinese in the driver's seat as the leading customers for many of the world's raw materials.

Depending upon how seriously China's ruling engineers view peak oil as a barrier to their internal growth and the degree of their concern about the threat to dynastic stability posed by rising food prices, they will move sooner, rather than later, to pull the plug on the U.S. economy. Deflating U.S. demand will reduce their sales, but also reduce their costs and enable them to reset oil and other commodity prices at lower levels.

If the Chinese do pull the plug on the U.S. economy, it will be because they recall the circumstances to which the Reverend Thomas Malthus alluded in lamenting the "but too frequent" bouts of bad weather that afflicted China where "millions of people" perished of hunger in "times of famine." There does appear to be an acute risk of unrest in China. That is what the Chinese government must think, as officials there maintained tight censorship on news of the Egyptian street protests against high food prices. When Mubarak's ouster was finally reported, it was disingenuously attributed to a military coup. As reported by the *Economist*, searches for the word "Egypt" in Sina Weibo, one of China's leading Twitter-like services, produces a warning that, "according to the relevant laws, regulations and policies, the search results have not been displayed." On Baidu, a big news portal, a prominent list of " 'hot search terms' includes 'the return of compatriots stranded in Egypt,' but nothing else."[46]

---

[45] For more information, see Gavyn Davies, "China Is Bigger than You May Think," *Financial Times*, February 15, 2011, http://blogs.ft.com/gavyndavies /2011/02/15/china-is-bigger-than-you-may-think/.

[46] "Build a Wall," *The Economist*, February 3, 2011, www.economist.com/node/ 18065655.

The Chinese authorities are predictably reticent about highlighting news of food riots gaining traction abroad when China has perhaps the highest food inflation rate in the world. The National Bureau of Statistics of China indicates that the average price of food in 50 Chinese cities in the January 21 to 31, 2011, period increased by 4.6 percent compared to the prior 10-day period (416 percent annualized).[47] This rampant food inflation in the economy of the leading creditor of the United States, where per capita income is on par with Tunisia's, poses serious risks to the global recovery and to the United States in particular.

Officially, China's urban unemployment rate is 4.1 percent. But the Chinese are more adept at confusing their unemployment picture with statistical smoke than even the U.S. Bureau of Labor Statistics. The 4.1 percent rate they report is the Urban Registered Unemployment Rate. It is an artifact of Maoist era internal controls on migration within the country and does not count the millions (no, hundreds of millions) of internal migrants from the countryside who are not officially urban residents. When these "discouraged workers" are considered, China's actual unemployment rate is a staggering 22 percent. Given China's size, that means that about 200 million Chinese lack work.

This is social tinder every bit as combustible as that in North Africa and the Middle East, where street rebellions lit a fuse under governments from Libya to Syria. Rather than let it ignite, China's leaders would much prefer to deflate the U.S. economy.

Note that the two most populous countries, India and China, are both on course to require significant food imports. China is rapidly urbanizing, a trend that is bound to reduce agricultural output, now the world's largest, in the decades ahead. The poor quality of China's freshwater resources also tells against a continuation of China's lead in farm output. Many experts believe that China's acute shortage of fresh water is its most pressing limit to growth. With some 350 million peasants expected to migrate from the countryside to urban settings that are still to be built, there is no obvious means to supplement degraded water supplies. China's largest waterway, the Yellow River, has been

---

[47] "Average Price of Food in 50 Cities, January 21–31, 2011," National Bureau of Statistics of China, February 9, 2011, www.stats.gov.cn/english /newsandcomingevents/t20110209_402701782.htm.

declining in recent years. In some months, its flow dribbles out before reaching the Pacific Ocean. Worse, according to Christina Larson, reporting for Yale University, "the river is now an estimated 10 percent sewage by volume."[48]

Meanwhile, in the past half century (from 1961 through 2007), while India's population tripled, its arable land per capita has been halved, from 0.35 hectares to 0.14 hectares. Agricultural productivity increased due to much higher energy inputs in farming, and increased irrigation from fossil aquifers. Neither of the world's two most populous countries is in a position to expand food production, quite apart from the likely consequence as Little Ice Age temperatures slash arable land worldwide. Now India, like China, is actively acquiring farmland abroad.

The debt-saturated advanced temperate-climate countries, are falling behind in this preparation for the future. I could be wrong, but I suspect that we're in the midst of one of history's biggest transition crises. If the advanced economies are flushed deeper into the solvency abyss in part because climate shifts us into Little Ice Age conditions, you can expect a global Malthusian resource panic, followed by a slow, protracted adjustment period that could prove fatal to hundreds of millions of people.

Now is the time for you to think about the fact that cold kills—in more ways than one. Unlike periods of warmer climate, like the Roman Warming and the Medieval Optimum, which were three to five degrees warmer than today, with plentiful food, colder periods are times of famine, want and more rapid extinctions. They are times of greatly increased war and struggle over decreased food and other resources.

Forget Global Warming. Global Darkening is upon us.

---

[48] Christina Larson, "Growing Shortages of Water Threaten China's Development," Yale Environment 360, July 26, 2010, http://e360.yale.edu /feature/growing_shortages_of_water_threaten_chinas_development/2298/.

Chapter 6

Deficit Attention Disorder

How the Perverse Logic of Debtism Promotes
the Illusion of Democratic Consensus
but Devastates the Economy

There is no means of avoiding the final collapse of a boom brought about by credit (debt) expansion. The alternative is only whether the crisis should come sooner as the result of a voluntary abandonment of further credit (debt) expansion, or later as a final and total catastrophe of the currency system involved.

—Ludwig von Mises

O ne of the least understood consequences of the abandonment of gold in the U.S. monetary system is its effect in transforming the United States from the world's most dynamic capitalist economy into a predatory system of debtism. As I defined in Chapter 2, debtism is the corrupt and pathological perversion of capitalism in which the greater part of the purchasing power of the country is diverted into the pockets of bankers and their best customers. Let's take a look at how this shift changed the world.

How Debtism Changed the World

Not to be vain about it, but I probably had a better grasp of the big picture twenty years ago than all but a few persons on the globe. Working with Lord Rees-Mogg, we correctly anticipated the fall of the Berlin Wall, the collapse of the Soviet Union, the rise of Islamic terrorism, and the failure of the state socialist experiment. It was precisely these insights that led to the founding of Anatolia Minerals (now Alacer Gold) and its stablemates among junior resource companies. Unlike most other analysts, we did not swallow the conventional wisdom that depressions were a thing of the past that had been superseded by clever manipulation of fiat money. I knew that another depression was likely in my lifetime. In addition to that, I knew from my eccentric research into past financial crises that they are inevitably bullish for gold.

What I failed to grasp, however, was that the onset of depression would not just entail a cyclical recurrence, but could represent a disastrous transformation of the whole nature of the economy. This was part and parcel of the little-noted transformation of the capitalist economy of the United States and other developed nations into debtist systems.

Why do I call the current economic system *debtism* rather than *capitalism*? For the simple and compelling reason that debt rather than capital lies at its heart. If you peel back the layers of the onion that shroud the dynamics of the current U.S. economy, you see that capital is no longer central. It is all about debt and the almost desperate angling by authorities to keep the debt aggregates expanding. All their policies aim toward stimulating private debt expansion. And failing that, things get messy.

When debt expands beyond the carrying capacity of consumers and economies, the natural tendency would be for debt to contract, as uncollectable obligations are written down; borrowers go bankrupt; and their remaining assets are auctioned off for the benefit of creditors. But this implies a deflationary collapse of the banking system and a sharp contraction of the economy. To avoid this purging of the system, the fallback position of the authorities is to perpetuate bad private debt by transplanting it onto the sovereign balance sheet. If you can't pay your mortgage, it will end up as part of the national debt to be borne by generations of desperate debt slaves so long as the status quo endures.

When Karl Marx criticized the capitalist (*Kapitalist*) mode of production in *The Communist Manifesto* (1848), he focused his attack on capital. According to Marx, the evil of capitalism was that it enabled the owners of capital to extract "surplus value" from workers. While all previous societies had extracted surplus labor, capitalism was new in doing so via the sale of produced commodities. Note that Marx's criticism was essentially an abstract complaint about the character of mass employment. The "exploitation" involved in debtism is far more predatory. It entails the wholesale diversion of the purchasing power of money into artificial asset bubbles for the benefit of a small sliver of the population.

Debtism has trumped capitalism as a mechanism for concentrating wealth. (I say this as someone who has never been an invidious egalitarian.) Inequality of income doesn't particularly bother me, per se. But I think it notable that the movement away from gold-backed (which is to say, asset-based money) to pure fiat money, based entirely upon debt, has led directly to increasing concentration of wealth.

You need only look at the dispersion of income in the United States before and after Richard Nixon repudiated the Gold Reserve Standard in 1971. As Kenneth Gerbino has pointed out, the shift from a quasi-asset based money to a pure fiat money, or unalloyed debtism, resulted in a drastic loss of income by those who work and save:

> It is the paper money created out of thin air that creates the unfair distribution of wealth that is making the middle class fall more behind and the poor more poor. Newly created money and credit in a paper money system benefits those that can access the money first and buy capital goods and real property at one price before the new money circulates and makes all prices go up. Wages also do not keep up with inflation and that creates another squeeze on the middle class . . . the bottom 90% of our citizens went from owning a big piece of the income gains (65%) in the 1960's to being squashed in the 2002−2007 period to 11%.[1]

---

[1] Kenneth J. Gerbino, "The Great Deceit," 321gold.com, May 28, 2010, www .321gold.com/editorials/gerbino/gerbino052810.html.

Part of the mechanism by which debtism impoverishes the masses is by transforming incentives and rewards for work and savings. To most outward appearances, the United States continued to seem like a free market, capitalist economy. But it changed in important ways that advantaged the few at the expense of the many.

The first perversion that arises from fiat money is the substitution of debt for capital as the mother's milk of economic growth. In a fiat system, such as that prevailing in the United States over the past four decades, production is not based upon savings and invested capital, it is spun out of money aggregates that expand as debt expands. Indeed, fiat money itself only comes into existence as debt. Extinguish the debt, and you extinguish the money supply.

Obviously, where money is borrowed into existence, the primary beneficiaries of the new money are those who have first access to it. Typically, it is those who are already well-heeled. It is they who have the good credit and collateral to borrow anew.

Another hidden expropriation of average people arises from the fact that a "pure credit" (fiat) money devalues earnings. With asset-backed money like the gold standard, the price level tends to fall as more goods and services are produced while the money aggregates rise slowly or not at all. With gold-based money, there is no way to produce a sustained credit expansion. The money supply only expands as a consequence of gold discoveries and increased mine output, or an improvement in the balance of trade that leads to the import of bullion. In short, with a real gold standard, the money supply expands very slowly.

Of course, to speak of a gold standard before the Civil War means trading in stylized facts, as the U.S. political system has rarely been hardy enough to sustain the rigors of sound money.

The nineteenth-century U.S. banking system was a confused proliferation of note-issuing banks, mostly chartered by states, with few or no branch offices. These banks tended to issue far more paper certificates for gold than their actual gold holdings would permit. Notoriously, note-issuing banks tended to locate their offices in remote corners of states, where it would be costly and inconvenient for customers to travel in order to redeem their paper notes for gold.

The reality was that the early nineteenth-century gold standard was diluted by the inflationary issue of bank notes that were purportedly redeemable for gold, but actually circulated in sometimes-generous excess to the underlying bullion. Furthermore, what passed for a gold standard was usually suspended during wars. This led to periods of more pronounced inflation, followed by contractions as credit tightened after the gold standard was reestablished in peacetime.

This happened in the United States after the Civil War. During that conflict, on February 25, 1862, Congress passed the Legal Tender Act, which forced Americans to accept paper money at par with gold and silver, thus allowing the government to pay its bills in paper money. After the war, the greenbacks were withdrawn from circulation. A long, deflationary phase began in 1873, and lasted until 1896. According to analyst Nikhil Raheja,

> During these years, production increased due to excessive savings/investments and high productivity, while the money supply grew at a slower pace, causing a mismatch between the total money available for consumption and the value of products on sale, and resulted in a fall in prices.[2]

I don't necessarily see the nineteenth century fall in prices as a mismatch but rather as an example of the free market dynamic at work, in which money tended to grow in value as productivity rose. This made the poor richer, as income they earned grew more valuable. According to economist Murray N. Rothbard, in A *History of Money and Banking in the United States: The Colonial Era to World War II*, general prices in the United States fell 1 percent on average each year during this period. In total, prices fell about 20 percent over 23 years. Note that with prices falling as a result of economic progress, the income of a person with stagnant wages grew 20 percent.

This was very different from what happens today under the debtist system of pure credit money, with concerted inflation of the money supply as debt proliferates. From 1970 through 2008, the money supply (M-2) in the United States skyrocketed by 1,314 percent, from $624 billion to $8.2 trillion. Meanwhile, real economic goods, the actual

---

[2] See Nikhil Raheja, "There is Nothing Wrong with Price Deflation," Seeking Alpha, October 19, 2009, http://seekingalpha.com/article/167225-there-is-nothing-wrong-with-price-deflation.

things that comprise the good life that people want to buy with money expanded barely at all. Naturally, prices increased when the dollar was cheapened as the debt orgy proceeded, with each new dollar of debt tending to result in an equivalent increase in the money supply.

If you have been tracking economic statistics with even one eye in recent years, however, you know that consumer prices have not increased by 1,314 percent in the past four decades. As measured by the government's slanted CPI calculations, you needed $5,549.05 in 2008 to attain the purchasing power of $1,000 in 1970. Obviously, a worker with stagnant wages lost quite a bit of purchasing power. But an even more powerful explanation for the growing inequality of wealth created by the debtist system becomes clear when you consider which prices were inflated disproportionately by all the trillions in new money borrowed into existence since 1970.

Put simply, the newly created money was put to use funding investment booms in both financial and hard assets. Wall Street analyst Kel Kelly is unusual in looking at this from the perspective of Austrian economic theory. He writes:

> the only real force that ultimately makes the stock market or any market rise (and, to a large extent, fall) *over the longer term* is simply changes in the quantity of money and the volume of spending in the economy. Stocks rise when there is inflation of the money supply (i.e., more money in the economy and in the markets). This truth has many consequences that should be considered.[3]

In other words, the currency was depreciated largely to stimulate investment booms. Kelly quotes Austrian economist, Fritz Machlup, saying,

> It is impossible for the profits of all or of the majority of enterprises to rise without an increase in the effective monetary circulation (through the creation of new credit or

---

[3] Kel Kelly, "How the Stock Market and Economy Really Work," Mises Daily, September 1, 2010, http://mises.org/daily/4654/How-the-Stock-Market-and-Economy-Really-Work.

dishoarding). . . . If it were not for the elasticity of bank
credit . . . a boom in security values could not last for any
length of time. In the absence of inflationary credit the funds
available for lending to the public for security purchases would
soon be exhausted, since even a large supply is ultimately
limited. The supply of funds derived solely from current
new savings and current amortization allowances is fairly
inelastic. . . . Only if the credit organization of the banks
(by means of inflationary credit) or large-scale dishoarding by
the public make the supply of loanable funds highly elastic, can a
lasting boom develop. . . . A rise on the securities market
cannot last any length of time unless the public is both willing
and able to make increased purchases.[4]

Of course, the issue is even more basic than that. Asset booms do not
arise solely because banks are prepared to lend funds "to the public for
securities purchases." Partly, they are a function of the fact that fiat
money makes it easier for many businesses to grow and earn a profit.
This is a policy that suits the fiscal imperatives of the state. Inflation
increases nominal profits and therefore increases tax receipts.

There is probably also a political imperative to ramp up GDP, which
happens automatically with inflation. Kelly puts it this way:

. . . a rise in GDP is mathematically possible only if the money
price of individual goods produced is increasing to some degree.
Otherwise, with a constant supply of money and spending, the
total amount of money companies earn—the total selling prices
of all goods produced—and thus GDP itself would all necessarily remain constant year after year. . . .

. . . [I]f there were a constant amount of money in the
economy, the sum total of all shares of all stocks taken together (or
a stock index) could not increase. Plus, if company profits, in the
aggregate, were not increasing, there would be no aggregate
increase in earnings per share to be imputed into stock prices. . . .

---

[4] Fritz Machlup, *The Stock Market, Credit, and Capital Formation* (New York:
Macmillan, 1940), 78, 90, 92.

In an economy where the quantity of money was static, the levels of stock indexes, year by year, would stay approximately even, or drift slightly lower—depending on the rate of increase in the number of new shares issued. And, overall, businesses (in the aggregate) would be selling a greater volume of goods at lower prices, and total revenues would remain the same. In the same way, businesses, overall, would purchase more goods at lower prices each year, keeping the spread between costs and revenues about the same, which would keep aggregate profits about the same. . . .

Under these circumstances, capital gains (the profiting from the buying low and selling high of assets) could be made only by stock picking—by investing in companies that are expanding market share, bringing to market new products, etc., thus truly gaining proportionately more revenues and profits at the expense of those companies that are less innovative and efficient. . . .

The stock prices of the gaining companies would rise while others fell. Since the average stock would not actually increase in value, most of the gains made by investors from stocks would be in the form of dividend payments. By contrast, in our world today, most stocks—good and bad ones—rise during inflationary bull markets and decline during bear markets. The good companies simply rise faster than the bad.[5]

If you consider the evolution of stock picking as an art during the twentieth century, it followed the indicated path of change informed by the changing character of money. Early in the twentieth century, when bank credit was far less elastic than at present, analysts tended to recommend stocks based on their dividend yields. As implied by Kelly's argument, there were not many capital gains to be had. The Dow Jones Industrial Average closed at 68.13 on January 2, 1900. It didn't rally decisively above 100 until 1920—after the inflation engendered by World War I had taken hold.

---

[5] Kelly, "How the Stock Market and Economy Really Work."

Unlike the recent period, when companies have tended to go public even before they became profitable, and many high-tech companies prided themselves in paying no dividends, in the days before debtism replaced capitalism as the organizing principle of the U.S. economy, it was hard to achieve a public listing. Companies could not file a prospectus around a business plan scribbled on the back of a napkin and raise hundreds of millions on the expectation of capital gains as they had during the dot-com boom.

Kelly argues that GDP growth, as measured in money and stock market values as reflected by broad indices like the S&P 500 and the Dow Jones Index, rises only as a result of the increase in money caused by the expansion of bank credit. Note that the DJIA went from 809 on January 2, 1970 to 12,800.18 on January 4, 2008, a gain of 1,582 percent, even greater than the increase in the (M-?) money supply in that period.

Clearly, a big percentage of the newly created money that was borrowed into existence during recent decades of growing wealth inequality went into increasing stock market values and bidding up other assets, including real estate. Who benefited most from these asset bubbles caused by the hydraulic force of credit expansion working its way through the economy? Obviously, persons who were already well-off, and had collateral to offer when borrowing money, gained the lion's share of the advantage of access to new credit.

Higher stock prices are not merely accidental or the coincidental consequence of credit expansion. Close analysis of Federal Reserve data shows that the authorities (also known as the Plunge Protection Team) have persistently pumped money into Wall Street. Phoenix Capital Research observes:

> . . . we have not had a period in which the Fed wasn't pumping tens of billions into the markets since 2007. Indeed, the only time the Fed wasn't officially pumping its brains out was between the end of QE 1 (April 2010) and the announcement of QE lite (August 2010). . . .
>
> However, despite the formal declaration that QE 1 was over, the Fed DID continue to pump north of $10—20 billion

into the markets every month, ALWAYS during options expiration week (this is pure coincidence of course).[6]

Business owners, managers, Wall Street bankers, and stockholders obviously gained more from the asset bubbles inflated by credit expansion than persons with stagnant incomes and no collateral.

Of course, I admit that it is difficult to abstract the impact of pure credit money in distorting the economy. Two aspects of rampant credit expansion are hard to grasp. According to Austrian economists, one of the crucial consequences of artificial credit expansion is a dramatic reduction in the efficiency of investment. Creating money out of thin air leads to a big surge of malinvestment, which both reduces the productivity of investment and leaves the economy vulnerable to collapse when the credit orgy inevitably comes to an end.

Equally, at first blush, it might not seem credible that rising GDP and escalating stock market indices are entirely epiphenomena of the expansion of bank credit. What of progress and improved productivity? Would not they account for growing wealth in society and stock appreciation?

The answer is yes and no. Without a doubt, real GDP rises when productivity increases and the economy produces more stuff that counts in material tallies of the good life. But Kelly's argument is that without artificial credit expansion society would become richer without an increase in the supply of money. Nominal GDP stays more or less flat, so that progress is reflected in falling living costs, as happened in the nineteenth century. Therefore, although there would be no explosion in the aggregate amount of profits earned, the real value of each dollar earned in corporate profits would rise.

Then what? A country with sound money in a bankrupt world would stick out like a supermodel in Huntington, West Virginia (widely recognized as America's fattest city). The value of the sound (or even semisound) currency would skyrocket. The conventional expectation would be that foreign sales for products priced in that currency would

---

[6] "Can Stocks Rally Without the Fed Juicing the Market?," Zero Hedge, June 17, 2011, www.zerohedge.com/article/can-stocks-rally-without-fed-juicing-market.

shrivel as currency movements raised the real costs of labor and all the factors that contribute to production.

Here you catch a glimpse of another reason that fiat money devalues labor. It fosters a race to the bottom. In a bankrupt world, where every economy is more or less addicted to debt, the geniuses who run central banks are all trying to make their currencies worth less. By contrast, the mechanism of progress with gold-backed money would be a steady increase in the value of the currency. Nothing of the kind could be tolerated in a debtist economy.

Witness the continued fulminations of the honorable members of Congress who have spent years trying to browbeat the Chinese into making the renminbi yuan worth more in foreign exchange markets. Consider the House-passed Currency Reform for Fair Trade Act of 2011, which would authorize the United States to slap duties on Chinese goods. Some 150 Congress-folk sponsoring the legislation are perturbed that the Chinese are buying tens of billions of U.S. dollars every month, thus keeping the value of the dollar from plunging as much as they would like.

"This unfair trade practice translates into a significant subsidy, artificially making U.S. products more expensive, and jeopardizing efforts to create and preserve manufacturing jobs in America," then-House speaker Nancy Pelosi (D-CA), said in a statement in support of the legislation in 2010.

There you see the animating principle of the debtist economy, namely that debt should be proliferated as far as possible, and fiat currency depreciated rapidly so as to lower labor and other factor costs, as well as lower the burdens of debt service. Little wonder that hard-working people get poorer with fiat money. Labor's share of U.S. national income has sunk lower than at any point in the past 60 years. As of June 2011 there were 44 million persons in the United States participating in the Supplemental Nutrition Assistance Program (SNAP) "food stamp" program, up from 27 million in October 2007—an increase of nearly 63 percent in less than four years.

In a better world, sound currencies based on gold would appreciate, rather than depreciate. Nominal GDP and stock market indices would grow slowly or not at all, while real wages and real wealth rose. And no one would mistake Nancy Pelosi for an economist. But note: the fact that she is helping to inform economic policy in the real world in which we live underscores an important, informing reason why debtism eclipsed capitalism as the organizing principle of the American economy. Debtism is better suited to the imperatives of politics.

Debtism Helps Politicians Manipulate You

Politicians want to manipulate economies. When they have the money illusion at their disposal, they can sell their favors to high bids from many factions angling for advantage in a politicized world. In addition to that, the surge in nominal GDP and asset booms that go hand-in-hand with remorseless credit expansion entail great advantages to politicians because they do concentrate income and wealth in the hands of a relative few.

Why does this help politicians?

For one thing, the impoverishment of the median voter puts him in a position of dependence on politicians. Of course, not one voter in a thousand recognizes that the collapse of real income growth is a direct consequence of the failed attempt to substitute debt for higher energy inputs in growing the economy. But it is far more popular to blame "Wall Street" greed and a lack of "regulation." In other words, give politicians more control.

In light of the analysis we have been exploring, the idea that better regulation could have prevented the Great Correction is superficial and implausible. Yes, certain types of regulation could have worked to keep the system from capsizing into collapse. But such regulations would have countermanded what the politicians wanted to see done. For example, can you honestly conclude that the politicians were prepared to authorize regulations that would have stopped the subprime crisis in its tracks? The politicians wanted to expand home ownership. In fact, they instituted specific regulations, like the Community Reinvestment Act to encourage banks to lend large sums to subprime borrowers in bad neighborhoods.

Equally, the exaggerated capital gains that arise from a rapid growth of nominal GDP create a lot of wealth that politicians can tap into and leverage for their own purposes.

A feature of credit-based money is that it has enabled politicians to more efficiently buy votes. For one thing, credit expansion enables constituents to at least temporarily live beyond their means. Since most politicians' terms are temporary, an ephemeral illusion of prosperity is often sufficient to secure their reelection.

Another, more complicated reward to politicians from runaway credit expansion is its effect in apparently concentrating the costs of government on a small fraction of the population, while spreading benefits to larger voting groups. The inflation of credit leads to higher nominal profits and outsized capital gains for those who are positioned to pocket them. Having helped to fill the pockets of the lucky few, the politicians then help themselves and pick those same pockets.

This is clearly illustrated by trends in Nancy Pelosi's California. In the 1970–1971 fiscal year, before Nixon repudiated the Gold Reserve Standard, the top 10 percent of California income earners paid a hefty 28.2 percent of California's personal income tax. By 2006, given the increased concentration income in the debtist economy, the top 10 percent were paying an astonishing 78.5 percent of California's Personal Income Tax.

While this made life for politicians easier so long as the party lasted, it is also high among the reasons that California is broke now. The politicians laid such a high percentage of the tax burden on a small fraction of the population that when the great correction began and easy capital gains disappeared, California's finances were devastated. Indeed, California was so dependent on a relative handful of rich persons to pay its bills that if even a few of them moved to Nevada, it threatened to undermine the state's bond rating.

What happened in California is a microcosm of what has happened to the U.S. federal government. California's budget situation is more desperate because the state's personal income taxes were more progressive going into the great correction. Also, let's not forget, California's task in borrowing money is more complicated than the federal government's. California must borrow money that already exists. The Feds can lend themselves cash by creating it out of the clear blue sky. And that is exactly what they have done, monetizing 140 percent of federal deficits during the process known as QE2.

The U.S. Budget Deficits Would Make Greece Blush

One of the more remarkable failures of the mass media in twenty-first-century America has been their silence in reporting the pathetic picture of U.S. federal finances. Notwithstanding the great economic accomplishments by private Americans in building wealth, the U.S. government currently finds itself with fiscal ratios so terrible that they have seldom been seen in even the most backward banana republics. Since 1970, federal spending has skyrocketed, rising more than 10 times faster than the median household income.[7] In inflation-adjusted 2010 dollars, median income rose from $39,732 in 1970 to $50,255 in 2009, a pathetically small gain of 27 percent over four decades. Meanwhile federal spending in 2010 dollars was $809 billion in 1970 and $3,551,000,000,000 in 2009, a surge of 299 percent.

In 2010, the United States found itself having borrowed (or printed) $0.55 of every dollar it spent since Lehman Brothers went broke in September 2008.

Think I am exaggerating? Here are the facts. Total net federal debt issued from September 2008 through July 2010 was $3.351 trillion. Gross individual tax receipts came to $3.185 trillion. Less refunds of $660 billion, the net individual tax take came to just more than $2.5 trillion. Add the corporate receipts of $250 billion, net of refunds, and total net tax revenue came to $2.775 trillion. In other words, the fiscal policy of the U.S. government was to borrow $0.55 for each $0.45 of receipts in the till.

This is the kind of deficit spending that has *always* been associated with hyperinflation and economic collapse in developing countries, and even in so-called advanced countries in the wake of wars.

The world's largest economy is fundamentally weak, much weaker than the economic and political establishment pretends. Indeed, I suspect that United States is so weakened that it is in peril of collapse.

---

[7] "Federal Spending Grew Nearly 12 Times Faster than Median Income," Heritage Foundation, chart entitled "Percent Change of Inflation-Adjusted Dollars (2010)," www.heritage.org/budgetchartbook/growth-federal-spending.

This may seem incredible in light of the announcement by the National Bureau of Economic Research (NBER) that the longest downturn since the Great Depression ended in June 2009. I am not alone in thinking that the determination that the recession ended may have been made rather hastily.

As you probably don't remember, but may have read, Herbert Hoover wore out his welcome with the American people by proclaiming, "Prosperity is just around the corner." Obama is less concise. He says he has taken "the beginning of the first steps to set our economy on a firmer foundation, paving the way to long-term growth and prosperity."[8] You see how politics has improved in the past 80 years. Obama is both walking on the street and paving it at the same time.

Hoover may have been the first president to put a telephone on his desk. But Obama is a pioneer in employing the Internet to tout his economic policies. Instead of an anachronistic promise of "prosperity . . . just around the corner," Obama launched a web site called recovery.gov that spotlights tales of recovery. It is far more advanced and interactive than the black and white newsreels of speeches that Herbert Hoover could offer.

But contrary to what the powers that be would have you believe, at an equivalent point in his term, Herbert Hoover actually had a more statistically valid basis for his claims that prosperity was soon to return than Obama had for his. Hoover not only spoke in more intelligible prose, he did a better job of combating depression than Obama.

Of course, unless you are a connoisseur of economic footnotes you may not realize that economic recovery after 1929 was arguably more robust under Herbert Hoover than it was under Obama's rule following the 2008 credit collapse.

Contrary to what you may suppose, the depression of the 1930s was not marked by uninterrupted declining quarterly GDP data every single quarter. In fact, the officially recorded downturn in the initial period of depression associated with the stock market crash stretched from the third quarter of 1929 to the third quarter of 1933, almost overlapping Hoover's term. In that initial four-year downturn, from 1929 to 1933, there were no fewer than six—*six*—quarterly bounces in the GDP

---

[8] President Barack Obama, April 17, 2009.

data. The average rate of economic growth in these up-quarters was 8 percent at an annual rate.

In case you're one of the Green Shoots bulls who imagine that politicians and their advisors have learned ever so much more than Hoover and his colleagues knew in 1929, pause and consider. With his trillions in stimulus spending, Obama engineered his quarterly bounces in real GDP, recording an average rate of economic growth of less than 3 percent at an annualized rate. In other words, while Hoover's economic performance has taken on mythic status as the worst in American history, the bounces off the bottom during the Hoover presidency were more than twice as vigorous as those under Obama.

If you care to read through old *Wall Street Journal* editions or trader's journals from the Hoover era, you see that most people were slow to get it. They did not see that trying to cushion, postpone, or turn back a credit cycle contraction, as Hoover did then and Obama has tried to do more recently, only protracts the inevitable period of adjustment.

A *depression*, unlike a *recession* of the kind seen 11 times previously since World War II, is not an inventory correction, but a wealth obliterating credit contraction that reduces leverage in the economy and compresses demand. Credit corrections don't yield to sustainable recovery until excess credit is unwound, bad debts are liquidated, and economic demand can be recalibrated on the basis of solvency.

You don't need to wonder whether genuine prosperity will be met around any corner toward which Obama is stepping, or on any nearby patch of pavement he is pouring. It is not likely for many years, perhaps decades to come. This is not a crowd-pleasing realization. Far from it. Denial is a common theme of life at all times in all places. Sometimes, as is the case now, a paradigm shift in conditions leads to a cluster of miscalculations that tend to compound errors of judgment informed by the natural human tendency toward optimism. I am all for optimism as a life strategy, but my prejudice is to believe that optimism is more constructive within a context of a realistic grasp of the facts.

Eighty years ago, when Herbert Hoover was a young president trying to turn back the tide of depression, investors repeatedly misread bounces off the bottom and random fluctuations as evidence that a return to prosperity was indeed imminent. Then as now, too many people thought that every green shoot was evidence that the economy was about to turn around. Not so.

The most extreme misreading was evidenced in the famous Sucker's Rally of 1930 when the market gained 50 percent on the widespread hallucination that the downturn was poised to end. It wasn't.

More lately, under Obama, infatuated investors bought the market on any flimsy hint of underlying economic strength, or just to ride along with the Federal Reserve's POMO operations wherein money is created out of thin air to monetize stock indices. Instead of reflecting genuine improvements in economic conditions and higher profit potentials because of repaired balance sheets, investors are gambling on the pump. They are expecting to profit from the overt effects of inflation on stock prices and from a continuing depreciation of the dollar.

Far from signifying improvement in the U.S. economic prospects, much market-moving news merely reflects deeper weaknesses abroad, and transparent statistical confections misrepresenting bottom-bouncing in the U.S. economy.

Given the fact that we are deflating the biggest credit bubble in the history of the world, genuine, sustained recovery won't be arriving soon. While the markets wax and wane over ticks up and down in an unemployment rate, the bigger picture is totally missed.

Consumption and debt growth have been strongly correlated since 1960. Rapid debt growth over the past half-century allowed consumption to grow faster than income. Conversely, if households were to go through a sustained period of deleveraging (retiring debt), then consumption growth would almost necessarily slow. That is what has happened since 2008.

The current deleveraging (credit contraction) is potentially more devastating than the Great Depression of the 1930s. This has been somewhat disguised by the introduction of food stamps and other welfare programs. These innovations in redistribution hold down the lines of hungry unemployed people that made such a vivid impression during the Great Depression. The National Bureau of Economic Research (NBER) may have determined that a recovery began in June 2009, but it has amounted to little more than Herbert Hoover's vaunted promise that prosperity was just around the corner.

It will be an effort of many years to mend balance sheets that have been severely stretched to accommodate outsized burdens of debt. The 55-year mean of Household Debt in the United States is 55.4 percent of GDP. To bring the debt back down to its mean levels implies shedding $6.33 trillion in debt. Hence, the U.S. economy is destined to remain depressed for the next 15 to 20 years. Perhaps longer.

Remember, the depression could linger for decades, as it has in Japan, where epic real estate and stock market bubbles collapsed in 1990. Japan still hasn't recovered, in spite of unremitting stimulus packages that involved trillions of deficit spending to build roads to nowhere.

Short of widespread liquidation and bankruptcy to wipe out excess debt in a hurry, there is really no option or magic potion for recovery. During the credit boom, the combination of higher debt and lower saving enabled personal consumption spending to grow faster than disposable income, providing a significant boost to U.S. economic growth. Reversing that means slower-than-expected growth, as spending lags behind income.

Shedding debt equal to 46 percent of GDP implies a much deeper and/or longer contraction than the Great Depression, when the nominal debt of U.S. households declined by one-third. The Japanese deleveraging involved shedding debt equivalent to 30 percent of GDP, so the current deleveraging process in the United States looks likely to be one of the most difficult and protracted in history. In other words, status quo expectations for resumption of debt-driven prosperity in the United States are delusional. The economy has reached debt saturation, and a large percentage of the newly created debt is devoted to refunding debts that have gone south.

The protracted political impasse in the U.S. Congress over raising the debt ceiling underscores the central role that ever-greater doses of debt play in promoting the illusion of economic prosperity. This highlights the vulnerability of the debtist economy.

As Ludwig von Mises so lucidly observed, artificial booms brought on by credit expansion cannot go on forever. He said,

> True, governments can reduce the rate of interest in the short run. They can issue additional paper money. They can open the way to credit expansion by the banks. They can thus create an

artificial boom and the appearance of prosperity. But such a boom is bound to collapse soon or late and to bring about a depression.[9]

In other words, taking debt expansion to the limit always ends badly.

Worse than the Great Depression

The vulnerability of the system arises from the ephemeral nature of fiat money. It can be destroyed almost as readily as it can be created out of thin air. Think of a house of cards. The sustainability of the artificial credit boom is jeopardized when the economy's weakest links encounter unfavorable winds. This was illustrated in the United States by the crisis in 2008 arising from the collapse of Lehman Brothers, and the gaudy end of the subprime mortgage boom. It remained on display with the continuing collapse in residential property values, as evidenced by record foreclosures. A June 14, 2011, report on CNBC stated that:

> The housing crisis that began in 2006 and has recently entered a double dip is now worse than the Great Depression. . . .
>
> Prices have fallen some 33 percent since the market began its collapse, greater than the 31 percent fall that began in the late 1920s and culminated in the early 1930s, according to Case-Shiller data. . . .
>
> Then there is the issue of underwater homeowners—those who owe more than their house is worth—representing another 23 percent of homeowners who cannot leave or are in danger of mortgage default.
>
> Indeed, the foreclosure problem is unlikely to get any better with 4.5 million households either three payments late or in foreclosure proceedings. The historical average is 1 million, according to Dales' research.[10]

---

[9] Ludwig von Mises, *Omnipotent Government* (New Haven, CT: Yale University Press, 1944), 251.

[10] Jeff Cox, "US Housing Crisis Is Now Worse Than Great Depression," CNBC, June 14, 2011, www.cnbc.com/id/43395857/US_Housing_Crisis_Is_Now _Worse_Than_Great_Depression.

If anything, the housing crisis deepened as 2011 drew to a close. Average new home prices fell in each of the last five months of the year (through November) at an annual rate of −25 percent. Meanwhile median prices deflated at a −24 percent annual rate. With 6 million homeowners either late on the payments or already in foreclosure, deflationary pressures continue to build.

A little appreciated facet of the foreclosure debacle is the fact that each property that is sold in foreclosure extinguishes debt and thus reduces the money supply. This deflationary impact is amplified by the fact that many foreclosed properties are sold for cash. The fact that buyers tend not to rely upon credit financing means that there is no counterbalancing growth in the money supply to offset the debt that is extinguished by the defaults.

Every artificial credit expansion is limited at points where weak players threaten to implode the tottering edifice of debt, touching off an avalanche of deflation. The imperative that drove the bailouts of Wall Street banks in 2008 and drove the European bailouts of Greece, Ireland, and Portugal more recently is the same. The authorities cannot permit the weak players to default without imperiling the whole system. As a result, you have a daisy chain of insolvent banks supporting insolvent governments and insolvent governments supporting insolvent banks.

The logic of fractional reserve banking (where trillions in debt are leveraged out of a thin sliver of bank capital) means that the whole banking system itself soon becomes insolvent when even a small fraction of existing debt goes sour. Without bailouts to re-fund the debt, the collapsing value of U.S. home mortgages or Greek government debt would soon undercut the claims of "innocent" counterparties in the banking system.

This creates both a fiscal and a monetary problem. The point where the two intersect is with deficit spending where governments issue IOUs as collateral for the creation of money out of thin air. In the early stages of a credit boom, the magic of deficits consists of the fact that the credit of the central government is generally unquestioned. This enables the government to escalate debt to a higher level (kick the can down the road or climb to a higher diving board) by taking on bad credits and re-funding them as part of the national debt. Yet even the good credit of the central government is not infinite, a point illustrated in different ways by the crises in the eurozone and the protracted political struggle in the United States over raising the debt ceiling.

Both crises illustrate an inescapable facet of reality, a point that Ralph Waldo Emerson developed in his "Essay on Compensation." Emerson wrote about the fundamental futility of trying to get something for nothing. He said,

> The absolute balance of Give and Take, the doctrine that every thing has its price,—and if that price is not paid, not that thing but something else is obtained, and that it is impossible to get any thing without its price,—is not less sublime in the columns of a ledger than in the budgets of states, in the laws of light and darkness, in all the action and reaction of nature.[11]

In the century and three-quarters that have elapsed since Emerson penned his classic essay, common sense has been perverted by the experience of credit bubbles fueled with fiat money and the Keynesian habits of modern politicians intent on spending from an empty pocket.

Consequently, the budgets of states, are no longer a standard of rectitude in comparison to a household ledger. Government budgets are now more ridiculous than sublime. Notwithstanding the fact that Greece has been in default for the majority of the time since it became independent of Turkey in the nineteenth century, the yield on Greek government debt fell to a level equivalent to that of Germany when Greece joined the eurozone.

By joining a currency union with Germany, Greece saw its debt suddenly priced like German debt. Of course, Germany had run one of the more conservative fiscal regimes in the second half of the twentieth century in the wake of hyperinflations after World War I and during World War II. The Greeks, on the other hand, had utterly no experience of fiscal rectitude. It was a stretch for the market to conclude that the mere association of Greeks with the Germans in the European Monetary Union would induce Greek politicians to forgo the considerable electoral advantages they could enjoy by exploiting lower interest rates on their national debt.

---

[11] Ralph Waldo Emerson, *Essays: First Series* (1841).

Borrowing funds that they were ill-prepared to repay may have assured long-term ruin, but it permitted Greek politicians to promote short-term illusions of democratic consensus by spending money the country could ill afford on lavish government salaries, early retirement programs and Northern European-style entitlements. The spending rewarded and gratified Greek government employees who could not otherwise have commanded such high incomes. And because these benefits were funded in large measure through debt rather than taxes, the success of spending constituencies in wresting unaffordable entitlements from the Greek treasury did not entail an equal and immediate loss to taxpayers.

A very similar dynamic promoting the illusion of democratic consensus through deficit persists in the United States. Witness the accumulation of underfunded liabilities that amount by some tallies to as much as $202 trillion. U.S. obligations are so many and varied that their sum is beyond calculation for most citizens.

What is calculable from the U.S. government's official GAAP accounting of its financial position, published annually, is that the accrual deficit of the United States has been expanding by roughly $5 trillion annually. This equates to a rate of increase in unfunded liabilities by more than 33 percent of GDP annually. In assessing the viability of the U.S. political economy in light of the rapidly escalating unfunded liabilities, you must consider the drastic slowdown in real growth of the private economy in the United States. When the annual cash deficit of the U.S. government is subtracted from GDP data, average annual economic growth in the United States since 1980 is actually −0.3 percent. Pretty grim.

Obviously, there is no combination of potential tax increases and spending cuts that could bring the U.S. federal budget into balance on an accrual basis (that is to say, with full accounting for the changes in assets and liabilities), just as Professor Laurence Kotlikoff observed in his Bloomberg article, the "U.S. Is Bankrupt and We Don't Even Know It."[12]

---

[12] Available at www.bloomberg.com/news/2010-08-11/u-s-is-bankrupt-and-we -don-t-even-know-commentary-by-laurence-kotlikoff.html.

But it should go without saying that the politicians prefer it when voters are unaware, and therefore, untroubled by worries over the dire fiscal position of the state.

It is probably worth recalling here that the Greek fiscal mess is not merely the culmination of usual social democratic largesse and Keynesian excess. For years during and after Greece's accession to the European Union, the country's fiscal accounts were consciously fraudulent. At one point, the entire Greek defense budget was taken off budget. The Greek government actually hired Goldman Sachs to help them fiddle their accounts with derivative trades. *Der Spiegel* (Europe's leading news magazine and Germany's top news web site) explains:

> Goldman Sachs helped the Greek government to mask the true extent of its deficit with the help of a derivatives deal that legally circumvented the EU Maastricht deficit rules. At some point the so-called cross currency swaps will mature, and swell the country's already bloated deficit.[13]

These frauds came to light early in 2010 as Greece first flirted with default. Greek politicians went hat in hand to the European Union (EU) and International Monetary Fund (IMF) begging for cash. After months of dithering a €110 billion bailout was cobbled together in May 2010, conditioned upon the promise by Greek leaders to slash their deficits. Only then did the illusion of social consensus in support of unaffordable spending break down in the crucible of austerity. Now taxes have been raised, spending has been slashed, and Greek economic growth has ground to a halt, with unemployment soaring to 15.9 percent.

In the process, Greece's operating shortfall expanded and was projected to rise even further in the fiscal years to come, demonstrating anew the apparently mysterious principle that you cannot cure a problem of unmanageable debt by adding still more debt. The EU and IMF bailouts of Greece merely enlarged the country's debt burden, making it still heavier and more difficult to bear.

Given that Greek debt is denominated in euros, but the Greek government cannot print euros, it lacks the option of gradually or

---

[13] Beat Balzli, "How Goldman Sachs Helped Greece to Mask its True Debt," *Spiegel* online, February 8, 2010, www.spiegel.de/international/europe /0,1518,676634,00.html.

not-so-gradually repudiating its obligations through inflation. Its only remaining choice is to default by unilaterally abrogating the terms of its debt obligations or not repaying at all. Although Greece has received yet another bailout in the amount of $170 billion, the country remains insolvent. It seems only a matter of time until Greece succumbs to a messy default.

The result to be expected is a deflationary shock to the system, possibly equivalent to the failure of Creditanstalt in 1931 as contagion effects raise yields on debts of other European countries and thus raise funding costs for their banks. And of course, banks and other holders of Greek debt (and other southern European sovereign debt) will be obliged to write off their losses, wiping out fiat money in the process. Moody's Investors Service warns that it may downgrade BNP Paribas S.A. and two big French banks because of their Greek debt holdings. In London, former UK treasury official Neil Mackinnon said, "[T]he probability of a eurozone 'Lehman moment' is increasing. The markets have moved from simply pricing in a high probability of the Greek debt default to looking at a scenario of it becoming disorderly and of contagion spreading to other economies. . . ."

The collapse of Lehman Brothers led to $2 trillion in write-downs and losses among the world's biggest financial institutions according to Bloomberg financial news. If something similar happens now, you can expect the world economy to notch down to a deeper level of depression similar to what happened after the failure of Creditanstalt. As Edward Harrison notes in "Thinking about Creditanstalt Today," the business news at this time in 1931 reflected "extreme levels of rebound confidence (in what we now realize was the middle of a terrific slide into Depression)."[14]

Among the sources he cites is a report that the Harvard Economics Society says

> gains in seasonal spring recovery this year have been far less widespread than a year ago, but, since they started from a much lower base, should be longer lasting. We anticipate that they

---

[14] Edward Harrison, "Thinking about Creditanstalt Today," Credit Writedowns, April 23, 2010, www.creditwritedowns.com/2010/04/thinking-about-creditanstalt -today.html#ixzz1PSQq3IEU.

will continue and spread and that an upturn of general business
is in early prospect.[15]

Note the similarity to today's confident forecasts of stronger growth.
The dynamic in the United States is somewhat different from that in
Greece. The United States has one great advantage that Greece lacks: its
debt is denominated in dollars, a currency the U.S. government can
print. The ability to create unlimited amounts of dollars at essentially no
cost would seem to give U.S. politicians the ability to enlarge deficits
without limit. But as Emerson suggested, this is an illusion. A matter of
"climbing to a higher diving board." He writes, "Always pay; for, first or
last, you must pay your entire debt. Persons and events may stand for a
time between you and justice, but it is only a postponement. You must
pay at last your own debt. If you are wise, you will dread a prosperity
which only loads you with more."[16]

The United States borrows a currency that it can depreciate, almost
at will. But the apparent consensus in support of spending trillions from
an empty pocket has begun to fissure as the prospective costs rise. The
issue as the United States grapples with the limits of sovereign debt
kiting is that it seems prepared to flirt with what von Mises described in
this chapter's epigraph as "the final collapse of a boom brought about by
credit (debt) expansion . . . as the result of a voluntary abandonment of
further credit (debt) expansion."

Events of 2011 showed that there were almost enough Tea Party
Republicans in the House of Representatives to block extension of the
debt ceiling or link it to meaningful spending cuts. In the event, the
Republicans and Democrats debated for months about whether a
$10 trillion increase in the national debt in a decade should be abated by
3 percent or 4 percent.

The debate discredits an optimistic forecast from 1886, when
Andrew Carnegie, then one of the world's richest men, wrote *Triumphant Democracy* to sing the praises of the United States. A big part of his
argument was focused on the heavy indebtedness that burdened Russia,
France, and other European nations. As Carnegie put it, "National debts

---

[15] Harrison, "Thinking about Creditanstalt Today."
[16] Ralph Waldo Emerson, *Essays: First Series* (1841).

grow troublesome. Year after year the burden they lay upon the pro-ductive energies of nations becomes harder and harder to bear."

Carnegie believed—wrongly, as it turned out—that democracy had defeated the temptation for America to burden itself with debt. "Our great advantage which the democracy has secured for itself in America is its comparative freedom from debt. The ratio of indebtedness to wealth is strikingly small."[17]

What a long way the United States has come in a century and a quarter. The United States was still the largest creditor nation in the world when I was a child. Today, it is the largest debtor nation in history.

The Collapse of the Boom

It will be interesting to see how long it takes for the markets to force the political authorities in the United States to adopt a plan to actually slash spending akin to the Plano Real instituted two decades ago by then-Finance Minister Fernando Henrique Cardoso in the administration of President Itamar Franco in Brazil.

Under the Plano Real, deficits were tamed because spending was curtailed on a real-time basis to match available revenues. To adopt such a policy in the United States today would mean reducing government outlays by $1.3 trillion, presuming that GDP did not fall precipitously. As I write, current U.S. government receipts are running at about the levels of 15 years ago while the National Debt has increased by roughly $10 trillion since fiscal year 1994.

In short, the U.S. economy has been more stagnant than is widely understood. Rapidly escalating deficits have disguised a slowdown or decline in real private economic activity. That being the case, if deficits were eliminated, nominal GDP would certainly plunge. If you subtract the annual government deficit from GDP data, average annual economic growth in the United States since 1980 is actually −0.3 percent.

---

[17] Doug Wakefield, "The Next Landslide: Lessons from Andrew Carnegie," Safehaven.com, May 29, 2009, www.safehaven.com/article/13462/the-next -landslide-lessons-from-andrew-carnegie.

Without government deficits to disguise the faltering growth of the real private economy, nominal GDP could plunge by 10 percent or more.

This would shift the full burden of kiting debt to the Federal Reserve. Chairman Ben Bernanke and his accomplices would almost certainly expand the Fed's balance sheet by trillions more in the attempt to ward off a deflationary collapse of the banking system. Whether this would be sufficient to avoid the final collapse of the boom is impossible to project. What is clearer is the likelihood that a sharp fall in nominal GDP and a surge in unemployment that would accompany drastic surgery to curtail the deficit would have decisive political effects. It would reveal the flimsiness behind the façade of democratic consensus in U.S. politics, one predicated on runaway deficits and continued kiting of the national debt.

In the next chapter, we take a look at the United States' path to bankruptcy and its similarities to the fall of Rome.

Chapter 7

"Rome" Falls, Again

Economic Closure and Financial Repression as the United States Faces Bankruptcy

The menacing specter of state bankruptcy drew ever nearer. The old remedy was prescribed: reduction in the value of the currency and increased taxation. . . . Thus began the fierce endeavor of the State to squeeze the population to the last drop. Since economic resources fell short of what was needed the strong fought to secure the chief share for themselves with the violence and unscrupulousness well in keeping with the origin of those in power. . . .

In these disturbed and catastrophic decades of the third century countless people, especially of the bourgeois middle class, were impoverished, even ruined, and these were precisely the men who had brought into being and maintained the economic prosperity of former times. The wasteful policy of the State, the constant interference with private economic life, and the inflations, amounted to a landslide beneath which a vast amount that was of value was crushed out of existence.

—*The Cambridge Ancient History*, Volume XI

Collapse may come much more suddenly than many historians imagine. Fiscal deficits and military overstretch suggests that the United States may be the next empire on the precipice. Many nations in history, at the very peak of their power, affluence and glory, see leaders arise, run amok with imperial visions and sabotage themselves, their people and their nation.

—Niall Ferguson, *The Rise and Fall of the American Empire*

To most people, the idea that we could be approaching the End of America is preposterous. After all, the United States has been the world's foremost economy for a century. Almost no one now living can recall a time when any country other than the United States was on top of the world. In fact, it requires a good education today to decipher Walter Lippmann's belief that "what Rome was to the ancient world, what Great Britain has been to the modern world, America is to be to the world of tomorrow."[1]

How quickly tomorrow has come and gone. It lasted for a generation or so after World War II, and while it did, American workers were far the most highly compensated people on earth.

Slip-Sliding Down the Road to National Insolvency

In 1960, German, Belgian, French, and British workers all earned less than one-third of the typical American income. At that time, the typical income in Japan was just one-tenth that of Americans. Swedes were exceptional in having attained 45 percent of the average U.S. wage.

Then in 1971, Richard Nixon repudiated the gold reserve standard. The countdown to national bankruptcy began in earnest as ticking time bombs destined to explode the American Dream were laid and set. The robust income growth that Americans had previously enjoyed came to a screeching halt, while incomes abroad soared. By 1978, American

---

[1] Quoted by Harold James, *The Roman Predicament: How The Rules of International Order Create the Politics of Empire* (Princeton: Princeton University Press, 2006), 28–29.

workers took home 20 percent less than Swedish and Belgian workers. German and Dutch workers also earned a premium over the U.S. income. Japanese income soared from 10 percent of the U.S. level to 68 percent in less than two decades.

Of course, it is important to recognize that much of the downward shift in the relative wealth of Americans came from a sharp decline in the exchange rate of the dollar. As William Easterly observed, the unweighted cross-country world average of gross domestic product (GDP) growth in 131 countries slowed from about 5 percent in the third quarter of the twentieth century to about 3 percent in the 1970s and 1980s. The worldwide average public debt to GDP ratio also rose steeply in the 1970s and 1980s.[2]

In other words, Nixon's unilateral revision of the world monetary system, scrapping the link to gold, preceded a dramatic drop in world average GDP growth. It also led an even sharper decline in relative U.S. wealth as the exchange value of the dollar plunged.

As I write, 40 years later, the U.S. balance of trade has been in deficit ever since. And the dollar has lost more than 80 percent of its 1971 value. (Seen in terms of gold, the dollar's depreciation is even more dramatic. At the current price of gold as I write, $1,506, the dollar retains just a little over 2 percent of its 1971 value in gold.)

As we discussed in Chapter 6, no one noticed it at the time, but the shift away from gold in the monetary system to pure fiat money led to debt-driven consumption as the main driver of economic growth. Indeed, as I mentioned, when Nixon abolished fixed exchange rates by severing the dollar's link to gold in 1971, the United States was the world's largest creditor. No longer. The move to fiat money resulted in a wholesale substitution of debt for capital in the U.S. economy. This was driven by the decline in per capita global energy output that undermined a key component in the growth recipe of the U.S. economy. It was amplified by the hydraulic force of the largest, cumulative trade deficit the world had ever seen.

---

[2] William R. Easterly, "Growth Implosions and Debt Explosions: Do Growth Slowdowns Cause Public Debt Crises?" *Contributions to Macroeconomics* 1, no. 1 (2001): 1.

From 1971 through 2010, the current account accumulated trade deficits of the United States totaled $7.75 trillion. By accounting identity, when the United States runs a trade deficit, it necessarily borrows an equivalent sum from foreign creditors. Four decades of accelerating trade deficits have hollowed out the capitalist system in the United States, concentrating wealth among the creditworthy and eliminating real income growth among average Americans.

Real average hourly wages in the United States peaked at $20.30 per hour (in today's dollars) in January 1973, on the eve of the first oil shock. Over the next 22 years, the average real hourly wage plummeted to $16.39. The only reason U.S. households have achieved higher real earnings is the influx of women into the workforce, which led to two-earner households. Of course, these data are subject to varying inter-pretations. Some economists argue that the fall in real income may be exaggerated by deficiencies in the government's calculation of inflation. No doubt there are such deficiencies—but whether they all tend to exaggerate inflation is more problematic.

We could argue the minutia of real income comparisons. Yet a dramatic change in trend in the early 1970s is indisputable. For the tens of millions of middle-class Americans classified as "non-supervisory production workers" in government statistics, the post–January 1973 stagnation in real hourly income represents a dramatic departure from the experience of preceding years.

Look at it this way. From 1947 to January 1973, average hourly pretax earnings, adjusted for inflation using current methods, grew at an average annual "real" rate of about 2.2 percent. If real income had continued to grow at that robust rate, average purchasing power would have doubled to more than $40 an hour by 2006. Instead, it fell to less than $18.00, almost 12 percent lower than at its peak a working lifetime ago.

More often than not the parents of my generation who expected their children to have more prosperous lives than their own were dis-appointed. I was born into the Golden Age of the Middle Class. Then, in February 1973, it suddenly and permanently ended.

When Nixon acted to sever the dollar's link to gold, domestic oil production had just peaked, and the United States was the world's manufacturing powerhouse. Factory jobs provided high income for rel-atively unskilled and less educated people. But the transition away from a capitalist to a debtist economy accelerated change in everything. It changed the focus of economic activity in the United States as measured by GDP, from genuine wealth creation to debt-driven consumption.

Unlike a capitalist economy where profits are based upon actually producing goods that consumers wish to buy in an environment of rising incomes, a debtist economy enshrines cost-cutting consumption in the face of stagnant or falling incomes. Americans exploited the dollar's status as the world's reserve currency to bully and borrow trillions through the current account deficit to live beyond our means. As the world's foremost military power, Americans forced oil producers to price crude in dollars. As consumers of last resort, Americans borrowed the money to enjoy a higher standard of living than they could afford, and that destined them to be cost-sensitive. As the process unfolded over 40 years, it was only a matter of time until underemployed Americans lined up to buy Chinese goods at Wal-Mart.

The Destruction of the Middle Class

For those Americans who lacked the skills to be appreciably more productive than Chinese peasants on an assembly line, the opening of low-wage economies implied the end of the middle-class lifestyle. Instead of a broad middle class where up to 90 million Americans were subsumed together as "non-supervisory production workers" whose prospects improved year in and year out, the prospects of the former middle-class diverged.

The less educated and less skilled segment who worked in the tradable goods sector sank toward poverty. As Harvard economics professor Edward L. Glaeser has shown, population growth in the least educated three-fifths of U.S. counties was less than 3 percent over the past decade. By contrast, in the one-fifth of U.S. counties where more than 21 percent of adults had college degrees in 2000, growth for the decade was over 13 percent.[3] A minority of skilled entrepreneurs, along with the highly educated, a total of about 13.2 million persons, became highly successful—earning more than $100,000 per year.

---

[3] Edward L. Glaeser, "Human Capital Follows the Thermometer," *New York Times*, April 19, 2011.

Another strand of the population continued to enjoy a middle–class lifestyle, but one financed at the general expense. Among those whose skills were not internationally competitive, government employees were exceptional in enjoying growing incomes along with such perks as defined benefit pensions and full-spectrum health care coverage.

Unfortunately, as the Romans discovered in the waning days of their empire, it is impossible for government spending to take up the slack in the shriveling private economy on a long-term basis.

For one thing, the resources to fund intervention at the necessary magnitude are not readily available. The weaker the economy becomes, the more tax receipts fall away. Although it is not widely recognized, by 2011 real per capita tax receipts in the United States had fallen to 1994 levels. In other words, GDP growth over the past 17 years was financed from deficits and debt. In fact, net private GDP has barely budged over the past decade.

While some of the gains in consumption since 1994 were funded on credit cards and through cash-out financing of appreciated real estate equity, the greatest contributor to consumption came from soaring government spending. For the decade since 2001 government spending added a total of $25.94 trillion to GDP.[4]

Pre-Industrial Growth Rates

Note another ominous aspect of the situation. Notwithstanding the invisibly low interest rates maintained by the Federal Reserve through the first decade of this century, the national debt compounded far faster than the growth of the net private economy upon which the hope of repayment lies.

GDP minus government spending grew from $9.314 9 trillion in 2001 to $9.721 5 trillion in 2010—a gain of just 0.043 percent over a decade.[5] At that truly medieval rate of growth, it would take the net private economy 167 years to double.

---

[4] Mike Shedlock, "Here's Why the 'Recovery' Feels so Much Like a Depression," Business Insider, September 29, 2010, www.businessinsider.com/heres-why-the-recovery-feels-so-much-like-a-depression-2010-9.
[5] Ibid.

That kind of growth rate predates the Industrial Revolution.

Prior to the Industrial Revolution, annual growth rates from 0 to 1 percent led to low incomes because they provided too little buffer against the inevitable negative shocks of war, famine, and pestilence. This appears to have been true in medieval England, where real farm wages, measured by half century, showed no improvement in the productivity of the economy from the years 1200 to 1249 to the years 1600 to 1649.[6]

While growth of the productive economy in the United States over the past decade was negligible, the national debt soared from $5.807 trillion in 2001 to $13.561 trillion in 2010[7]—a gain of 133 percent.[8] The burden of the national debt compounded more than 3,000 times faster than the productive economy grew.

Those who draw their bearings by looking at the gross GDP numbers to justify a vibrant economy have lost the plot. GDP attributable to government spending, especially deficit spending, is bogus. It is not real prosperity but debt-financed consumption with unpleasant implications for your future.

Are You Ready for Taxes to Double?

The U.S. government is doomed to bankruptcy. Indeed, it is already bankrupt. Never in the history of the world has any government owed as much money as the U.S. Treasury owes today.

As mentioned previously, Professor Laurence Kotlikoff of Boston University, an economist expert in government debt, has calculated that the true indebtedness of the U.S. Treasury is greater than the combined GDPs of all countries. Yes, it is true that the debts of the United States are denominated in U.S. dollars—a currency that the government can create at little or no cost. This only means that the dollar is destined to

---

[6] Gregory Clark, "Markets and Economic Growth: The Grain Market of Medieval England," www.econ.ucdavis.edu/faculty/gclark/210a/readings/market99.pdf.

[7] "Historical Debt Outstanding—Annual 2000–2010," TreasuryDirect, www.treasurydirect.gov/govt/reports/pd/histdebt/histdebt_histo5.htm.

[8] Calculated as $13.56 - 5.807 = 7.753$; $7.753 \div 5.807 = 133\%$

collapse. If your income and wealth are inexorably tied to dollars, you could be wiped out.

Kotlikoff suggests that the IMF has already endorsed a remedy—the doubling of taxes in the United States:

> . . . you will find that the IMF has effectively pronounced the U.S. bankrupt. Section 6 of the July 2010 Selected Issues Paper says: "The U.S. fiscal gap associated with today's federal fiscal policy is huge for plausible discount rates." It adds, "Closing the fiscal gap requires a permanent annual fiscal adjustment equal to about 14 percent of U.S. GDP."
>
> The fiscal gap is the value today (the present value) of the difference between projected spending (including servicing official debt) and projected revenue in all future years. . . .
>
> To put 14 percent of gross domestic product in perspective, current federal revenue totals 14.9 percent of GDP. So the IMF is saying that closing the U.S. fiscal gap, from the revenue side, requires, roughly speaking, an immediate and permanent doubling of our personal-income, corporate and federal taxes as well as the payroll levy set down in the Federal Insurance Contribution Act.[9]

The problem is that any attempt to double taxes would crush the economy. And, of course, it is clear that there is little appetite for spending cuts as drastic as would be required to even balance the budget on an accrual basis that, as Federal Reserve Bank of San Francisco President and CEO John C. Williams has calculated, is trillions of dollars out of whack on an accrual basis.

Forget about achieving an appreciable surplus that would retire some of the national debt. U.S. government debt will never be repaid except for whatever part of it may be extinguished by inflation. That will come directly out of your hide.

Face it: you are an extra caught in the remake of a bad movie.

---

[9] Laurence Kotlikoff, "U.S. Is Bankrupt and We Don't Even Know It," Bloomberg News, August 10, 2010, www.bloomberg.com/news/2010-08-11/u-s-is -bankrupt-and-we-don-t-even-know-commentary-by-laurence-kotlikoff.html.

Welcome to the Second Decline and Fall of "Rome"

There is an ominous precedent for the destiny of the United States in the fall of the Roman Empire. We are far poorer than we think. The irresponsible fiscal and monetary policies of the United States government are primed to make Americans poorer still.

Contrary to what many may naively suppose, more energetic efforts to tax the rich are likely to result in an even tighter squeeze on those of lower means.

Consider this from Bruce Bartlett's work titled "How Excessive Government Killed Ancient Rome." Bartlett is a columnist for the *Economix* blog of the *New York Times*, the *Fiscal Times*, and *Tax Notes*:

> As the private wealth of the Empire was gradually confiscated or taxed away, driven away or hidden, economic growth slowed to a virtual standstill. Moreover, once the wealthy were no longer able to pay the state's bills, the burden inexorably fell onto the lower classes, so that average people suffered as well from the deteriorating economic conditions. In Rostovtzeff's words, "The heavier the pressure of the state on the upper classes, the more intolerable became the condition of the lower classes." (Rostovtzeff 1957: 430). . . .
>
> Although the fall of Rome appears as a cataclysmic event in history, for the bulk of Roman citizens it had little impact on their way of life. As Henri Pirenne (1939: 33-62) has pointed out, once the invaders effectively had displaced the Roman government they settled into governing themselves. At this point, they no longer had any incentive to pillage, but rather sought to provide peace and stability in the areas they controlled. After all, the wealthier their subjects the greater their taxpaying capacity. . . .
>
> In conclusion, the fall of Rome was fundamentally due to economic deterioration resulting from excessive taxation, inflation, and over-regulation. Higher and higher taxes failed to raise additional revenues because wealthier taxpayers could evade such taxes while the middle class—and its taxpaying capacity—were exterminated. Although the final demise of the

Roman Empire in the West (its Eastern half continued on as the Byzantine Empire) was an event of great historical importance, for most Romans it was a relief.[10]

Of course, the United States is not going to be pillaged by Germanic tribes. But what you can expect, as suggested in the passage quoted from the *Cambridge Ancient History*, volume 11, is a Roman-style response as "the menace of state bankruptcy" draws nearer.[11]

You will see a replay of "the fierce endeavor of the State to squeeze the population to the last drop." The amount of squeezing will be prodigious as the United States is well and truly insolvent. The first danger is that taxes will be raised to confiscatory levels—on the wealthy.

Like the original Alternative Minimum Tax, the new, higher rates will apply at first only to a small segment of the population. But as the continued emissions of new dollars conjured out of thin air inevitably devalue the currency, the price level will skyrocket, and you will end up earning, millions or even hundreds of millions of dollars, making you one of the "wealthy" to whom the new "taxes on the rich" will apply.

The greatest danger to your living standard therefore is the looming menace of hyperinflation and the death of the dollar. We are approaching what I previously mentioned Ludwig von Mises describing as "the crack-up boom" and I expect "a final and total catastrophe of the currency involved" . . . namely the dollar.

Standard & Poor's "downgrade" on U.S. credit during August 2011 merely underscored the underlying weakness that has been evident for years now. Many more people than you may have already begun to believe in the coming bankruptcy of the United States. This is reflected in something I heard from an American living in Geneva. He had just been visiting with some consular official who works in the American Embassy in Bern. The woman from the embassy told him something astonishing—that the wait for the exit interviews required to renounce

---

[10] Bruce Bartlett, "How Excessive Government Killed Ancient Rome," *Cato Journal* 14, no. 2 (Fall 1994).

[11] Peter Garnsey, Dominic Rathbone, and Alan K. Bowman, eds., *The Cambridge Ancient History, Vol. XI: The High Empire, A.D. 70–192* (Cambridge, UK: Cambridge University Press, 2000).

U.S. citizenship now exceeds three years. This statistic reflects a swelling recognition by successful Americans that U.S. citizenship is a major liability.

The fact that it requires a formal exit interview at the embassy to escape from U.S. tax liabilities reflects the enactment of increasingly draconian restrictions on emigration from the United States. U.S. citizenship carries more fiscal burdens than that of any other country. U.S. citizens alone, among leading economies, must pay U.S. taxes whether they reside in the United States or not. An April 5, 2010, article by the Dow Jones News Service explains,

> Unlike most jurisdictions, the U.S. taxes the income of citizens and green-card holders no matter where in the world it is earned.
>
> In order to give up U.S. citizenship, a person must obtain or have citizenship in another country. The person surrenders their passport or green card during an interview with a consular officer in their new home country. He or she must also submit a form, including a list of assets, to the IRS to complete the process.
>
> Chris Kavanagh of the American Institute in Taiwan, which represents U.S. interests in Taiwan, said 43 people gave up their U.S. citizenship in Taiwan in 2009, the highest that figure has been since 2003. He cautioned against drawing conclusions from that data, however.
>
> The IRS says some of the swelling of numbers of expatriations towards the end of 2009 occurred because the agency made a push to notify people that had already surrendered their passport, but had not completed the process by submitting the IRS form. Until that form is received by the IRS, these people are still subject to U.S. tax. "There is some catch-up going on," said IRS spokesman Bruce Friedland.
>
> The stock market plunge of late 2008 and early 2009 may also have played a role in the spike in expatriations. Since 2008, Americans with net worth greater than $2 million have had to pay an exit tax assessed on their assets. With gains reduced or wiped out by the market collapse, those seeking to give up their

U.S. citizenship had an opportunity to do so with less exit tax required.[12]

The New Berlin Wall

So-called exit taxes, the fiscal equivalent of the Berlin Wall, have been imposed to prevent successful Americans from escaping a lopsided tax burden in which 73 percent of income taxes are paid by the top 10 percent of earners, while the bottom 40 percent actually receive "refunds" having paid nothing.[13]

Recall the attitude of the Roman Empire as it faced bankruptcy, succinctly summarized in the quote from *Cambridge Ancient History* at the beginning of this chapter: "Thus began the fierce endeavor of the State to squeeze the population to the last drop."

A little-appreciated provision of President Barack Obama's "highway legislation," Senate Bill 1813, Section 40304, says that "Revocation or denial of passport in case of certain unpaid taxes . . ." grants the IRS the power to prevent any American citizen merely alleged to owe taxes from leaving the United States. Under this agenda of financial repression, what was once "the land of the free," figures to be the world's largest debtor's prison.

While it may seem obvious to you that the U.S. government is hopelessly insolvent, it is my opinion that the United States will become a full-fledged police state before it collapses, destined to be the Argentina of the twenty-first century. It won't be pretty.

With a system so heavily tilted toward income redistribution, the pressures to close off emigration came naturally. The growth of predatory taxation and the multiplication of legal restrictions on emigration make it costly and complicated for a successful person to leave the United States. They require anyone attempting to resign U.S. citizenship to pay capital

---

[12] Martin Vaughan, "Increasing Number of U.S. Expats Give Up Citizenship as IRS Gets Aggressive about Overseas Asset Reporting," Cuenca High Life, April 7, 2010, www.cuencahighlife.com/post/2010/04/07/Increasing-number-of-US-expats -give-up-citizenship-as-IRS-gets-aggressive-with-overseas-bank-accounts.aspx.
[13] "Nearly Half of US Households Escape Fed Income Tax," CNBC.com, April 8, 2010, www.cnbc.com/id/36241249/Nearly_Half_of_US_Households_Escape _Fed_Income_Tax.

gains on appreciation of his worldwide wealth. But it gets worse. The United States could possibly continue to demand tax payments for up to a decade after you leave. And of course, if you are prohibited from leaving the U.S., you are effectively doomed to be a debt slave. Alternatively, if you try to flee, it could make it difficult for you to establish residence in a new country and qualify for citizenship there.

The growth of predatory taxation and the multiplication of legal restrictions on emigration have made it costly and complicated to join the 742 Americans leaving the United States each hour.[14]

The Roman Empire tried to keep taxpayers from fleeing, too. "Exit taxes" and restrictions on expatriation are modern-day analogs to the "tax reforms" of Diocletian, the Roman emperor (284–305) who wiped out what remained of the urban middle class (curiales). By the time Diocletian undertook his "reforms," in 297, Rome was on the verge of collapse under the weight of ceaseless wars and the largest, most bureaucratic government the world had ever seen.

When Diocletian acted to raise taxes, the urban middle class was already fleeing in large numbers to escape the crushing burden of taxation. To frustrate that ambition, he made the curiales responsible for collecting taxes. If their collections fell short of the government assessment, they had to make up the difference from their own pocket, or be forced to sell their property. Many curiales tried to flee, but leaving was also against the law. It is not a coincidence that one of the most popular questions asked of soothsayers in the late Roman Empire was "should I flee?" Those who waited too long came to regret it. The middle class was financially ruined.[15]

It does not take a soothsayer to see that a similar fate awaits Americans with assets as financial repression escalates. While Roman taxpayers were legally prohibited from leaving, Americans are not yet chained to the fisc, but that is uncomfortably close to becoming a reality. The passage of President Obama's highway bill will give the IRS the

---

[14] Bill Bonner, "Subprime State of Mind," *The Daily Reckoning*, April 19, 2012, http://dailyreckoning.com/subprime-state-of-mind.

[15] Lynn Harry Nelson, "The Later Roman Empire," WWW Virtual Library, www.vlib.us/medieval/lectures/late_roman_empire.html.

power to prevent any American from travelling abroad. It will become even more complicated to escape.

In particular, the requirement to hold another passport before legally quitting the U.S. tax regime makes legal expatriation a process of years rather than simply going to the ticket agent and booking a passage as it was in the late nineteenth century, when passports were not even required for most international travel.

Americans as the New Illegal Emigrants

Just as there are illegal immigrants to the United States, so there are also now growing numbers of illegal emigrants from the United States. While statistics are necessarily sketchy, evidence suggests that there has been a dramatic upsurge in the number of U.S. persons living abroad. Although it has been little reported in the media, a growing number of native-born Americans are fleeing financial repression at the hands of the Obama administration. As indicated earlier in this chapter, they have been departing at the rate of 742 per hour. According to the Association of Americans Resident Overseas, (AARO) apart from the military and other U.S. government employees, 5.08 million U.S. citizens reside abroad, about a two-thirds increase since 2008. "Among the benefits the study cites of a life abroad are statistics that show expats earn more, pay less tax, have a better work/life balance, have an improved quality of life, enjoy broader cultural opportunities, and enjoy better job prospects."[16]

In the opinion of the U.S. State Department, the AARO estimate is 25 percent too low. The State Department suggests that about 1.34 million Americans have become "illegal emigrants," which is to say, they have gone abroad and fallen off the radar.

The Association of Americans Resident Overseas suggests that there was a surge of persons leaving the United States after the onset of the Second Great Contraction in December 2007. If, indeed, it amounted to a two-thirds increase in the number of Americans living outside the United States, it marks a major inflexion point. According to the Center for Immigration Studies, a think tank that agitates for tighter border

---

[16] The Association of Americans Resident Overseas, www.aaro.org.

controls, the number of illegal immigrants living in the United States declined to 11 million in 2008 from 12.5 million in 2007.[17] For the first time since the depths of the Great Depression in the early 1930s, more persons appear to have left the United States than moved in.

Only time will tell how many of the new expatriates fall off the radar. My expectation is that quite a few will. Probably, only a small percentage left with the intention of actually renouncing U.S. citizenship. I suspect that most would prefer to simply disappear. The Obama administration seems to think so, too. That is why they are increasing financial repression, using heavy-handed tactics to make it difficult for Americans to open bank accounts outside the United States, even if they live abroad.

An element of this new repression is a requirement that all Americans file Form 8938 if they have more than $50,000 in foreign financial assets. Note that "financial assets" are defined to include "all rental property." According to the Federal Register, "The IRS will use the information to determine whether to audit this taxpayer or transaction, including whether to impose penalties."[18] For those who are not multimillionaires, and therefore unlikely to be pursued by the IRS, the drastic step of renouncing citizenship might seem unwarranted.

Unlike the situation a century ago as British hegemony waned, there is much more visibility about what lies ahead. Today, it is not only young, low-skilled and semiskilled workers who have an incentive to get out while they still can (or not to come in the first place, as even illegal immigration has slowed as economic opportunity in the United States recedes). There is also ample reason for the older, wealthier person to emigrate.

Here the British experience is instructive. Falling relative income is associated with large out-migration. Since 1901, more people have emigrated from the UK than immigrated. By 1997, a net exodus from

---

[17] Steven A. Camarota and Karen Zeigler, "Homeward Bound: Recent Immigration Enforcement and the Decline in the Illegal Alien Population," Center for Immigration Studies, July 2008, www.cis.org/trends_and_enforcement.

[18] John C. Fredenberger, "Tell the IRS What You Think of Their New Financial Report Form!," Association of Americans Resident Overseas, http://aaro.org /component/content/article/50-fyi-taxation/296-tell-the-irs.

the UK of 15,600,000 had occurred.[19] A similar exodus is destined to occur in the United States. Indeed, it may already have begun.

One of the more important investment decisions you will face in the coming years is whether you should begin to pack your bags. In my view, the U.S. economy is destined to grow slowly, or not at all, as leverage is subtracted from the system and taxes are increased to draconian levels.

You may not think of yourself this way, but if you are a U.S. citizen you are one of the "assets" of the fisc. You are not yet a complete slave as the Roman urban middle class became, but you face ruin nonetheless, as the dollar collapses and the inevitable bankruptcy of the United States looms.

The dollar will be a much smaller fraction of an ounce of gold. Look out below.

Next up, we discuss Brazil's appeal in a post-dollar world.

[19] Joe Hicks and Grahame Allen, "A Century of Change: Trends in UK Statistics since 1900," A House of Commons research paper, www.parliament.uk/documents/commons/lib/research/rp99/rp99-111.pdf.

Chapter 8

The Sunny Side of the Leverage Cycle

How Brazil's Legacy of Hyperinflation Prepared It to Prosper in a Post-Dollar World

None of the Brazilian banks has come under the suspicion of being weak. The balance sheets are very strong. The Brazilian corporate sector is extremely underleveraged. The Brazilian citizen is underleveraged. The credit to [gross domestic product] ratio in Brazil is just above 30 percent. It used to be in the low 20 percent range, and 30 percent is still quite a low figure. Despite all that, what we're witnessing with European and American banks has made everybody more cautious and has brought [the credit markets] to a halt here.

—Candido Bracher, Chairman, Banco Itau, December 18, 2008

I t is a cliché— indeed, an article of faith—among most Americans that the United States is the richest country in the world. But, alas, this is no longer true. Unfortunately, most of us appear to have missed an important bulletin that dates back to 1494—two years after Columbus discovered America. That's when the Tuscan friar Luca Bartolomes Pacioli surprised the world with his *Summa de Arithmetica*, the first book in print to explain the mysteries of double entry bookkeeping.

Fra. Pacioli's work sparked a realization that in order to accurately appraise your wealth it is not enough to just add up your assets. You must also subtract your liabilities. Hence the bad news for those who still believe that the United States is the richest country in the world.

I am reminded of a charming story told about Donald Trump during the downturn of the early 1990s, when his leveraged real estate empire had come to grief with the banks. One night, Trump was walking in the Upper East Side of Manhattan with his beautiful girlfriend when they encountered a vagrant. Trump surprised his girlfriend by saying that the homeless man was worth a billion dollars more than he was. She said, "But he doesn't look like he has a penny."

"He doesn't," Trump replied.[1]

Equally, while the U.S. standard of living remains high by any reasonable standard of accounting, the United States is one of the poorer countries in the world—if not the poorest. After a multidecade borrowing binge, we owe over $14 trillion to the rest of the world. The national debt is just the tip of the iceberg, the portion of our overseas borrowings that has been converted into U.S. Treasury securities.

We used to beguile ourselves that it didn't matter how high the debt grew because "we owe it to ourselves." Not so much. According to the Treasury statistics, (current as of August 2011) the U.S. government owes approximately $865 apiece to each and every citizen of China and $1,034 to each Brazilian. Other vast sums are owed just about everywhere. We should have known better. And so should the Chinese, the Brazilians, and the others.

The United States government not only sports a national debt exceeding 100 percent of GDP, but has also created unfunded liabilities in astronomical sums, likely exceeding the total value of world output. As mentioned, Professor Laurence Kotlikoff puts the sum at $202 trillion by citing congressional figures.[2] More conservative, or perhaps less

---

[1] This story was confirmed to me by Donald Trump.

[2] More recent calculations by Professor Kotlikoff put the total obligations of the U.S. government at $211 trillion. See http://theeconomiccollapseblog.com /archives/shocking-charts-and-statistics-that-prove-that-america-is-no-longer-a -wealthy-nation.

comprehensive, estimates of U.S. unfunded liabilities range as low as *USA Today*'s $62 trillion[3]—a "low" guess which is barely below *The Economist*'s estimate of world GDP at $65 trillion in the 12 months to May 2011.[4]

When state and local government debt are added, the total U.S. debt picture is so ugly that it would make young children cry—if they had any inkling what it implies for their future. But it is rather much to expect the kids to be bawling as if they understood accounting better than their parents and grandparents when even hedge fund and money managers seem to have been hoaxed by the fairyland accounting U.S. banks use to pad their earnings.

As reported in the *Financial Times*, 80 percent of the $16 billion in quarterly net profits (almost $13 billion) recently reported by big U.S. banks, including Citigroup, Bank of America, J.P. Morgan, and Goldman Sachs, came from the banks claiming that the fall in the value of their own debt was income. Sounds crazy doesn't it? But that's what happened.

The banks claimed that their creditworthiness had fallen, enabling them to write down the value of what they owe to reflect the greater risk that they will not pay it all back. They then claimed the difference as income.

These are hints to the wise: the insolvency of the U.S. government and the U.S. banking system should not go unnoticed. They tell you that life has changed. The rules of the world you grew up in are different. A major phase of economic history is coming to an end.

The age of American prosperity is over. I say that deliberately. The average American races on a hopeless treadmill where he or she must go faster and faster to stay in the same place. What to make of it? My sometime friend, Bill Clinton, warns: "People have been betting against America for 200 years and they all wound up losing money."[5] As a

---

[3] Dennis Cauchon, "U.S. finding for future promises lags by trillions," *USA Today*, June 6, 2011, www.usatoday.com/news/washington/2011-06-06-us-owes-62-trillion-in-debt_n.htm.

[4] "World GDP: In Search of Growth," *Economist* online, Graphic Detail (blog), May 25, 2011, www.economist.com/blogs/dailychart/2011/05/world_gdp.

[5] Quoted in Simon Schama, "Bill Clinton talks to Simon Schama," *FT Magazine*, October 14, 2011, www.ft.com/intl/cms/s/2/e0c1418c-f526-11e0-9023-00144feab49a.html#axzz1sanF4sIO.

description of the past, Bill Clinton's observation is accurate. But I don't recommend that you pay him for investment advice; I doubt it will hold true in the future.

It is not just the government whose liabilities are cascading while its assets fall. The typical American's home has doubled in size since 1970. But a big house doesn't mean Americans are any wealthier. Those new McMansions have plunged in value, causing Americans to lose an aggregate of $7 trillion.

Even though our assets have shriveled, the net liabilities of Americans have grown.

You Are in Steerage on a Sinking Ship

Notwithstanding hopeful hype about recovery, mainly driven by unsustainable monetary and fiscal stimulus, the U.S. economy is headed for a wrenching adjustment that will push living standards down over a period of many years or even decades. I expect to see half a century's worth of economic progress wiped away.

This is not really so bold a statement as it may appear. From the perspective of the average American, there has been precious little progress over the past four decades. The average American male with full-time employment has lost $800 in annual purchasing power over this period.

Living standards seemed to continue rising, albeit erratically, principally for two reasons:

1. Many women entered the workforce so that multiple-earner households became commonplace.
2. Household debt increased 20 times over, as many families added leverage in order to spend more. Now the United States is in the midst of a protracted period of deleveraging.

As the *Economist* reported in "Deleveraging: You Ain't Seen Nothing Yet," a study by the McKinsey Global Institute

noted that combined public and private debt burdens had reached historic highs in many rich countries. Based on previous episodes of debt reduction, it reckoned that once deleveraging began, countries would on average spend the next six to seven years whittling those debt ratios back by around 25 percent.[6]

This implies slower growth for the United States, culminating in a sovereign credit crisis, probably before 2015. Already, the U.S. fiscal ratios are worse than those of Portugal, which entered a solvency crisis with sovereign debt totaling 93.3 percent of GDP. And the U.S. ratios are worse still than those of Spain, where government debt stood at 61 percent of GDP in 2011. Gross U.S. federal debt exceeded 115 percent of GDP. And that just records explicit debt. Unfunded obligations in the United States are staggering. U.S. medical liabilities exceed total world GDP. The present value of unfunded Medicare liabilities at the beginning of 2010 was a whopping $75.167 trillion. Add another $18.901 trillion for prescription drugs benefits, and unfunded medical liabilities on the U.S. balance sheet are $94.068 trillion—a sum about 25 percent greater than the total annual output of the world economy, put at $70.16 trillion by the CIA ($5 trillion above the estimate of the *Economist*).[7]

Deleveraging is a particularly painful process when it depends upon the slow, incremental retirement of debt. Much of the progress of U.S. households toward debt reduction through December 2011 was the result of mortgage defaults. Write offs were "running at around 2 percent of banks' secured loans" in the United States.[8]

Typically, governments go more deeply into debt as households and nonfinancial corporations reduce indebtedness. This is because, as Richard Nixon famously said of himself and his fellow politicians, "We are all Keynesians now." Nixon's uncharacteristic homage to a defunct economist was a confession of profligacy and open admission of the otherwise unspoken policy by which all advanced economies have operated since World War II.

John Maynard Keynes rationalized a turn to profligacy in his *General Theory of Employment, Interest and Money* (1936). This became holy writ for politicians in advanced countries. The central argument of the

---

[6] "Deleveraging: You Ain't Seen Nothing Yet," *The Economist*, July 7, 2011.
[7] CIA World Factbook, https://www.cia.gov/library/publications/the-world -factbook/geos/xx.html. Updated June 7, 2012.
[8] "Deleveraging: You Ain't Seen Nothing Yet."

General Theory is that the level of employment is determined, not by the price of labor as the neoclassical economists argued, but by the spending of money (aggregate demand). Keynes wrote that government could improve economic prospects by spending money in almost any ridiculous fashion. He famously advised burying money in abandoned mine shafts so entrepreneurs would have an incentive to hire workers to dig it up. Politicians were only too delighted to discard the old-fashioned requirement to balance budgets. Consequently, after World War II all the advanced economies ran chronic deficits, bringing them to the point of insolvency. Among them, the United States has achieved the distinction of becoming the most thoroughly indebted country in the history of the world.

In the Keynesian perspective, attempts by households to reduce their debt mean a withdrawal of spending, which leads to a decline in aggregate demand. Australian Keynesian Billy Mitchell puts it this way: "As the private sector withdraws spending (aggregate demand) and starts reducing its debt levels, the only way that GDP can continue growing is if there is an external trade boom (unlikely overall) and/or fiscal support."[9]

It is unclear that this is true, however, even in Keynesian terms. The largest contribution to deleveraging in the United States household sector has arisen from debt default. Underwater homeowners who determined to stop paying their mortgages would in most cases have increased aggregate demand by diverting their mortgage payments to other uses. The backlog of foreclosure cases in the United States has been so great that homeowners who stopped paying their mortgages could, on average, live in their homes rent free for about a year and a half.

In any event, deleveraging is underway, and the typical response of governments is to run larger deficits to keep GDP rising. Over the long run, this is unsustainable. At some point, the government's good credit is exhausted. Without economic growth, the government's ability to borrow ever-growing amounts on the security of its taxing power is eclipsed. The Keynesian end point brings retrenchment that aggravates other deflationary forces.

---

[9] Billy Mitchell, "Private Deleveraging Requires Fiscal Support," The Billy Blog, September 14, 2010, http://bilbo.economicoutlook.net/blog/?p=11545.

As the end point approaches, credit markets jam up, a forewarning that the system is stressed and something big is coming. The U.S. economy peaked in 2007. But notwithstanding the fact that the financial system was imploding under the weight of oil prices that approach $150 per barrel, the stock market continued to rally. There was a recurrence of this precrisis environment as 2011 drew to a close. This time, the problem was worse. It was not just a question of subprime American homebuyers finding that they bought more house than they could afford. Entire countries are going bust. The heavily exploited fiction that the sovereign debt of countries in the Organization for Economic Cooperation and Development (OECD) is riskless is being exposed as a fantasy.

Stopping Runaway Spending

"If you've seen one, you've seen them all," would be an apt description for most of the world's banking and monetary systems. Given that they are all fiat systems with fractional reserve banking, Brazil's is distinguished by some subtle, yet important differences informed by the Brazilian experience with hyperinflation as recently as the mid-1990s. "From 1980 when the IMF price level series began to 1995 the price level in Brazil increased by a factor of 1 trillion. That which cost one real in 1980 cost 1 trillion reals in 1997."[10]

Economists at Brazil's largest private bank, Bradesco, looking over a longer period, asserted that accumulated inflation in Brazil between 1961 and 2006 was 14.2 quadrillion percent. That is 14,200,000,000,000 percent—the highest in the world over that 45-year span. Decades of hyperinflation provided Brazil with an expensive tutorial. This led Brazil to realize at least two distinct advantages:

1. Hyperinflation spurred Brazil to pioneer advanced online banking. With the value of money declining at a 2,000 percent annual rate, everyone wanted to get rid of cash as quickly as possible. Consequently, the lackadaisical check clearance characteristic of the

---

[10] Thayer Watkins, "The Hyperinflation in Brazil, 1980–1994," www.sjsu.edu /faculty/watkins/brazilinfl.htm.

United States would have been intolerable for Brazilians whose checks clear within 24 hours. As a result, Brazil pioneered Internet home banking and electronic funds transfer. As Virginia Philip, an analyst at Tower Group, Needham, Massachusetts, specializing in financial services and technology says, "I definitely would put the major Brazilian banks in the very elite in the world of online banking. Banks across the world look to them as models."[11]

2. Hyperinflation not only gave Brazilians cutting-edge banking technology, it taught them that financial crises were not just theoretical possibilities or footnotes from the past, but vivid realities. Consequently, Brazilian leaders somehow found the stomach to impose highly conservative regulation that reduced leverage for banks to protect depositors and prevent the banking system from becoming an accomplice to quantitative easing.

The second achievement is far the more important. The story of how it was done has been told by its architects, one of whom was Gustavo Franco, former governor of Brazil's central bank and a key player in the economic team that struggled for a decade to come up with "a policy that could stabilize the economy."[12]

Dr. Franco's account of the obstacles that the reformers overcame includes the intellectual challenge of sorting out the actual cause of the problem. Not surprisingly, perhaps, the hyperinflation itself so thoroughly skewed economic accounting that it obscured cause and effect relationships. Eventually, however, Franco and his colleagues, led by the then-finance minister, and later the thirty-fourth president of Brazil, Fernando Henrique Cardoso, determined that runaway spending was the underlying cause of hyperinflation. Franco said, "The Brazilian state had begun to spend twice as much as its ability to collect taxes. But it was difficult to see this from the numbers. Hyperinflation then produced

---

[11] David Lipschultz, "Advanced Online Banking, Born of Necessity; Hyperinflation Prompted Brazil to Find Ways to Clear Checks Quickly," *New York Times*, March 25, 2001, www.nytimes.com/2001/03/25/business/business-advanced -online-banking-born-of-necessity.html.

[12] Leslie Evans, "How Brazil Beat Hyperinflation," Los Angeles: UCLA International Studies & Overseas Programs, February 22, 2002, www.econ.puc-rio.br/ gfranco/How%20Brazil%20Beat%20Hyperinflation.htm

many funny theories about its causes. It took us 10 years to work through these to an actual solution."[13]

To successfully implement a remedy to runaway spending required the reformers to circumvent and defy the special interests that ordinarily dominate consideration of budget questions. Cardoso came to the task well-armed as a professor of political science at the Universidade de São Paulo. In the event, a primary reason Franco cited for the ultimate success of the reformers was the fact that they were able to act during a unique interlude,

> [W]here none of the political forces of the country were able to intervene in the process to promote the special interests that the state had been committed to supporting in the preceding decades. Pres. Fernando Collor de Mello was impeached in December 1992 and replaced by his vice president, Itamar Franco.[14]

Franco recalls the good luck that his namesake, President Franco "was not interested in economics and signed anything the ministers would bring him. This was unbelievable, but it depoliticized the process."[15]

Equally, Brazil's Congress was luckily weakened by a major scandal "in which 26 members of Congress and three state governors were implicated in diverting millions in federal funds into their own accounts." This facilitated needed reforms because it "kept them out of the discussion. This gave us a window of opportunity when the politicians did not interfere."[16]

Putting a "politically incorrect" gloss on it, Franco said, "We empowered the treasury and the central bank to subvert democracy." (For democracy here, read, the unfettered operation of special interest politics.) The problem was that special interest groups and political representatives beholden to them had voted to give themselves things the country could not afford. The reformers answer: "The finance ministry, treasury, and Central Bank, using a constitutional amendment

---

[13] Evans, "How Brazil Beat Hyperinflation."
[14] Ibid.
[15] Ibid.
[16] Ibid.

passed in 1994 simply did not implement the budget."[17] They closed off-budget spending while the Treasury exercised de facto line-item vetoes on the congressional budget. "While Congress had passed a budget that authorized, say, 800 million reals for a project, the treasury chose to actually expend only $200 million."[18]

Curtailing spending out of an empty treasury was a giant step toward reforming the system. But it was not enough. The reformers also took aim at the banks who had become accomplices in financing runaway spending: "The flood of bad loans from banks to fund the government projects the government itself was no longer underwriting was stopped by imposing criminal penalties."

As Franco recalls,

> [W]e prohibited—made it a crime—for a bank to lend money to one of its own shareholders. Bank officials in the private sector did not even maintain checking accounts in their own banks, for fear of being prosecuted if their check guarantee cards lent them funds to cover an overdraft. But the state banks could lend to the government. Under the Real Plan we enforced the same rules on the state banks and threatened the bank officials with jail if they lent money to the government. We criminalized a major source of inflation, especially where regional banks frequently bought government bonds. We made that illegal.[19]

As of mid-1994, 40 or more Brazilian banks were actually insolvent because of their lending to government projects: "We began in December 1994 with the intervention in Banespa (Bank of the State of São Paulo) and other state banks. Banespa was the largest state bank in the country with claimed assets of $30 billion—but with real assets of a negative $25 billion."[20]

The rate of price inflation in Brazil dropped dramatically after July 1994 in response to the Plano Real. By 1997 price increase rates had subsided to low single digits. The hyperinflation was over. Franco,

---

[17] Evans, "How Brazil Beat Hyperinflation," 2.

[18] Ibid.

[19] Ibid.

[20] Ibid.

Cardoso, and colleagues had succeeded through a process that "departed not only from the accepted theories, but also the accepted political process." As Franco recalled, "The key was to create an impersonal mechanism, not to get into negotiations with parties and unions—or housewives associations. You need market mechanisms. Dialogue doesn't work in this kind of situation."[21]

In short, the authors of the Plano Real cut the Gordian knot of political impasse by ignoring and/or sidelining the special interest groups that as a matter of course dominate the corporate state. "The assumption here was that each constituency, if consulted, would fight for its particular entitlement, driving the state budget back up and keeping the price spiral virulent."[22]

The paradox is that Brazil has thrived as a deleveraged economy and consequently does not face the quandary of figuring out how to borrow its way to a higher savings rate that perplexes American and British policy makers in the current depression. The deleveraged state of the Brazilian economy is partly an artifact of punishingly high real interest rates in the recent past. As of June 30, 2002, Brazilian government loans yielded 17.7 percent. Business loans yielded an average of 38.28 percent. And the average annual yield to banks on consumer loans was a punishing 60.57 percent. Taking out a consumer loan in Brazil made about as much economic sense as borrowing from a Mafia loan shark.

One of my mentors, the late Mancur Olson, was fond of saying that "values reflect what used to pay." Or not pay, as the case may be. With the average annual interest rate on consumer loans bumping above 60 percent just a few years ago, it is easy to imagine why Brazilian consumers have tended to shun credit, although that is changing as millions of new consumers attain middle-class incomes.

Important Lessons from Hyperinflation

I believe that the relatively recent history of hyperinflation in Brazil, which ended only in the late 1990s, has acted almost like the mechanism

---

[21] Evans, "How Brazil Beat Hyperinflation," 2.
[22] Ibid., 4.

of the gold standard. It has informed incentives for highly conservative banking regulation, along with sound fiscal and monetary policy.

Banking crises have historically spilled into Brazil from abroad—as they did on several occasions near the turn of the millennium. Brazil caught contagions from the "Asian flu" in 1997, the Russian crisis of 1998, and still another contagion from Argentina in 2002. There was also a financial crisis in 1999, when Brazil ended the peg of its currency, the real, to the dollar.

Candido Bracher, president and CEO of Banco Itau, summarized the Brazilian experience: "During the 1990s and various crises—the Asian crisis, Russian crisis, every crisis—Brazil was hit severely. We were so dependent upon foreign savings. Our foreign-exchange rate was devalued very quickly. We had to send our interest rates through the roof to attract capital. In all these cases, if there was a liquidity crisis abroad, we would be very severely hit."[23]

With those recent crises in mind, Brazilian bank regulators were alert to the prospect of further crises and bank failures in the offing.

In most countries, banks are obliged to maintain some minimum capital ratios—capital as a percentage of their assets (loans)—as recommended by the Bank for International Settlements in the so-called Basel standards. Rather than establish a simple leverage ratio, however, those standards were fudged with a risk-weighted approach. In practice, this meant that some of what proved to be the biggest and riskiest banks in the world were leveraged to the hilt. Inevitably, supposedly AAA credits, like subprime loans and sovereign debt proved to be far less blue chip than regulators in the advanced economies pretended.

Part of the problem with the risk-weighted approach was that it tended to rest on historic track records that purported to show little or no prospect of sharp downgrades or default in debt instruments. Unfortunately for many international banks, particularly those in the United States and Europe, the Basel standards enshrined the anachronistic fiction that the sovereign debt of OECD countries is riskless.

---

[23] "Banco Itaú BBA's Candido Bracher: 'The Party Will Not Be as Fancy as Before,'" Knowledge@Wharton, December 18, 2008, http://knowledge.wharton.upenn.edu/article.cfm?articleid=2117.

Other absurdities abound in the Basel standards. For example, ratings agency Moody's "Transition Matrix for Withdrawn Ratings" based on experience between 1920 and 1996, showed only a 0.03 percent chance of an Aaa-rate bond falling after one year to a rating of Baa. This is the perspective that leads gamblers to play Russian roulette. ("The track record shows I haven't blown my head off yet.") More to the point, it helps explain why AIG sold hundreds of billions of cheap credit-default swaps that devastated that company.

Imagine AIG's amazement when an avalanche of AAA-rated subprime mortgage securities swooned into default.

Minimal Bank Capital Ratios: A Crisis Waiting to Happen

U.S. banking regulators swallowed the same cocky assumption about systemic risk. They designed banking regulations the way AIG wrote credit-default swaps: on the mistaken faith that there would never be a credit collapse.

In the U.S. banking system, before the subprime crisis, the effective capital ratio was often as low as 4 percent, though it had to be no less than 5 percent to meet the standard for well-capitalized banks owned by bank holding companies—a group that includes the top 20 U.S. banks. Their capital ratios at the onset of the crisis varied between 5 percent and 8 percent.

Although U.S. and British bank regulators played a major role in negotiating the Basel II Accords (initially issued in June 2004 to help protect the world banking system from risks arising from bank failures), they choose to adopt the minimum permissible capital ratios as their regulatory norm. Brazilian bank regulators went the other way entirely. They insisted on limiting the leverage in the banking system to minimize the risks and costs of a future banking crisis.

All Brazilian banks must maintain minimum capital ratios of at least 11 percent. But many Brazilian banks have capital ratios of 16 percent or more—double, or even triple, the levels in the United States and Britain.

There has been a lot of jabber in political circles about the Great Correction and the supposed difficulty of keeping banking regulation up to date in the face of rapid technological change. Don't believe it. The U.S. authorities were wrong about this as they were about so much else. Evidence suggests that authorities in the United States, Britain, and other rich industrial countries actively abetted and encouraged explosive leveraging of debt in their economies by minimizing capital ratios.

U.S. Reserve Requirements: A System Failure

They did the same thing when it came to reserve requirements. Reserve requirements for Brazilian banks have been dramatically higher than those in the United States, Britain, and other advanced economies. The purpose of bank reserves is to absorb losses and provide liquidity to stabilize the financial system in times of crisis. The drawback of high reserves, from the perspective of politicians and aggressive bankers, is that they deleverage the system.

In Brazil before the crisis in 2008, banks were required to sequester 30 percent of their deposits with the central bank. In the United States, the notional level of reserves was 3 percent. But in reality regulatory interpretations allowed U.S. banks to operate free of any reserve requirements.

Due to "deposit reclassification" and other slippery interpretations instituted by the authorities to increase leverage in the banking system, U.S. banks were permitted to count their vault cash toward their reserve requirements, rather than actually depositing reserves with the central bank. This may not be quite as silly as counting the cost of the bank safes, desks, and furniture in the lobby toward reserves. But it's close. Even without any notional reserve requirements, banks would have to hold vault cash in any event—for use in their day-to-day operations in ATM machines and to satisfy customer withdrawals.

U.S. reserve requirements have been effectively nil for many years. Ironically, the Fed took a dramatic step on October 6, 2008, to make holding reserves more attractive to banks. On that date, the Fed began paying interest on banks "required and excess reserve balances." This is better understood as part of the multifaceted, multitrillion-dollar bailout of the banking system than as a step toward more measured regulation. As of November 2011, U.S. bank reserves had swollen to $1,591,900 million, as essentially insolvent banks opted to make deposits with the

Federal Reserve rather than lend to customers.[24] You can gain a better perspective on the precrisis effectiveness of U.S. reserve requirements from the fact that at the end of 2008, total reserve balances on deposit with the Federal Reserve amounted to less than $9.5 billion—a trivial sum compared to a banking system whose total liabilities totaled $13.5 trillion.

When Lehman Brothers went bankrupt and the global credit crisis hit its most severe moment to date, U.S. banks had virtually no reserves upon which to fall back. The amounts they could have swept out of their ATM networks could not have come close to backstopping their liquidity needs.

The Political Roots of the Economic Crisis

By waving bank reserve requirements, the U.S. authorities determined that taxpayers would provide the reserves for U.S. banks. It has long appeared to political authorities that abetting the growth of leverage improved the ability of consumers to generate wealth and obtain the good things that wealth affords, such as a new car, the latest fashions, or, more importantly, a home.

Even if this implied long-term ruin to a degree they failed to grasp, it was politically irresistible for politicians of both the right and the left to employ credit and leverage to facilitate even a temporary appearance of prosperity. The same political impulse that impelled politicians in the United States and Britain to scrap the gold standard also impelled them to favor easy money and ever greater leverage in the economic system.

As a result of this consensus, banking systems in both countries have been skirting the consequences of insolvency since 2008. In my view, there is a high likelihood that living standards that were inflated by decades of easy money will be deflated in the years to come as the North Atlantic economies are deleveraged. (Note that multi-trillion-dollar Treasury- and Fed-sponsored bailout programs supported up to 73 percent of the balance sheet of U.S. banks; the costs of these bailouts have only begun to be tallied.)

---

[24] Federal Reserve Statistical Release H.3, "Aggregate Reserves of Depository Institutions and the Monetary Base," www.federalreserve.gov/releases/h3/current/.

In Brazil, by contrast, the authorities were much less cocksure that they could control systemic risk. They were more concerned about avoiding the potentially ruinous consequences of a banking crisis. Consequently, they adopted more measured and conservative banking regulation. Having experienced recurring crises as they sought to distance themselves from the hyperinflation of the 1980s and early 1990s, they were more sensitive to the downside of leverage.

Rather than vitiating reserve requirements, Brazilian authorities successfully restrained the growth of debt by mandating high bank reserves.

When the global economic crisis triggered by the subprime collapse suddenly hit Brazil in September 2008, the authorities were in a position to respond. Of course, the crisis in Brazil was minimized because the Brazilian banking system was solvent. Brazil had no subprime problem. It scarcely had any mortgage debt at all. And far from indulging the fantasy that lending to government is riskless, Brazil had seen its state banks lose tens of billions that way, and prohibited such loans altogether.

The conservative regulation of Brazilian banks assured that unlike American and British banks, Brazilian banks were not highly leveraged.

During the liquidity strains caused by the flight of billions of dollars in hot money, the Central Bank of Brazil simply allowed the banks to access their reserves deposits to absorb losses and increase liquidity. In other words, Brazilian taxpayers were not called upon to backstop the banks because they had adequate reserves.

How Brazilians Became the New Scots

Speaking soon after the crisis, Banco Itau's Bracher made his pronouncement quoted at the head of this chapter:

> None of the Brazilian banks has come under the suspicion of being weak. The balance sheets are very strong. The Brazilian corporate sector is extremely underleveraged. The Brazilian citizen is underleveraged. The credit to [gross domestic product] ratio in Brazil is just above 30 percent. It used to be in the low 20 percent range. And 30 percent is still quite a low figure.[25]

---

[25] "The Party Will Not Be as Fancy as Before."

By contrast, total government corporate and individual debt in the United States was guesstimated by the Federal Reserve at 371 percent of GDP in 2009 about the time of Bracher's comments.

Another statistical mirror of Brazil's different position in the leverage cycle is the fact that only about one-third of the home sales in Brazil in the middle of the past decade were assisted with mortgage finance of any kind. Leverage was as low as it can be when you have to make a 100 percent down payment to buy a house. And the mortgage credit that has heretofore been available in Brazil was more akin to that available in the United States in the 1920s than the terms that became familiar during the subprime boom, with the Alt A, or "Liars' Loans," when borrowers frequently took cash back from mortgaging residential real estate for more than 100 percent of its value, without even documenting their income. By contrast, Brazilian mortgages are typically extended for only 10 years on a fraction of appraised value at punishingly high interest rates.

Through an ironic twist of history, Brazilians have become the new Scots. They abhor debt the way my Scots ancestors once did. No, the Brazilians did not suddenly become Presbyterians. The Brazilian distaste for debt was formed in the crucible of economic trauma. With an average of 60.5 percent interest rates on consumer loans as recently as June 30, 2002, it's little wonder that consumers in Brazil have tended to shun credit.

This all happened recently—within living memory even for young Brazilians—in the wake of a trillionfold increase in the price level after 1980. That hyperinflation coincided with complete stagnation in real income growth in Brazil. This underscores one of the many paradoxes in economics. Although hyperinflation rewards debtors by wiping out the value of money, it also wipes out credit, so no one can borrow money.

In the aftermath of hyperinflation, credit usually becomes scarce, and the costs of borrowing rise. Largely as a consequence of hyperinflation, Brazil has had the world's highest real interest rates for the past decade. High real interest rates encourage savings and punish borrowing. High real interest rates have kept Brazil relatively free of excess private sector debt.

Crash-Proofing the System Brazilian Style

The fact that the U.S. government was considered unquestionably creditworthy encouraged U.S. officials to take a cavalier attitude about protecting the nation's balance sheet. Brazilian officials, on the other hand, conscious that Brazil's ability to borrow internationally had been repeatedly called into question during crises as recent as 2002, took much more care to strengthen their fiscal and monetary posture.

Four major planks in Brazil's financial framework dramatically underscore the more measured and conservative approach Brazil has taken:

1. The Brazilian constitution contains a provision prohibiting quantitative easing. The Brazilian central bank, the Banco Central do Brasil, is *constitutionally prohibited* from granting loans to the federal treasury. Nor can it lend to government agencies or purchase primary issue Brazilian government securities.

2. Since 1999, Brazil has instituted a Fiscal Surplus Rule, which has resulted in an average annual primary budget surplus of 4 to 5 percent of GDP.

3. The passage of the Fiscal Responsibility Law approved in Brazil in May 2000, committed Brazil to recognizing the skeletons in the closet—the off-budget unfunded and contingent liabilities that have become so menacing in the United States. When these came to light, the Brazilian treasury realized that the net present value (NPV) of public debt—today's value of future costs and benefits—should be increased by about 6 to 8 percent of GDP due to unavoidable future payments for pension entitlements, public guarantees, and judicial settlements.

4. An important aspect of the Fiscal Responsibility Law is a provision forbidding the federal government of Brazil from bailing out any subnational government. This means lavish pensions and other spending commitments cannot be made by states and municipalities and pawned off on the federal treasury.

America's $104 Trillion Problem

Contrast this with the United States where unfunded liabilities have been ballooning to a fantastic degree. The president of the Federal Reserve Bank of Dallas, Richard Fisher, has lately seemed something of an optimist as his once-lofty estimate—$104 trillion—of U.S. unfunded liabilities made late in the last decade barely exceed 50 percent of Kotlikoff's more recent reckoning at $202 trillion. Take your pick. They are equivalent to a choice between drowning in 104 feet or 202 feet of water.

Left *unreported* was the fact that the discounted present value of entitlement debt, over the infinite horizon, reached $104 trillion. This is almost eight times the annual gross domestic product of the United States—and almost 20 times the size of the debt our government is expected to accumulate between 2009 and 2014.

And while the announcement that the Social Security trust fund will begin its decline one year earlier is an important fiscal event, the swelling of overall entitlement debt to more than one hundred trillion dollars has far more serious implications for economic growth—implications we are poorly positioned to address given the budget deficits we face today.

One spoilsport budget analyst reacted to Fisher's comments by calculating that meeting the unfunded liabilities of the U.S. government will require a 68 percent increase in U.S. federal taxes.

Clearly, U.S. politicians were thinking ahead when they established the peculiarly predatory system of taxation that made income taxable by citizenship rather than residence. If the U.S. taxed as almost every other country does, by domicile, the airports and ports would be crowded with people heading for the exits.

Even so, I still think there may be a strong argument for getting out. Unless you are convinced that the fiscal and monetary framework, the tax regime, and the prospect of monetary disruption are almost completely irrelevant to your prospect of success, you have to recognize that the United States faces dire straits in the years to come. "Weimer Republic, the Sequel" is almost a best case scenario. (One aspect of the unfunded entitlement liabilities to which Fisher refers is that they are not susceptible to being erased by hyperinflation; Social Security and other government pension funds are indexed to inflation.)

Brazil and the Taylor Rule

In April 2010, my colleague Charles Del Valle suggested in a comment that Brazil is the New America. His conclusion is informed by Brazil's deleveraged position in the credit cycle. The difference in leverage between the United States and Brazil has been truly startling. The United States and Brazil are on opposite extremes of the leverage cycle.

Mortgage debt in the United States stood at 75.7 percent of GDP. In Brazil, all mortgage debt amounted to less than 2 percent of GDP. Other debt aggregates are similarly lopsided. In 2008, the average credit card debt of an American consumer was 41 times higher than that of his Brazilian counterpart.

As we explore in this book, Brazil's emerging middle class shows signs of taking up the bad habits of U.S. consumers, embracing fast food and credit card debt. By 2012, Brazil's consumers were both fatter and more leveraged than they were when the Great Contraction struck.

Meanwhile, both obesity and insolvency are rarer among Brazilian consumers than those in the United States. In addition to conventional statistical measures of the different position of Brazil and the United States in the leverage cycle, there is further evidence that will more vividly strike the eye of a visitor to Brazil: the relationship between fashion and the credit cycle.

As a man, I would much rather see a young woman in a skimpy Brazilian bikini than draped in a generous *burqa*. Roughly speaking, two Brazilian bikinis could be fashioned from the fabric in a single handkerchief. This makes Brazil's the most efficient fashion for covering a female form since manufactured clothing replaced pelts and feathers.

Hence, the pertinence of the famous observation, first made in the 1920s by Wharton economist George Taylor, known as the "hemline effect." Taylor observed that in times of prosperity women's hemlines rise and more bare skin shows. But when hemlines tumble and women's clothes cover more body surface, it's time to hold on to your wallet.

After the Wall Street Crash in 1929, women turned the short skirts of the 1920s into dishrags. Hemlines tumbled to the ankles, where they remained throughout the Great Depression. The fact that Brazilian women are adorned in some of the world's most revealing fashions underscores my central observation about Brazil: it is in a different phase of the leverage cycle than the major Northern Hemisphere economies.

Because Brazil's consumer economy is relatively nonleveraged, Brazil's adjustment to the credit crisis—known as the *terremoto* (Portuguese for "earthquake")—did not necessitate deleverage, much less lead to covering the bodies of Brazil's well-tanned women.

Leverage and Growth

The startling differences between indebtedness in a highly leveraged economy like that of the United States and an underleveraged economy like that of Brazil flows through into practically every dimension of the economy.

Unfortunately for economic prospects in the United States, when leverage is compounding, growth accelerates, but tends to recede when leverage declines. In fact, ever since Nixon closed the gold window, economic growth in the United States has seemed totally dependent on compounding leverage rather than income growth. See Table 8.1.

Median real per capita income in the United States was higher in 1973 than it is now. It topped out almost 40 years ago, soon after Nixon repudiated the Gold Reserve Standard. As Table 8.1 shows, total household debt in the United States has exploded by twentyfold since then.

While we tend to think of U.S. prosperity as driven by free market vitality, a case could be made that in recent decades GDP growth has been driven not by income growth but by financial engineering to inject increased leverage into an ever-less competitive economy.

To the extent that is true, you can expect the U.S. economy to painfully contract as leverage in the system recedes. In my view, as one who wasted decades of his life trying to draw attention to the peril of national bankruptcy posed by spending vast sums out of an empty pocket, I see little hope that a collapse can be avoided. It is hopelessly utopian to expect any decisive fiscal or monetary reform until the United States experiences the traumatic consequences of the coming solvency crisis. Any attempt at reform by accelerating the deleveraging

Table 8.1   Leverage in the U.S. Economy Soars

Year	Total ($Trillion)	Total Household	Total Business	Total State and Local	Total Federal	Total Financial	Total Foreign
1974	2.408	0.680	0.823	0.208	0.358	0.258	0.081
Q1 2009	52.859	13.795	11.156	2.259	6.721	17.021	1.907

Source: U. S. Federal Reserve, "Credit Market Debt Growth by Sector," www.federalreserve.gov/releases/z1/Current/z1r-2.pdf.

process would engender tantrums from powerful lobbies that would make the Greek protests seem measured and responsible.

The trillionfold or even 14 quadrillionfold inflation coincided with complete stagnation in real income growth in Brazil. This underscores one of the many paradoxes in economics. Although hyperinflation rewards debtors by wiping out the value of money, it also wipes out credit.

GDP Gains Based on Income Growth

This points to another strength of Brazil, namely that it owes its growing prosperity to actual income growth rather than just credit expansion.

Per capita GDP in Brazil more than doubled in the past decade in U.S. dollar terms, in a low leverage economy. This happened in the face of the highest real interest rates in the world. While Greenspan and Bernanke were inflating a credit bubble with invisibly low rates in the United States, Brazil was growing robustly in spite of interest rates on consumer debt that were at times higher than 60 percent—so high they would stop the U.S. economy dead in its tracks.

Part of the reason that rates were so high is that laws were not configured to maximize lending. Until recently, for example, creditors absorbed the risk of insolvency because only in the past decade were Brazilian bankruptcy laws changed to give creditors priority claims on collateral if a borrower became insolvent. Naturally, this discouraged lending and magnified the spillover effects.

High real interest rates reward savers. If you are a saver, you will realize higher returns on your savings in Brazil than in the United States, or any of the highly leveraged advanced countries where interest rates are kept invisibly low to stimulate recovery and bail out insolvent banking systems.

Of course, high real and nominal interest rates also assure that Brazil will retain a tool of economic stimulation in its arsenal long after the advanced economies run out of scope to easily promote stalled growth. As of November 30, 2011, the SELIC rate in Brazil, (the equivalent of the U.S. discount rate), was 11 percent. It was reduced twice in the second half of 2011 in recognition of a growing danger of a global slowdown. The Brazilian SELIC rate can be trimmed many times from

11 percent before it becomes as nugatory as the 0.25 percent level of the equivalent discount rate in the United States.

If the world slips into a deeper state of depression, as seems entirely possible, with governments in the advanced countries wrestling with the prospect of total collapse, they will also be starting more or less from scratch as they grapple for effective ways to stimulate growth. As Charles Hughes Smith observed,

> Despite all the brave talk of the manipulators on the Board of the Federal Reserve, they've run out of manipulative tricks. With interest rates already near zero, their most basic toolbox is empty. Now they're reduced to bleating about all the phantom tools in their possession and playing around with long-term bond yields and mortgage rates interventions that cannot possibly create jobs or organic (i.e. real, unmanipulated) demand for stocks and housing.[26]

Brazilian politicians and central bankers are certainly not above manipulating markets. But because Brazil has high nominal and real rates authorities, there will retain a conventional mechanism for rekindling economic activity. They will cut interest rates from the sky-high 11 percent range into single digits, although not necessarily into fractional decimal points as has been the case with the United States, Great Britain, and Japan.

Unlike the United States, Greece, Portugal, and Spain, Brazil has sufficient financial reserves for a rainy day, or *anos de vacas magras* ("years of the skinny cows") as they would say in Portuguese. The country's total net debt as a percentage of GDP is only a bare fraction of that of the United States, and Brazil is sitting on a fat stash of $350 billion in currency reserves, while the United States has none.

I think the case for Brazil as the most attractive of the BRICs is overdetermined. I have previously indicated a prejudice, in that I married a beautiful Brazilian lady who has deepened my appreciation of

---

[26] Charles Hugh Smith, "Another Reason for Stocks to Tank in 2012: Jobs," Of Two Minds.com December 8, 2011, www.oftwominds.com/blogdec11/stocks-jobs12-11.html.

the good things Brazil has to offer. Like many things in life, my marriage did not work out. But that doesn't diminish the attractions of Brazil.

There is much more to Brazil's appeal than what you see in *The Victoria's Secret Catalogue* and a low degree of leverage throughout the economy—although that alone will account for a lot of growth potential as compared to highly leveraged economies like Greece and the United States that are destined to endure painful deleverage in the decades to come.

Next, we take a look at liquidity in another sense—the world's water situation and Brazil's liquid riches, part of its unique position as the world's first tropical agricultural superpower.

Chapter 9

A Bounty of Water and Land

Brazil as History's First Tropical Superpower

The Lord shall open unto thee his good treasure, the heaven to give the rain unto thy land in his season, and to bless all the work of thine hand: and thou shalt lend unto many nations, and thou shalt not borrow.

—Deuteronomy 28:12

In these forests the multitude of insects that bite, sting, devour, and prey upon other creatures, often with accompaniments of atrocious suffering, passes belief. The very pathetic myth of "beneficent nature" could not deceive even the least wise being if he once saw for himself the iron cruelty of life in the tropics.

—Theodore Roosevelt, on nature in Brazil,
Through the Brazilian Wilderness, 1913

Brazil and Water

One of the perennial confusions in economics is that between monetary inflation and relative price increases. This was in play again with the early January 2012 announcement that in December 2011, Chinese inflation had jumped by 4.1 percent over its rate a year earlier.

Sustainability

On its face, that seems to represent about a 25 percent improvement over the average Chinese inflation rate of 5.4 percent in 2011. But look more closely. The same report reveals that Chinese food prices jumped 9.1 percent year on year in December. This is quite ominous for China, but very bullish for Brazil.

Here is why. In recent years, China has been the world's largest agricultural power, producing more food than any other country. The trouble is that China's farm output is unsustainable. Soil erosion as a consequence of overplanting, land mismanagement, and an acute shortage of water for irrigation are undermining the productivity of Chinese cropland.

Satellite photos compared to those from 40 years ago show a huge new dust bowl crossing western China and western Mongolia. Wang Tao, a leading Chinese desert scholar, has estimated that each year, 1,400 square miles of former cropland in northern China turn to desert. Grain harvests in northern China and Mongolia have shrunk by half or more in the past 20 years.

The problem is not isolated to the Mongolian border region. In China's grain-growing plains, as well as in large parts of the grain-growing areas of India, there is not nearly enough natural rainfall for rechargeable aquifers. This means that irrigation-supported crop growth over the second half of the twentieth century has been fed by water pumped up from deep underground fossil aquifers in addition to water channeled from river systems.

In those areas of China without access to the river systems, irrigation water is pumped from underlying fossil aquifers filled over hundreds of millions of years. As these aquifers do not readily recharge when they are drained annually for irrigation, they rapidly run dry.

More than 70 percent of the world's population, including billions living in China and India, is being supported by crops irrigated from falling water tables. As a result, thousands of square miles of former cropland are turning to desert annually. In China, overpumping in the fossil aquifers in the north is rapidly turning into desert a region responsible for half of China's wheat production and more than one-third of its corn production.

In China as a whole, almost four-fifths of its total grain harvest comes from irrigated land. Symptomatic of the increasingly arid conditions is the drying up of multiple lakes in China. In western China, Quinhai Province, through which the main branch of the Yellow River flows, once had 4,077 freshwater lakes. But in the past two decades, more than 2,000 of those lakes there have disappeared. In Hebei Province, which surrounds Beijing, 969 of 1,052 freshwater lakes have vanished in the past 20 years.

According to *Issues Online in Science and Technology*:

Water tables are falling as aquifers are pumped at rates exceeding their ability to recharge. Even the water in deep-fossil aquifers, laid down millions of years ago and which can't be recharged, is being depleted. Nearly 90 percent of all fresh water used by humans goes for irrigation. According to the United Nations Food and Agriculture Organization (FAO), just 16 percent of the world's cropland is irrigated, but this 16 percent produces 36 percent of the global harvest.

The stripping of forest and grassland and the cultivation of sloping land have led to rapid runoff of rainwater that normally would help recharge near-surface aquifers. In many regions, inadequate drainage has increased the salt content of the soil, leading to a loss of productivity and sometimes abandonment of agriculture altogether. The once-fertile crescent of the Middle East is a striking example, and similar salinization is accelerating in the United States, China, and elsewhere. It is certainly possible and imperative to increase the efficiency of agricultural water use, but it is not clear whether this will fully compensate for water losses or increase yields of annual crops enough.

Dust bowls and desertification are serious in many parts of the world. Depletion of the fossil aquifer under the North China plain, for example, has led to huge dust storms that choke South Koreans every year.[1]

---

[1] Peter C. Kahn, Thomas Molnar, Gengyun G. Zhang, and C. Reed Funk, "Investing in Perennial Crops to Sustainably Feed the World," *Issues* online, Summer 2011, www.issues.org/27.4/kahn.html.

Dust bowls and desertification are not just problems for South Korean air quality. Rapidly rising food prices pose a threat to stability in China, as elsewhere. Remember, per capita income in China is on par with Tunisia's. What appeared to be a stable dictatorship in Tunisia was overthrown early in 2011 when food prices surged. China has a long history of dynasties overturned during times of dearth.

The epigraph that starts this chapter, from Deuteronomy, suggests a link between rainfall and deficit spending. In the modern context, the imperative to deplete fossil aquifers when rainfall is inadequate closely parallels the political imperative to borrow in order to finance spending when tax revenues are inadequate. In both cases, the overriding importance of achieving near-term goals—in this case, greater prosperity for farmers as well as lower food prices—trumps the threat of long-term ruin.

A World of Water Shortages

Note that China is not the only country that is rapidly depleting its fossil aquifers. Shortages of water for irrigation are undermining the productivity of one-third of the world's cropland.

At least 18 countries now have food production bubbles based on the depletion of water from nonrechargeable fossil aquifers. Between 1968 and 1998, India's food production surged due to unsustainable pumping of groundwater aquifers. Experts estimate that over 15 percent of India's population is being fed wheat, rice, and barley irrigated with water pumped from fossil aquifers. In India's breadbasket—the regions of Punjab and Haryana—water tables are falling three feet a year. In the western Indian state of Gujarat the water table has fallen from 50 feet below the surface to 1,300 feet below the surface in 30 years.

The situation in the Midwest of the United States is not much better. As you'll remember if you read John Steinbeck's *The Grapes of Wrath*, large sections of the United States were transformed into a dust bowl due to inadequate rainfall during the Great Depression.

This problem was "solved" not by increased precipitation but by the development of more powerful diesel and electric pumps capable of mining water from the Ogallala fossil aquifers deep below the surface.

In the words of water alarmist Lester R. Brown,

. . . the world has a huge water deficit. Using data on over-pumping for China, India, Saudi Arabia, North Africa, and the United States, Sandra Postel, author of *Pillar of Sand: Can the Irrigation Miracle Last?*, calculates the annual depletion of aquifers at 160 billion cubic meters or 160 billion tons. Using the rule of thumb that it takes 1,000 tons of water to produce 1 ton of grain, this 160-billion-ton water deficit is equal to 160 million tons of grain or one-half the U.S. grain harvest.[2]

Unfortunately, current and looming water shortages are not a figment of Lester Brown's imagination. It is particularly notable that much of America's grain crop is irrigated with water mined from the Ogallala fossil aquifer. While Americans tend to take for granted the superiority of American farming, agricultural prosperity in the United States may prove to be as unsustainable as the federal deficit. As reported in the *New York Times*, "the [Ogallala] aquifer is dropping lower and lower, and some geologists fear it could dry up in as soon as 25 or 30 years. This is a major issue confronting not just those eight states but the entire country."[3]

According to United Nations estimates, the population of the world will expand to 9.1 billion by the year 2050. But long before that happens, a global shortage of fresh water is likely to push food prices to destabilizing heights.

While water is potentially one of the world's most valuable commodities, because of its importance in the cycle of life, water is not easily exported. For one thing, water is heavy. It is heavier than all but the heaviest grades of crude oil, (also known as bitumen), with an API gravity of less than 10.

Although fresh water is not suitable as a long-distance export, at least not directly, the virtual export of water is destined to be a major informing factor in the prosperity of Brazil. While the onrushing specter of water and food shortages threaten economic and political disruption in failing states

---

[2] Lester R. Brown, "Population Growth Sentencing Millions to Hydrological Poverty," The Policy Institute, June 21, 2000, www.earth-policy.org/plan_b _updates/2000/alert4.

[3] Katherine Q. Seelye, "Aquifer's Depletion Poses Sweeping Threat," Green (blog), May 4, 2011, http://green.blogs.nytimes.com/2011/05/04/aquifers-depletion -poses-sweeping-threat.

across the globe, and even emerging market powerhouses India and China are threatened, one country stands alone as likely to benefit.

Renewable Water

In 2010, *The Economist* detailed the advantages possessed by Brazil with renewable water as follows:

> According to the UN's 2009 World Water Assessment Report, Brazil has more than 8,000 billion cubic kilometres of renewable water each year, easily more than any other country. Brazil alone. . . has as much renewable water as the whole of Asia. . . . And again, this is not mainly because of the Amazon. Piaui is one of the country's driest areas but still gets a third more water than America's corn belt. . . . Brazil has almost as much farmland with more than 975 millimeters of rain each year as the whole of Africa and more than a quarter of all such land in the world.[4]

Speaking of the Amazon, more than 20 percent of the world's fresh water flows through the Amazon basin alone, about 133,000 cubic meters per second. And this is only the most spectacular part of the world's most dense hydrological system.

Brazil's embarrassment of riches where water is concerned was highlighted in August 2011 by a presentation at the International Congress of the Society Brasiliera Geophysical in Rio de Janeiro. Researchers described a heretofore unknown "underground river," the Rio Hamza, that flows to the Atlantic Ocean four kilometers beneath the Amazon. Some scientists disputed that the Rio Hamza is actually a river rather than a porous aquifer through which a substantial volume of water is trickling. According to *Wired* (UK) "a flow rate calculated to be around 3,000 cubic metres per second—which is a mere three percent of the Amazon River itself. That's still plenty, though—more than 46 times the flow of the Thames."[5]

---

[4] "The Miracle of the Cerrado," *The Economist*, August 26, 2010.

[5] Duncan Geere, "Underground river discovered below Amazon," Wired.co.uk, August 26, 2011, www.wired.co.uk/news/archive/2011-08/26/underground-river-amazon.

So while the aquifers supplying other important economies, including the United States, dwindle toward the vanishing point, Brazil has 8,000 cubic kilometers (or 1,919 cubic miles in the U.S. system of enumeration) of renewable water each year.

For one thing, it suggests that Brazil's recent prominence as a driver of world growth will continue. From 2007 through 2010, Brazil contributed 10.03 percent of total world market growth at current exchange rates—more than the United States, which added 8.2 percent (due mainly to exchange rate gains for the dollar)—and infinitely more than Europe, which subtracted 9.2 percent from the world growth. Together, China and Brazil contributed 43.4 percent of world growth from 2007 through 2010. Brazil's lavish natural endowment of fresh water, in combination with China's receding ability to feed itself, guarantees a deepening of the trade ties between the two countries.

As you look ahead to the middle of this century, Brazil is destined to increase its virtual exports of water in the form of grains and proteins. No other country has both in the freshwater and the spare farmland required to convert water into food at the scale that Brazil can. According to the UN's Food and Agricultural Organization (FAO) Brazil's total potential arable land is more than 400 million hectares, of which only about 50 million are currently in use.

This is incredibly bullish for investors in Brazilian government debt. The simple truth stated in the epigraph from Deuteronomy will be as valid in the future as it was when the Bible was written, "The Lord shall open unto thee his good treasure, the heaven to give the rain unto thy land in his season, and to bless all the work of thine hand: and thou shalt lend unto many nations, and thou shalt not borrow." In an increasingly crowded, urbanized, and hungry world, Brazil's terms of trade are destined to improve dramatically. Almost uniquely among all the globe's economies, Brazil will have the capacity to export food at a scale capable of filling the deficits destined to emerge elsewhere.

The 2011 revolutions of the Arab Spring, in which four dictators whose regimes stretched back for decades were overthrown, underscores the imperative that politicians everywhere will feel to purchase Brazilian food at prices that would seem staggering in comparison to those of the old normal.

In that light, Brazil seems destined to become one of the globe's leading creditor countries, profiting from what appears to be inflation elsewhere and ultimately lending "unto many nations." That should make longer-term, Brazilian government debt denominated in real, and currently paying 12.5 percent potentially one of the world's greatest investments.

Brazil Reinvents Agriculture

A century ago, leading agronomists thought they had pinpointed the factors informing optimum conditions for farming. At that time and for generations afterward, there was a smug perception that success in agriculture was predicated upon a past history of glaciation. This, of course, implied that only countries with temperate climates could compete in farming.

A representative statement of this view was spelled out in 1914 by O. D. von Engeln, a professor of physical geography at Cornell. He wrote:

> Pleistocene continental glaciation was a phenomenon centering essentially about in the North Atlantic Basin. Around the North Atlantic Basin are centered, also the leading nations of the modern world . . . it is sometimes suggested that the leadership of such nations is largely accruing from natural advantages they have derived from continental glaciation. Without question many of the natural resources of these nations are owing to the invasion of the ice.[6]

von Engeln went on to spell out an elaborate argument supporting the view that success in farming was predicated upon exploiting glaciated rather than nonglaciated land. Part of this view was based upon analysis of the effect of ice sheets on the deposition of minerals in the soil. According to von Engeln, glaciation improved soil quality in most cases by crushing minerals and thoroughly mixing them to form a richer topsoil for growing crops. Drawing on U.S. data for the value of

---

[6] O. D. von Engeln, "Effects of Continental Glaciation on Agriculture," *Bulletin of the American Geographical Society* 46, no. 4 (1914): 242–243.

farmland in 1910, he showed that variations in value between and within states reflected patterns of glaciation.

For example, a map on page 249 of volume 46 of the *Bulletin of the American Geographical Society* shows the relative value of farmland by counties in Indiana, with land in the glaciated counties worth up to 10 times more than land in the more southerly, nonglaciated counties. Von Engeln spelled out his thesis according to the lights of the day:

> Geographical factors other than glaciation, moreover, may be determinant in this general grouping of modern, virile peoples around the North Atlantic, and historical considerations may not be wholly set aside. Moreover, it must not be forgotten that France, Italy, New Zealand and Australia, to name examples without the glaciated regions, are also in the van of modern progress.[7]

Of course, von Engeln erred in stating that France, Italy, and New Zealand and Australia were without glaciated regions. According to *U.S. Geological Survey Professional Paper 1386–E.–1*, "Glaciers of Europe," France has 350 square kilometers of glaciated territory and Italy 608 square kilometers under glacier. While only a small area of Australia in the vicinity of Mount Kosciuszko was glaciated in the past, the whole of the Southern Alps in New Zealand were covered by a sheet of ice. Presumably, von Engeln meant to say that these "virile nations" did not feed themselves on formerly glaciated lands.

Putting aside the somewhat sloppy iteration of the facts, the implications of this line of analysis were not overtly bullish for Brazilian agriculture. Just about the only limited potential that could have been envisioned for Brazil joining the van of modern progress where farming is concerned was confined to the potential for growing wheat and other cereal crops in the temperate climate in the south of Brazil, below the Tropic of Capricorn (23° 27' S. latitude), which crosses Brazil at the latitude of the city of São Paulo. This is the South region, known for its cattle-raising gaucho culture. Uncharacteristically of Brazil, it is subject to frosts and snowfall during the austral winter, from June through September.

---

[7] Von Engeln, "Effects of Continental Glaciation," 243.

Azorean settlers who came to Rio Grande do Sul after 1752 introduced wheat farming there, and it remained the main export of the state until well into the nineteenth century. Today, approximately 90 percent of Brazil's 5.3 million metric tons of wheat is produced in the states of Parana and Rio Grande do Sul. The three southernmost (and coldest) states of Brazil, Parana, Santa Catarina, and Rio Grande do Sul, comprise 576,409 square kilometers—an area larger than France, but only 6 percent of Brazil's total territory of 8,514,877 square kilometers.

The New Breadbasket of the World

The received opinion of experts until the very end of the twentieth century was that farming in the tropics was a losing proposition. In part, this was a simple matter of precedent. Before the emergence of Brazil as, in the words of The Economist, "the first tropical food-giant," the leading farming locales were all temperate producers.[8] Even at the turn of the millennium, it was difficult for skeptics to see that Brazilian farm production was destined to increase in the dramatic way it has. Agronomists, thoughtful observers, and official bodies relying upon production statistics compiled through the mid-1990s would have had to look very closely to see a reason to alter the conventional wisdom indicating that temperate farming was approximately 50 percent more productive than farming in the tropics.

A part of this difference, as von Engeln implied, was attributable to soil conditions. In addition to lacking the advantages of glacial deposition, tropical soils are notoriously fragile and subject to rapid leeching of organic compounds. Unlike soils in temperate zones where winter frosts contribute to the buildup of richer topsoils over time, tropical soils tend to be rapidly depleted of nutrients.

Another factor that has tended to weigh against the productivity of farming in the tropics is the rich array of pests and parasites that contribute to post-harvest food losses. Christopher Wheatley and fellow experts at the International Center for Tropical Agriculture, known as CIAT (after its Spanish initials), estimate tropical harvest losses of food grains, "from mishandling, spoilage and pest infestation at 25 percent;

---

[8] "The Miracle of the Cerrado."

this means that one-quarter of what is produced never reaches the consumer for whom it was grown, and the effort and money required to produce it are lost forever."[9] Meanwhile, fruit, vegetables, and root crops tend to suffer even greater losses. "Some authorities put losses of sweet potatoes, plantain, tomatoes, bananas and citrus fruit sometimes as high as 50 percent, or half of what is grown."[10]

Economist Jeffrey D. Sachs analyzed the enhanced vulnerability to spoilage in the tropics in his December 2000 paper, "Tropical Underdevelopment":

> B. Pests and parasites. A second major feature of tropical ecosystems is the high prevalence of crop pests and parasites. Tropical ecosystems generally are characterized by a high degree of biodiversity, which in a very general sense resists the monoculture systems that characterize temperate-zone food production. Monocultures in the tropics are prone to devastation through plant diseases, pests, and other forms of competition with highly biodiverse ecosystems. Just as with human diseases, the year-round high temperatures of the tropics, and the absence of freezing winter months to kill parasites and pests, are the root of the high-burden of plant diseases and crop losses due to spoilage. The high prevalence of tropical animal diseases, such as trypanosomiasis, has long hindered animal husbandry and the mixed crop-cattle agricultural systems characteristic of temperate ecozones.[11]

The factors that Jeffrey Sachs cites as contributing to high losses of the crops in the tropics to pests and parasites are real. They are not figments of the temperate-centric imagination. Equally, as Sachs was shrewd enough to recognize in his analysis from the year 2000, there are

---

[9] "Prevention of Post-Harvest Food Losses: Fruits, Vegetables and Root Crops. A Training Manual," International Center for Tropical Agriculture, FAO Corporate Document Repository.

[10] Christopher Wheatley, "Adding Value to Root and Tuber Crops," International Center for Tropical Agriculture, FAO Corporate Document Repository.

[11] Jeffrey D. Sachs, "Tropical Underdevelopment," Center for International Development at Harvard University, Working Paper no. 57, December 2000.

ecological barriers to technological diffusion. He proposed the convincing hypothesis,

> that the rate of technological innovation in the temperate-zone economies was much higher than in the tropical-zone economies in the nineteenth and twentieth centuries, while the rate of technological diffusion between the two zones was very limited because key technologies could not cross the ecological divide.[12]

Sachs astutely framed the issues. Yet, I believe that his lucid analysis draws the wrong conclusion because at the very time when he was writing a fundamental change was taking place that has continued to gather momentum.

Thanks to research conducted over the last quarter of the twentieth century by Embrapa (Empresa Brasileira de Pesquisa Agropecuaria), the Brazilian Agricultural Research Corporation, a technical firm affiliated with the Brazilian Ministry of Agriculture, Brazil is now capitalizing on innovations unprecedented in the history of tropical farming. Dr. Silvio Crestana, the director-general of Embrapa, confirmed Sachs's perspective on the difficulty of transporting key technologies across the ecological divide. He recounts, "We went to the U.S. and brought back the whole package [of cutting-edge agriculture in the 1970s]. That didn't work and it took us 30 years to create our own."[13]

Yes, there are ecological barriers to the diffusion of agricultural innovations between temperate and tropical regions. Heretofore, most of these have tended to favor producers in the temperate zone. And, yes, during the nineteenth and twentieth centuries the rate of innovation was much higher in the temperate zone. But no longer.

What Jeffrey Sachs and few others apparently suspected was that as the twenty-first century opened, a remarkable surge of technical innovations in tropical farming was poised to make Brazil the new breadbasket of the world. The innovations include the following:

---

[12] Sachs, "Tropical Underdevelopment."
[13] "The Miracle of the Cerrado."

1. Embrapa devised a systems approach to improving the acidic soils of the vast Brazilian Cerrado, previously regarded as unfit for farming. Famed American botanist Norman Borlaug the so-called father of the Green Revolution, opined, "nobody thought the soils were ever going to be productive."[14] But by spreading millions of tons of lime (over five tons of lime per hectare) Embrapa dramatically reduced the acidity of soils in the Cerrado.

2. Embrapa created new breeds of grass that greatly increased pasture yields, supporting a vast expansion of Brazil's cattle herd—from 78 million head of cattle in 1970 to over 200 million today. The time required to raise a bull for slaughter fell by 60 percent from four years to as little as 18 months.

3. Embrapa created a tropical version of soybeans, otherwise a temperate climate crop. Embrapa also formulated varieties of soybeans that could thrive in acidic soils. Given Brazil's greater factor endowment of sunlight, Embrapa's customized soybeans were designed to grow faster than typical temperate-climate varieties. These short cycle plants mature 8 to 12 weeks faster, making it possible for Brazilian farmers to produce two crops a year. Whereas previously second crops were much smaller, they have now become as large as the year's first crop.

4. Embrapa pioneered no-till farming in which the soil is not plowed before sowing and the crop is not harvested at ground level. Instead, the remains are left to rot in the fields, preserving and enhancing the nutrients in the soil. As of 2010, Brazilian farmers used no-till techniques for over 50 percent of their grain crops, a system applauded by the Sierra Club and other vocal environmentalists. No-till has many advantages for tropical agriculture including reduced soil erosion, a greater efficiency in water use, and a decrease in vulnerability to pests.

5. Embrapa has other, far-reaching research initiatives to build on Brazil's growing agricultural prowess. They include developing a system to capture methane emissions from pig manure to make biogas and employing engineered strains of nitrogen-fixing bacteria to reduce the need for nitrogen fertilizer.

---

[14] "The Miracle of the Cerrado."

6. Embrapa's genetic resources and biotechnology Center (Embrapa-CENARGEN) is developing insect- and/or disease-resistant crops and also focusing on strains with lower postharvest storing losses. To date, they have registered successes in creating common beans with transgenic resistance to bean viruses, "papaya resistant to *Papaya ringspot virus*, passion fruit resistant *passionfruit Woodiness virus* and soybean resistant to herbicide."[15]

Diversification

As *The Economist* declared in "Brazilian Agriculture: The World's Farm":

> Over the past 35 years Brazil has transformed itself from a food importer into one of the world's largest exporters. It is the first tropical country to join the big farm-exporting ranks (the rest have temperate climates). The country is now the world's biggest exporter of five internationally traded crops, and number two in soy beans and maize. None of the other big exporters has anything like this degree of diversification. Perhaps the most striking achievement has been the growth of soybeans: soya is a temperate crop and Brazilian research scientists had to breed new varieties that would grow in the tropical Cerrado, the savanna-like land where the farm miracle has taken place.[16]

This is evident in a 132 percent increase in Brazilian soybean production from 2000 to 2010. During that time in the state of Mato Grosso, according to the UN Food and Agricultural Organization (FAO), the cost of producing soybeans fell to about $6.23 per 60 kilogram bag, just 53 percent of the U.S. level of $11.72. Furthermore,

> In 2002, for the first time in history, the overall average yield of soybeans in Brazil (2.6 t/ha) was higher than the average yield in the United States of America (2.4 t/ha). It is reasonable to state

---

[15] M.G. Cardoso Costa, A. Xavier, and W. Campos Otoni, "Horticultural Biotechnology in Brazil," ISHS Acta Horticulturae 725: Fifth International Symposium on in Vitro Culture and Horticultural Breeding.

[16] "Brazilian Agriculture: The World's Farm," *The Economist*, August 27, 2010.

that in the Centre West region, Brazilian farmers are practicing one of the most advanced and sustainable agricultural systems in the world.[17]

The FAO and other experts are effusive in their estimates of the potential for farming in Brazil.

In a world suffering from declining marginal returns along a broad horizon, it is notable that Brazil's surge in productivity exemplified by a 3,000 percent increase in soybean output over the past 35 years is overwhelmingly attributable to rising returns. According to the prominent Brazilian economist, Antonio Delfim Netto, over 90 percent of the increase in Brazilian agriculture over the past three decades has been due to improvements in total factor productivity with less than 10 percent attributable to increased use of land, labor, and capital.

Remarkably, Brazil produces a quarter of the world's soybean exports on just 6 percent of the country's arable land. Brazil has ample room to expand production. According to the FAO, Brazil has more potential farmland than any other country—up to 400,000,000 hectares, of which only 50 million are currently in use. As canvassed earlier in this chapter, Brazil also has more fresh water than any other country: 8,000 cubic kilometers (1,919 mi^2) of renewable water each year, more than the whole of Asia.

Irrigation

In *Pillar of Sand: Can the Irrigation Miracle Last?* Sandra Postel argues that irrigation miracles cannot last. She states that a key lesson from history is that most irrigation-based civilizations fail. Postel writes:

> One out of every five hectares of irrigated land is losing productivity because of spreading soil salinization. And as water becomes scarce, competition for it is increasing—between neighboring states and countries, between farms and cities, and

---

[17] "Fertilizer Use by Crop in Brazil," Land and Plant Nutrition Management Service, Land and Water Development Division, www.fao.org/docrep/007/y5376e/y5376e0b.htm.

between people and their environment. . . . Water scarcity is now the single biggest threat to global food production.[18]

While irrigation in many areas is drawn from rapidly depleting fossil aquifers, Brazil enjoys more freshwater than any other country. One of Brazil's great strengths as a growing agricultural power is that most of the country's crop production is rainwater fed. Brazil has more than a quarter of all the farmland in the world that gets 975 millimeters or more of rain annually. Long after the fossil aquifers underpinning production in China, India, and the American Midwest have been depleted, Brazil will continue to be bathed in an average of 1,919 cubic miles of renewable freshwater annually. If, as projected, the world's population reaches 9 billion by 2050, the main hope of avoiding a Malthusian crisis will lie with the farmers of Brazil.

Paul Collier, Professor of Economics at Oxford and author of *The Bottom Billion: Why the Poorest Countries are Failing and What Can Be Done about It*, points out that "after many years of stability, world food prices have jumped 83 percent since 2005—prompting warnings of a food crisis throughout much of the world."[19] Collier scolds the governments of OECD countries on several scores,

> . . . encouraging beggar-thy-neighbor restrictions, pressure for yet larger farm subsidies, and they retreat into romanticism . . . the subsidy hunters have, unsurprisingly, turned the crisis into an opportunity; for example, Michael Barnier, the French agricultural Minister, took it as a chance to urge the European commission to reverse its incipient subsidy-slashing reforms of the common agricultural policy. And finally, the Romantics have portrayed the food crisis as demonstrating the failure of scientific commercial agriculture which they have long found distasteful. In its place they advocate the return to organic small-scale farming—counting on abandoned technologies to feed a prospective world population of nine billion.[20]

---

[18] Sandra Postel, *Pillar of Sand: Can the Irrigation Miracle Last?* (New York: W.W. Norton & Company, 1999), 6.

[19] Paul Collier, "The Politics of Hunger: How Illusion and Greed Fan the Food Crisis," *Foreign Affairs* (November/December, 2008).

[20] Ibid.

Collier continues by stating that "the world needs more commercial agriculture, not less" and arguing that Brazil's model could be translated in areas where land is underused.[21]

Of course, the credit for the surging productivity of Brazilian agriculture upon which the hopes of a hungry world depend does not go equally to the proprietors of all of Brazil's 5 million farms. Roughly 2.5 million of these earn less than R10,000 a year and account for just 7 percent of total Brazilian farm output. In other words, these are still the unproductive tropical farmers who by and large have not incorporated the technical innovations from Embrapa. Almost all the gains in Brazil's agricultural productivity are attributable to 1.6 million large commercial operators toward whom Embrapa's research and technical innovations are directed and who account for more than 75 percent of Brazil's farm output.

On a per crop basis, the productivity premium of what the FAO describes as Brazil's "good farmers" over the old-fashioned, tropical subsistence farmers is vast. For example, in 2004 the average yield for maize in Brazil was 3 tons per hectare. For the large commercial farmers, the yield was 10 tons per hectare. For beans, the average yield was 0.7 tons per hectare. Yields for good commercial farmers were five times higher (3.5 tons per hectare). Average wheat yields were 1.6 tons per hectare, while large commercial producers got 6 tons per hectare. The problem of low productivity among small producers who pulled down average yields for the whole country was not due to a lack of relevant agricultural technologies, but by the failure or inability of small farmers to apply them.[22]

A History of Small and Large Farms

The division between Brazil's large, capital-intensive, export-oriented farms and the smaller operations of subsistence farmers has origins deep in Brazil's past.

---

[21] Collier, "The Politics of Hunger."

[22] Land and Plant Nutrition Management Service, Land and Water Development Division, "Fertilizer Consumption of Some Basic Food Crops and Export Crops in 2002," Chap. 10 in *Fertilizer Use by Crop in Brazil* (Rome: Food and Agricultural Organization of the United Nations, 2004), 30–39, ftp://ftp.fao.org/agl/agll/docs/fertusebrazil.pdf.

Through the first four centuries of Brazilian history, the country's prosperity was based largely on tropical agricultural. For many years, Brazil's main export was cane sugar, produced on large plantations located within 15 miles of the coasts or along navigable rivers. Sugar plantations, harnessing slave labor, enjoyed considerable economies of scale. Larger plantations tended to be more profitable. And the economic logic underpinning sugar farming on a large scale was reinforced by the political culture of Portuguese colonialism.

Between 1534 and 1536, Portuguese King John III created a system of hereditary captaincies dividing the "official" Portuguese territory east of the Treaty of Tordesillas line along lines of latitude. Although Brazil would eventually expand far to the west of the Tordesillas line (drawn to divide Portuguese from Spanish territory by the corrupt, Spanish-born Pope Alexander VI), the initial hereditary captaincies were cautiously defined according to the Tordesillas treaty's terms.

The donataries were rich men, chosen not only because they had capital, but also because they were expected to sail thousands of miles and negotiate under challenging conditions with Indians from completely alien cultures. The hope was that the captaincies would succeed in developing Brazil at their own expense, thus saving the crown from undertaking the development outlays. Only 2 of the 15 captaincies proved profitable, based upon production and export of sugar. The more successful of these was Pernambuco, where Duarte Coelho prospered from the success of his sugarcane mills. However, other than São Vicente, the other 13 captaincies proved to be busts. The donataries either had no success dealing with the Indians or had not bothered to make the necessary investments to develop these huge tracts of land that spanned degrees of latitude and exceeded the size of European countries.

In response to the failure of the captaincies, the Portuguese crown undertook to sponsor the colonization of Brazil on its own. While the donations of crown land were downsized, they were informed by a similar perspective. The Portuguese crown wanted to accelerate the settlement and development of Brazil as rapidly as possible with the least investment on its part. At the time, Brazil was competing for capital and attention with the eastern Asian and African colonies of the Portuguese empire. With Portuguese capital stretched thin, and the powers that be nervous that French, British, Dutch, and other ships were visiting the Brazilian coast, the decision was reached to give large tracts of Brazilian land to grandees who were considered wealthy enough to develop them rapidly. This entailed the donation of crown land (*sesmarias*) in large blocks to wealthy Portuguese as well as to military personnel.

In theory, any settler could apply for these land grants, but he had to demonstrate that he had capital and access to slaves to operate the plantations.

Brazil was thus divided into gigantic tracts, called *latifundia* in the Roman style, which, although smaller than the captaincies, tended to be far larger than even the most prosperous estates of English colonists in North America. Unlike production of grain and hay that predominated in England's North Atlantic colonies, where a higher production scale provided no appreciable advantages, monocropping of sugarcane over extensive areas of land did tend to reduce production costs.[23] Large plantations also tended to be more profitable because they could better match their output to the capacity of sugarcane mills. A small sugarcane farm could not amortize the cost of building a mill. And needless to say, given the transportation conditions in sixteenth- and seventeenth-century Brazil, it was prohibitively expensive to move unprocessed sugarcane very far from the spot where it was harvested.

As suggested earlier, the large-scale economies of sugarcane farming underpinned a highly unequal land tenure system that tended to be self-reinforcing. To quote from the FAO's summary history of the development of agriculture in Brazil, "in this way, the territory of Brazil was divided into immense properties, with very little land remaining without an owner in the areas where the Europeans lived, mainly along the coast."[24] The limited scope for small farmers led to accommodation of the small population of free whites, ex-slaves, and

---

[23] Land and Plant Nutrition Management Service, Land and Water Development Division, *Fertilizer Use by Crop in Brazil* (Rome: Food and Agricultural Organization of the United Nations, 2004), 11.
[24] Ibid.

mestizos as sharecroppers occupying small strips of land on large estates for subsistence production and food for the local market. And perhaps more significantly, small farmers pioneered the Brazilian tradition of squatting on unoccupied land along the sparsely populated frontier. The very high transportation costs due to Brazil's challenging topography discussed earlier kept the frontier close to the coast for a long time. In fact, by the beginning of the eighteenth century, 200 years after Brazil's discovery, the country had a total population of only 300,000.

Obviously, with the monocropping of sugarcane predominating on the large plantations, someone had to produce the food required for consumption by the landlord class, the slaves, priests, the military, and the other government functionaries. But the Portuguese legal system as imposed in Brazil did not provide a framework of property rights to protect small holdings. With rare exceptions, up to 1822, when Brazil became independent, the increase in the number of small properties in Brazil was due to squatting and illegal ownership, as property could not be acquired except by donation personally from the Portuguese monarch.

This history is important because it informed a very different trajectory for Brazilian landholdings in the middle of the nineteenth century than that in the United States. In the United States, the Homestead Act of 1862 made land grants to small farmers who promised to cultivate the land. This encouraged an influx of migrants from Europe seeking the opportunity to own land, which was typically planted in grain. In Brazil, by contrast, farming in the plantation system produced high-value crops for export, which generally offered few prospects for participation by smallholders.

The *sesmarias* system of allocating property through royal land grants was abolished when Brazil became independent in 1822. But strangely, no new process for allocating legal title to property was put in place for the next 28 years. In effect, there was no regularized process for allocating land titles for almost three decades in Brazil. The only method to acquire new land was by squatting—taking physical possession. This enabled some small holders to stake tentative claims on the sparsely populated frontier. But the main beneficiaries of the 30-year anarchy in Brazil's land title system were the owners of the latifundia, the great estates. As economic historians Lee Alston, Gary Libecap, and Bernardo Mueller observed, the owners of the large estates "had the capital and other resources to occupy and defend additional land claims."[25]

By the mid-nineteenth century, the relative importance of sugar had declined in Brazil. It then comprised just 26.7 percent of Brazil's exports, while coffee had surged to more than 41 percent, (on the way to becoming approximately 70 percent of exports). After three decades in which Brazil really had no legal process for establishing property rights in its vast reserves of unused land the dramatic growth in world demand for coffee precipitated a crisis. The proximate problem was that small producers could compete in coffee production, which did not require high fixed capital investments. Therefore, it suddenly became a matter of urgent importance for the large holders to call a halt to the acquisition of unused land (of which Brazil had plenty) by squatting. The potential competition from small holders threatened to undermine profitability.

The fact that the international slave trade had been suspended and slavery was in its twilight created an additional problem that the owners of the large plantations sought to resolve. They wanted to attract free labor by increased immigration from Europe, and at the same time, make sure that the new immigrant laborers would hang around to work on the plantations rather than settling on the abundant, unused land and farm it for themselves.

Hence, the Land Law of 1850. The law legalized informal squatter claims prior to 1850, while conditioning formalization upon payment of a substantial tax. It also revalidated the *sesmarias'* land titles. At the same time, the law forbade further acquisitions by squatting. It stipulated that thereafter, unused land in Brazil could only be acquired by purchase. Thomas E. Skidmore rightly observed, "the chief purpose of the law was to promote the large plantation system."[26]

---

[25] Lee J. Alston, Gary D. Libecap, and Bernardo Mueller, *Titles, Conflict, and Land Use: The Development of Property Rights and Land Reform on the Brazilian Amazon Frontier* (Ann Arbor: University of Michigan Press, 1999), 34.

[26] Thomas E. Skidmore, *Brazil: Five Centuries of Change*, 2nd ed. (New York: Oxford University Press, 2010), 59.

A Stunning Increase

Brazil's very different approach to land tenure was at least partially dictated by its tropical climate and the relatively high-scale economies involved in the production of sugar during the early centuries of settlement. The fact that for the first 322 years of Brazil's history land titles could only be acquired under the *sesmarias* system in a personal grant from the king of Portugal significantly limited the emergence of a middle class in Brazil. This was particularly true because farming was the principal means to acquire wealth in the centuries when Brazil's main exports were tropical commodities.

As *The Economist* put it,

> The increase in Brazil's farm production has been stunning. Between 1996 and 2006 the total value of the country's crops rose from 23 billion reias ($23 billion) to 108 billion reias, or 365 percent. Brazil increased its beef exports tenfold in a decade, overtaking Australia as the world's largest exporter. It has the world's largest cattle herd after India's. It is also the world's largest exporter of poultry, sugar cane and ethanol. . . . Since 1990 its soyabean output has risen from barely 15m tonnes to over 60m. Brazil accounts for about a third of the world soyabean exports, second only to America. In 1994 Brazil's soyabean exports were one-seventh of America's; now they are six-sevenths. Moreover, Brazil supplies a quarter of the world soyabean trade on just 6 percent of the country's arable land.[27]

In the next chapter, we explore an emerging advantage closely associated with the Brazilian economy: its role as an energy superpower in the era of peak oil. While the advanced temperate zone economies are hard-pressed to prosper as the price of BTUs soars, Brazil is leveraging its unmatched agricultural capabilities to become a leader in biofuels, as well as a nation rich in oil.

---

[27] "The Miracle of the Cerrado."

Chapter 10

Reversing the Gap

Brazil as the World's Emerging Energy Superpower

We know the country that harnesses the power of clean, renewable energy will lead the twenty-first century.

—U.S. president Barack Obama

We still do not know exactly how much oil is in the presalt layers. . . . We have strong evidence that God is Brazilian.

—Brazilian president Dilma Rousseff

The translation in this chapter's epigraph does not do Dilma's comments justice. A better rendition might read, "While we still do not know exactly how much oil is in the presalt layers, preliminary indications are that the oil is so plentiful that it proves Lula's assertion that 'God is a Brazilian.'"

According to Representative Doc Hastings, chairman of the Natural Resources Committee of the U.S. House of Representatives, Brazil's

221

offshore oil reserves "contain a combined 58 billion barrels of oil,"[1] a providential amount, considering that proven oil reserves in the United States were 21 billion barrels (3.3×10^9 m^3) in 2006 according to the Energy Information Administration.

This represents a major turnabout in the fortunes of Brazil, if not in theology. In his intelligent and nuanced analysis from the turn of the millennium, "Tropical Underdevelopment," Jeffrey D. Sachs argues that the income premium enjoyed in temperate zone economies during the nineteenth and twentieth centuries was at least partially attributable to their greater ability to mobilize energy resources. Sachs points out, "with regard to hydrocarbons (oil and gas), global production in 1995 . . . the per capita hydrocarbon production in the tropical countries was only 28 percent of the per capita hydrocarbon production in the non-tropical countries."[2] In other words, the lagging economic development of tropical countries, of which Brazil is now the emerging counterexample, seemed to have closely paralleled their deficit in the production of BTUs.

The Zero Sum Growth Game

Only a decade into the twenty-first century, however, there is growing evidence that Brazil is no longer an energy-poor, tropical country, but rather a new energy superpower whose future growth will be much less constrained by high oil prices than will the leading temperate zone economies.

Whereas politicians in the United States have been jabbering about the importance of energy independence since the 1970s, actual progress in that direction has been negligible, with oil imports rising from about 30 percent of consumption to as much as about 70 percent. Partly, the paltry U.S. progress toward energy independence reflects a conflict between energy and monetary policy. Given that oil is priced in dollars,

---

[1] Representative Doc Hastings, "U.S. Needs Brazilian Approach to Energy Policy," The Hill, January 24, 2012, http://thehill.com/blogs/congress-blog/energy-a-environment/206067-rep-doc-hastings-r-wash.

[2] Jeffrey D. Sachs, "Tropical Underdevelopment," NBER Working Paper No. 8119, 22.

a currency the United States can manufacture at little or no cost, the massive purchases of imported oil have helped maintain the bid for dollars, thus enabling Americans to live at a higher standard than they earn on the back of the world's reserve currency.

Brazil, on the other hand, has no reserve currency conflicts and has made dramatic progress in achieving energy independence. In 1974, Brazil imported almost 80 percent of its oil. Today, Brazil's net percentage of oil imports is less than zero. Brazil became an oil exporter in 2009.

Earlier in this book, I offered reasons to suppose that you are now living through the endgame of the rapid growth phase of economic history based upon cheap oil. This is a problem with both a demand and a supply dimension. Demand for oil grew sharply while supply growth stagnated. The emergence of the BRIC economies, along with other emerging market fellow-travelers dramatically increased oil demand.

Real world GDP rose by 5 percent annually in 2006 and 2007. This led to surging oil consumption. China alone increased oil consumption by 840,000 barrels a day between 2005 and 2007. Over a longer term, China increased oil consumption at a 6.3 percent compound annual rate in the decade after 1998 [3] If China's growth in oil demand continues over the next two decades it would imply oil consumption in that country of double the current U.S. levels by 2033.[4]

As oil production has plateaued, the only way to accommodate a sharp increase in the consumption of some countries is by a reduction in the consumption of others. That implies sharply higher prices. In the words of economic historian James D. Hamilton, "with no more oil being produced, that meant other countries had to decrease their consumption despite strongly growing incomes. The short run price elasticity of oil demand has never been very high . . . meaning that a very large price increase was necessary to contain demand."[5]

The advent of peak oil implies still more abrupt price rises in the decades to come. The incumbent Organisation for Economic

---

[3] James D. Hamilton, "Historical Oil Shocks," prepared for the *Handbook of Major Events in Economic History*, revised, February 1, 2011, 19.

[4] Ibid., 19.

[5] Ibid., 22.

Co-operation and Development (OECD) economies, which led the world for years based upon growth fueled by cheap oil, face crises as the world experiences a major energy transition. Here is the crux of the issue from the World Economic Outlook (WEO) 2010 Executive Summary, "All of the net growth [in oil demand] comes from non–OECD countries, almost half from China alone . . . demand in the OECD falls by over 6 mb/d [million barrels per day]."[6]

As unlikely as it may seem on first glance, this take from the WEO is implicitly optimistic. Why? Because the WEO's projection of oil production in 2035 puts oil output at 99 million barrels per day. While that is considerably lower than WEO projections from 2007, it represents a 12 percent increase in output from production levels in 2011. In other words, the WEO report suggests that oil output will rise rather than fall. But if oil output peaked in 2005, as it appears, output will not grow from here. Indeed, it is already apparent that oil discovery peaked way back in 1965, although some analysts argue that step-out discoveries associated with existing production should be counted as new finds.

However you slice it, it is beyond question that the easy production from existing oil fields does come to an end. This was evident in the history of oil production in Pennsylvania associated with Drake's original oil well in Titusville. His success there attracted other operators to develop large wells in other parts of the Appalachian field in Pennsylvania. By 1890, oil production from Pennsylvania and nearby New York was five times what it had been in 1870.[7] Yet, after oil prices fell to $0.56 a barrel during the recession of 1890–1891, annual oil production from the Appalachian field peaked, falling by 14 million barrels by 1894. Production there never recovered. As economic historian James Hamilton put it, "indeed even with the more technologically advanced secondary recovery techniques adopted in much later decades, [it] never again reached the levels seen in 1891."[8]

---

[6] Cameron Leckie, "Economic Growth: A Zero Sum Game," *Energy Bulletin*, November 25, 2010, www.energybulletin.net/stories/2010-11-25/economic -growth-zero-sum-game.
[7] Hamilton, "Historical Oil Shocks," 4.
[8] Ibid.

It is pertinent that production records from Texas and the North Sea show quite similar patterns of falling output after peaks—in 1972 in Texas, and 1999 in the North Sea. Texas production fell at a rate of 3.5 percent a year from 1972 to 1982 resulting in 1982 production being 31 percent below the 1972 level. North Sea production fell at a rate of 4.5 percent per year from 1999 through 2009. Production in 2009 was 38 percent below the level in 1999.[9]

It is likely that other major conventional oil fields initially tapped 40 or more years ago will follow similar trajectories. With each year that passes, production potential from those older fields declines. Production from many smaller new fields is required to offset the annual depletion of the giant conventional oil discoveries that have been exploited for decades.

In spite of oil prices at $100 per barrel, and much improved technology, the huge finds of earlier decades are proving difficult to duplicate. So it is likely that you face a zero sum game in which the uptick in net demand for oil from non-OECD countries is met not by new net production but by displacement of demand from within the OECD. Here "displacement of demand" should be understood as "demand destruction" where rising prices make previous uses of energy financially infeasible in crumbling OECD economies. U.S. oil consumption, which surged above 21 million barrels per day in 2006, has plunged to 18.8 million barrels per day

In short, we've reached the zero sum stage of peak oil. This is bad news for the established users who are demanding oil for legacy systems designed when oil was cheap. They will probably be unable to grow if they cannot afford to out bid the emerging users who can pay higher prices at the margin for high-value applications of oil. As a general matter, it is obvious that the emerging economies will be better able to afford the higher prices and therefore will bid away the oil that the OECD economies need in order to grow.

---

[9] Jeffrey J. Brown, Samuel Foucher, and Jorge Silveus, "Peak Oil Versus Peak Net Exports—Which Should We be More Concerned About?" Association for the Study of Peak Oil and Gas—USA, October 7, 2010.

Grim Prospects

Analyst Jeffrey J. Brown, one of the originators of the Export Land Model, argues that the prospects for oil-importing economies are even more grim than the statistics suggest at first glance.

He argues that the net export decline rate tends to exceed the production decline rate and that the net export decline rate tends to accelerate with time.[10] From a close analysis of the relationship between growing domestic consumption, production depletion, and export records in 16 oil exporting countries, Brown and his colleagues suggest that an ominous future awaits oil-importing countries (meaning most of the OECD economies, including the United States):

> If we extrapolate the 2005 to 2009 rate of increase in consumption by the exporting countries out to 2015 and if we extrapolate Chindia's (China plus India) 2005 to 2009 rate of increase in net imports up to 2015, and if we assume a very slight production decline among the exporting countries (0.5 percent/year from 2005 to 2015), then for every three barrels of oil that non-Chindia countries (net) imported in 2005, they would have to make do with two barrels in 2015.[11]

This scenario has grim implications for economic growth in the United States and the other leading OECD economies. The underpinning of this concern is strong enough that the U.S. military issued its own warning of an impending oil production shortfall in 2010. " 'By 2012, surplus oil production capacity could entirely disappear, and as early as 2015, the short fall in output could reach nearly 10,000,000 barrels per day,' says the report, which has a foreword by a senior commander, General James N. Mattis."[12]

The U.S. military projection is actually five times more bleak than Brown's export extrapolations. World oil production stood at 86 million barrels per day at the time of the U.S. military's crisis alert,

---

[10] Brown, Foucher, and Silveus, "Peak Oil Versus Peak Net Exports."

[11] Ibid.

[12] Terry McAlester, "U.S. Military Warns Oil Output May Dip Causing Massive Shortages by 2015," *Guardian*, April 11, 2010.

and they were forecasting production to fall by 10 million barrels a day by 2015, or an annual production decline of 2.5 percent, five times the 0.5 percent decline projected by Brown. If Brown's adjustments are overlaid on the U.S. military's more pessimistic forecast of falling oil production, the OECD economies would face a potentially catastrophic crisis from a collapse in energy inputs (and an accompanying spike in the price of those supplies that remain available).

But this raises the question of whether economies must decline when energy inputs fall. Unhappily, the answer seems to be yes.

As energy analyst Cameron Leckie points out, the International Energy Agency, the Paris-based intergovernmental energy group associated with the OECD, has conjured up a scenario under which a 6 million barrels per day decline in OECD oil demand will not result in a corresponding drop in OECD GDP. The IEA is simply projecting that "the oil intensity of the OECD economies will improve significantly over coming decades."[13]

Oil intensity is a measure of total oil equivalent per thousand dollars of GDP at market exchange rates. The projection that the advanced economies will suddenly become much more efficient at employing energy to achieve economic growth begs a lot of questions. Yes, it is always possible to improve efficiency. But most of the easy and obvious steps in that direction were undertaken years ago in response to the first or second oil shocks. A close read of recent energy intensity measures shows that the advanced economies "have high energy consumption per capita, between 100 and 350 GJ, and high GDP per capita, between $10,000 and $43,000 (consisting of Western European countries and North American countries, Australia, and New Zealand)."[14]

A hint of the difficulty entailed in rapidly improving legacy inefficiencies in energy use comes from the countries of the former Soviet Union. Notwithstanding high oil prices that exceeded $146 a barrel in 2008, the former Soviet republics continued to have very high energy consumption per capita and very high energy consumption per GDP when

---

[13] Leckie, "Economic Growth: A Zero Sum Game."

[14] T.V. Ramachandra, Yves Loerincik, and B.V. Shruthi, "Intra and Inter Country Energy Intensity Trends," *Journal of Energy and Development* 31. no. 1 (2006): 43–84.

compared with other Eurasian countries.[15] They had significant incentives to improve efficiency, but it was just not that easy to accomplish.

The past record does not encourage optimism that any economy can readily prosper when oil intensity declines.

Pulling the Plug

Declining oil intensity in the United States over the past four decades has coincided with the export of energy-intensive manufacturing jobs and the stagnation of real income for the middle class. The dot-com and housing bubbles reduced energy intensity in the United States, as did all forms of financialization that have increased the percentage of GDP pocketed by bankers whose activities are generally much less energy-intense than farming, construction, or manufacturing. By 2005, on the eve of the Great Correction, the finance industry accounted for one in every four dollars of profits earned by U.S. companies.

Even accounting for the higher percentage of the U.S. economy absorbed by the financial sector, the U.S. employs much more energy relative to GDP than Brazil. According to 2011 figures from the IMF, U.S. GDP was $48,187 per person while that in Brazil was only about $11,845, roughly one-quarter of the U.S. level. But energy consumption (in millions of barrels of oil equivalent) was 17,260 in the United States and only 1,750 in Brazil, a ratio of 9.86:1. Overall, the United States uses more than twice as much energy relative to per capita GDP than Brazil. While some improvements in energy efficiency are conceivable, they are not likely.

As Cameron Leckie puts it,

> the difficulty of this challenge should not be underestimated particularly given current circumstances. Many OECD nations have aging populations, are heavily in debt, virtually all are dependent on oil imports with some notable exceptions (Norway and Mexico) and have in many instances outsourced much of their manufacturing industries to developing nations.

---

[15] Ramachandra, Loerincik, and Shruthi, "Intra and Inter Country Energy Intensity Trends."

Reducing the oil intensity of an economy will require significant capital investment, something that in the weakened economic state of many OECD nations is unlikely. . . . Reducing
oil intensity is also subject to diminishing returns, each increment of improvement in oil intensity will become increasingly
expensive and difficult to achieve. In this context, significantly
reducing the oil intensity of the economy would be a monu-
mental achievement.[16]

The challenge of reducing energy intensity without undermining
the basis of prosperity is even more daunting than Leckie's lucid summary suggests. This is because the economy is a complex system with
emergent properties. Economist James Rickards explains:

Complex systems design themselves through evolution or the
interaction of myriad autonomous parts. The second principle is
that complex systems have emergent properties, which is a
technical way of saying the whole is greater than the sum of its
parts—the entire system will behave in ways that cannot be
inferred from looking at the pieces. The third principle is that
complex systems run on exponentially greater amounts of
energy. This energy can take many forms, but the point is that
when you increase the system scale by a factor of ten, you
increase the energy requirements by a factor of a thousand, and
so on. The fourth principle is that complex systems are prone to
catastrophic collapse. The third and fourth principles are related.
When the system reaches a certain scale, the energy inputs dry
up because the exponential relationship between scale and
inputs exhausts the available resources. In a nutshell, complex
systems arise spontaneously, behave unpredictably, exhaust
resources and collapse catastrophically.[17]

Short of catastrophic collapse, you should be prepared for an
increase in more familiar symptoms of economic distress. As we touched

---

[16] Leckie, "Economic Growth: A Zero Sum Game."
[17] James Rickards, *Currency Wars: The Making of the Next Global Crisis* (Penguin
Group, Kindle Edition: Kindle Locations 3095–3104).

upon in the start to our peak oil discussion in Chapter 4, the United States has created a huge hostage to fortune by becoming the most deeply indebted nation in history. You cannot indenture yourself to others and expect your creditors to always act with your convenience in mind. With yours and my financial well-being closely tied to the prosperity of the United States, we may be prejudiced to suppose that what is good for the United States is good for the world economy.

With that in mind, it is perhaps too tempting to suppose that the Chinese would not be willing to foreclose on their wayward debtor, even at the risk of precipitating another down leg in the current depression. After all, U.S. consumers are China's best customers. Usually, you can count on trading partners not to bankrupt their customers.

But this is an argument reminiscent of claims before World War I that there could be no war because all the countries had a strong incentive to preserve the world's open trading system and the prosperity that went with it. Remember that China's leaders are Malthusian engineers. They are focused on long-term planning to secure access to the resources they need to grow their own economy. Their one child policy clearly shows they are inclined to take drastic action in an effort to minimize what they may see as the potentially destabilizing impact from population pressures on resources that cannot be expanded at the same geometric rate as unchecked population.

With peak oil a focus of growing concern, I suspect it is only a matter of time before the Chinese use their financial clout to take away some more of the roughly 18.8 million barrels per day of precious petroleum that the United States currently consumes. Contrary to the breezy assertions of alternative energy shills the energy density of oil is crucial to the economy of abundance, particularly when there are imbedded commitments to mobility. Without sufficient access to oil, economies like that of the United States would grind to a halt.

Depending upon how seriously China's ruling engineers view peak oil as a barrier to their internal growth and the degree of their concern about the threat to dynastic stability posed by rising food prices, they will move sooner rather than later to pull the plug on the U.S. economy. Deflating U.S. demand will reduce their sales, but also reduce their costs and enable them to reset oil and other commodity prices at lower levels.

Short of the rediscovery of Aladdin's lamp, it is highly unlikely that the OECD countries will be able to grow in an environment where their oil inputs seem destined to fall by 6 million barrels or more per day for a protracted period.

You need only recall Jeffrey Sachs's analysis mentioned at the start of this chapter from a little over a decade ago that correlated the underperformance of tropical economies with relatively smaller energy inputs. What was true in the nineteenth and twentieth centuries for tropical economies is likely to be no less true of the temperate economies in the twenty-first century era of peak oil. And how ironic, then, that Brazil, the world's largest tropical country, looms large as the new energy superpower of the twenty-first century.

Submerging Economies

Steeply higher energy prices will prove ruinous to the United States and other heavily indebted advanced economies. The Great Correction is only the brightest visible star in a constellation of economic crises associated with the repricing of hydrocarbon energy that implies the end of growth in the OECD countries.

Oil analyst and energy sector investor Gregor Macdonald (http://gregor.us) explains why higher oil prices hurt advanced economies, soon to be known as submerging economies, more than emerging ones:

> High oil prices are more painful to the OECD/developed world user than the developing world user. In the developing world coal accounts for the largest chunk of BTU consumption, and the marginal utility to the new user of oil is high. In other words, the OECD user is embedded in a system where the historical consumption pattern has been to use much more oil per capita. But in the developing world, just a small amount of oil to the new user of oil is transformational. It will be the developing world therefore that will take oil to much, much higher prices in the next decade. They will use small amounts per capita, but the aggregate demand will be scary high. After all, the developing world's systems are not leveraged to oil.

They are new users of oil—and unlike us aren't married to a system that breaks from high oil prices.[18]

The crucial passage here is "after all, the developing world's systems are not leveraged to oil. They are new users of oil—and unlike us, aren't married to a system that breaks from high oil prices." Here "breaks" is used in the same sense as in "bankruptcy." The word "bankruptcy" comes from the term *broken bench* or *banca rotta*, a use that originated in medieval Italy, where the practice of the day was to physically break the bench of an insolvent trader as a visible sign that he could no longer meet his obligations.

Think of California, a state designed around a highway system installed on the premise of $0.30 gasoline that prevailed in the 1950s. California's suburbs, like those in the rest of the United States, sprawl over the landscape, necessitating long, bumper-to-bumper commutes in every direction. Not incidentally, California consumes three times more energy than it produces. When the Chinese and Indians bid the price of oil into the stratosphere, they're bankrupting Los Angeles and San Diego, not Shanghai or Mumbai—where housing patterns do not incorporate the assumption of cheap gasoline. Much more could be said about the dependence of the United States on cheap oil. The horizontal rather than vertical development of U.S. metropolitan areas is only one dimension of the story. Another is the fact that the average American family has three automobiles, many of which are SUVs that guzzle fuel. China has now replaced the United States as the world's largest market for new cars. The cars the Chinese buy are tiny by U.S. standards. Much the same can be said for India's car market.

The adjustment to higher oil prices in China and India involves a choice of what to buy and how to build. The adjustment in the United States is destined to be much more wrenching. Scary-high oil prices imply the devaluation of the North American suburbs, a development that would obliterate much of what remains of the real estate equity of the suburban middle class, depreciating the largest investment of most Americans while simultaneously deepening insolvency of the banking system. The problem is not a cyclical decline in real estate values but a

---

[18] Gregor Macdonald wrote this excerpt in a comment posted on *The Oil Drum*.

secular decline in earnings capacity of Americans, combined with peculiarly punishing consequences of skyrocketing oil prices on the infrastructure of middle-class America.

You are waiting in line to witness and participate in a stress-induced transition to the next stage of economic history. It could be a parallel to the initial stages of the Industrial Revolution, precipitated by peak wood, with the difference that it spells collapse for the complex systems of the advanced economies that are overextended on the basis of cheap oil.

Meanwhile, the venue for any deepening of prosperity is likely to be not the OECD countries, but emerging economies, such as China, India, and particularly the country of the future, Brazil.

Rio Is the New Houston

Phase transitions to new energy sources have traditionally had far-reaching and disruptive consequences. The chill that settled in with the Maunder Minimum we explored in Chapter 4 was exactly that, although in some respects it later proved to be a blessing in disguise. If you remember, colder weather provided a stress-induced trigger to the greatest surge of prosperity in human history. It began with a doubling in the price of wood, from 6 grams of silver per million BTU to 12 grams of silver per BTU.[19] Peak wood, precipitated by colder weather that reduced the growth of European forests, led to higher prices that, in turn, helped stimulate a switch to a higher-density energy source—coal. Richard Wilkinson pointed this out in his argument that the initial stages of the Industrial Revolution were stress-induced.[20]

Unlike other instances of shifts to a colder climate, the Little Ice Age in Europe did not precipitate the collapse of complex societies and a descent into a dark age. As discussed in Chapter 4, instead of collapsing, Europe expanded and acquired energy subsidies through colonies, and

---

[19] Gregor Macdonald, "Stagnation and Descent," excerpted at http://gregor.us/annual/gregor-us-monthly-2010-annual.

[20] Richard G. Wilkinson, *Poverty and Progress: An Ecological Model of Economic Development* (London: Methuen, 1973).

also started using energy-dense coal to power the Industrial Revolution. The surge in energy led to unprecedented growth in the mid-eighteenth century; growth that parallels the later growth from peak coal before World War I to peak oil in the nineteenth century. However, realizing there may not be a higher density energy to exploit in the coming years, the collapse of the advanced economies like the United States is imminent. By contrast, the fortunes of Brazil will not be as deeply dented by peak oil as will be economies that import large percentages of the oil they use—at least for now and depending on Brazil's overall, future energy strategy. In 2012, Brazil was the world's eleventh oil producer, and it is poised to become one of the top five oil-producing countries by 2020, as oil prices soar.

At the beginning of this chapter, I quoted the chairman of the Natural Resources Committee of the U.S. House of Representatives, Representative Doc Hastings, as claiming that Brazil's offshore oilfields contain "a combined 58 billion barrels of oil." A report by Bloomberg filed January 19, 2011, suggests that Representative Hastings was being conservative. He may have underestimated Brazil's presalt oil reserves by half. Bloomberg reported that, "Brazilian oil deposits below a layer of salt in the Atlantic Ocean hold at least 123 billion barrels of reserves, more than double government estimates."[21]

The Bloomberg report was based on a university study that set out to show that the Brazilian government's reserve estimates were too optimistic, but reached the opposite conclusion, putting a 90 percent probability on the 123 billion barrel reserve estimate. That is a high level of confidence. Whether or not it proves true, Petroleo Brasileiro SA, or Petrobras (NYSE: PBR) has already done more than any other oil company to discredit peak oil. Whether the new offshore reserves amount to 123 billion barrels, 58 billion barrels, or only 33 billion barrels of oil, as optimists in Brazil's Energy Ministry hinted for several years, the find would still be the largest oil find in three decades and one of the largest in history.

Note that those who resist the notion of peak oil point to the presalt discoveries to underpin their hope that world oil production will not

---

[21] Peter Millard, "Brazil Oil Fields May Hold More Than Twice Estimates," Bloomberg, January 19, 2011, www.bloomberg.com/news/2011-01-19/brazil -oil-fields-may-hold-more-than-twice-estimated-reserves.html.

decline. But Sergio Gabrielli, the CEO of Petrobras, has put the world's prospective oil deficit in perspective. In a presentation in December 2009, he showed world oil capacity, including biofuels, being unable to offset world oil decline rates. Gabrielli stated in his presentation that "*the world needs oil volumes the equivalent of one Saudi Arabia every two years to offset future world oil decline rates*" (emphasis added).

In a January 2009 interview with *BusinessWeek*, Gabrielli suggested that the company's internal projections were slightly more optimistic. He said,

> according to the company's projections, production from existing fields will fall from a little over 18 million barrels a day to maybe half of that even if new techniques are used to slow the rate of decline. So just keeping global production flat is going to require lots of new fields and *requires the world to replace one in Saudi Arabia per three years*[22] (emphasis added).

In fact, if the 123 billion barrel estimate proves correct, Brazil's new presalt fields would be larger than even Saudi Arabia's massive Ghawar Field, thought to have contained 100 billion barrels before production began in 1951. Since then, an estimated 65 billion barrels of oil have been produced at Ghawar. If Brazil's presalt production province proves to be even half as productive, it would guarantee Brazil's emergence as one of the world's preeminent energy powers. That is the role Brazil seems destined to fill, even with much more modest success in exploiting its deep offshore energy resources.

According to *Forbes*, the world oil and gas industry is converging on Brazil in a big way, with the intention of investing an estimated $1 trillion exploring and drilling for oil there. Petrobras alone is scheduled to invest $224.7 billion over five years drilling and producing oil from the presalt region deep off the coast of Rio de Janeiro.[23]

---

[22] Peter Coy, "Petrobras Makes a Big Bet," Bloomberg Businessweek, January 27, 2009, www.businessweek.com/bwdaily/dnflash/content/jan2009/db20090127 _390876.htm.

[23] Kenneth Rapozo, "Petrobras as Brazil's Moon Landing," *Forbes*, September 29, 2011.

Some investment analysts have suggested that if Petrobras succeeds in its production targets, it could become the first public company worth $1 trillion. Petrobras already accounts for 22 percent of the world's deep water oil production. Its presalt investment program is projected to push annual production to 3.9 million barrels of oil by 2014. And natural gas production is also expected to reach 130,000,000 cubic feet per day by the same year. Company projections call for production by 2014 to bring annual sales to almost $250 billion, with profits exceeding $30 billion. Similar growth is projected for the following four years. If reached, analyst Ryan Fuhrmann, projects that "Petrobras has a good chance at having a market cap of $1 trillion" within the decade.[24]

The Petrobras story is a component in the bright future of Brazil. Its $224 billion investment plan is just the first installment in over $1 trillion of investment in the next 10 years to develop vast offshore oil deposits.

"This could be the largest private-sector investment program in the history of mankind—more than actually putting a man on the moon," says Pedro Cordeiro, head of the oil and gas practice at Bain & Company consultancy in São Paulo.[25] On an inflation-adjusted basis, this is a greater sum than the Marshall Plan that rebuilt Europe after World War II.

As reported in *The Economist*, the early indications encourage optimism that Brazil will succeed in bringing in vast quantities of offshore oil and gas. Gabrielli proclaimed, "[I]n the presalt area, our exploration has a success rate of 87 percent compared with a world average of 20 percent to 25 percent for the industry."[26]

The vast oil deposits will compound the growing prosperity of Brazil. The expensive oil that will be extracted will make Petrobras one of the world's more important and profitable companies. Remember, before 1995, when the dot-com boom skewed historic investment statistics, the oil industry earned a higher rate of return on invested capital than any other industry. That was during a period when oil was generally cheap and its real price only briefly rose above $40 in today's

---

[24] Ryan Furhmann, "This Could Be the First $1 Trillion Stock," StreetAuthority, December 7, 2010, www.streetauthority.com/growth-investing/could-be-first-1 -trillion-stock-457883.

[25] Joe Leahy, "Platform for Growth," *Financial Times*, March 16, 2011, 9.

[26] "Brazil's Oil Boom: Filling Up the Future," *The Economist*, November 5, 2011.

terms. Petrobras will be earning returns at $200 to $300 per barrel. The profits should overshadow anything earned by oil companies in the past. Note that Petrobras is not the only Brazilian oil company expecting to bring in vast amounts of production from offshore fields. OGX Petroleo e Gas Participacoes, the oil group controlled by Brazil's richest billionaire, Eike Batista, forecasts that it will produce 1.4 million barrels a day by 2020, which would account for about one-quarter of Brazil's projected production.

Brazil became a net oil exporter in 2009, after investing lavishly in domestic oil and gas exploration for decades. In 2012, Brazil's oil production was running at about 3 million barrels per day. Credible plans call for output to expand to 5.5 million barrels per day by 2020. About 1.5 million barrels a day will initially be earmarked for export.

Brazil may be able to reduce rather than increase its internal oil consumption, even if it grows rapidly between now and 2020 because almost uniquely among the world's economies, Brazil has a growing portfolio of both economic and effective renewable energy.

The grave difficulty that the leading temperate zone economies have experienced in deploying rather than just talking about alternative energy sources testifies to the reversal of the tropical underdevelopment deficit that Jeffrey Sachs highlighted in 2000.

Notwithstanding a drastic 469 percent increase in the real price of BTUs, since 1945 (calculated in terms of the annual average inflation-adjusted price of oil), alternative energy continues to provide no more than a trivial contribution to meeting the world's need for power, especially in the advanced, temperate zone economies. For example, as of July 2011 solar power produced only 661,339 billion BTUs or 0.002 percent of total world production of 267,757,600 billion BTUs. Wind power produced 0.012 percent while geothermal accounted for just 0.0007 percent.

This implies that Malthusian resource panic lies ahead as countries scramble to reserve as much precious hydrocarbon fuels, especially petroleum, for themselves, as they can secure. As a rule of thumb, it would not be wrong to assume that, barring recession, the market supply for oil-importing countries will more or less recede from year to year.

The world consumes far more oil each year than is discovered, a trend that has persisted for decades. Therefore, a reasonable basis for forecasting the future prosperity of different economies is their relative capacity to sustain or even expand current energy use. For reasons I spell out next, Brazil has more capacity than most other economies to increase energy inputs per capita in a way that increases the return on energy invested.

Leading the Way in Renewable Energy

While renewables and alternative energy seem to be a lost cause in many economies, *Renewable Energy World* magazine raves, "With almost half of its energy supply generated by renewable sources, Brazil increasingly looks like a positive example for the rest of the world."[27]

Equally, the United States is ill-suited to effect a seamless transition to alternative sources of energy. For one thing, the United States lacks many of Brazil's natural advantages. Nowhere is that better epitomized than in the pathetic results of George W. Bush's cellulosic ethanol project. You may remember this grand declaration from his 2006 State of the Union address: "We'll fund additional research in cutting-edge methods of producing ethanol, not just from corn but from wood chips and stalks or switchgrass. Our goal is to make this new kind of ethanol practical and competitive within six years."

Subsequently, Congress passed an energy bill that provided a tax credit of $1.01 per gallon for this new cutting-edge fuel. Congress and Presidents Bush and Obama also showered loans, grants, and subsidies to producers, as well as guaranteeing them a market by mandating the purchase of 250,000,000 gallons in 2011. Unfortunately however, actual production in 2011 was a mere 6.6 million gallons. Faced with a 97 percent shortfall in supply, oil companies were forced to purchase waiver credits for failing to comply with the purchase mandate. In 2010 and 2011 oil companies in the United States paid some $10 million for failing to buy a product that doesn't exist. A report on biofuels by the National Academy of Sciences issued in October 2010 concluded that

---

[27] Robin Yapp, "Brazil Soars in Clean Energy Rankings," *Renewable Energy World*, September 28, 2011.

"currently, no commercially viable bio refineries exist for converting cellulose biomass to fuel."[28] In the words of the *Wall Street Journal*,

> Congress subsidized a product that didn't exist, mandated its purchase though it still didn't exist, is punishing oil companies for not buying a product that doesn't exist, and is now doubling down on the subsidies in the hope that someday it might exist. We'd call this the March of Folly, but that's unfair to fools.[29]

Meanwhile, Brazil produced 6.92 billion U.S. gallons of ethanol in 2010, production that directly substitutes for oil. Reuters reported, " 'Brazilian ethanol output, and biofuels as a whole, continue to constitute strong sources of non-OPEC supply growth that warrant increased analytical scrutiny,' the IEA said in its monthly oil market report. 'For 2010 and 2011, we see annual Brazilian ethanol production growing on average by 50,000 barrels per day, to 475,000 bpd and 520,000 bpd, respectively.' "[30]

Furthermore, Brazil's unsubsidized sugarcane ethanol has an energy balance about seven times greater than U.S. ethanol produced from corn. The energy balance is the difference between the energy required to produce and deploy an energy source and the amount of energy gained from using it. It is generally accepted that Brazil's sugarcane ethanol produces eight times more energy than is required to make it. The energy balance from U.S. corn-based ethanol seems to be about one unit of current energy equals 1.25 energy units of corn ethanol. But some critics of corn ethanol production in the United States, such as Tad Patzek, a geological engineer from the University of California, Berkeley, contend that ethanol and biofuels in general (as pursued in the United States) are "energy negative," meaning that they require more energy to produce than is contained in the final product.[31] Given the perhaps negative or at

---

[28] "The Cellulosic Ethanol Debacle," *Wall Street Journal*, December 13, 2011, A20.

[29] Ibid.

[30] Ikuko Korakone, "Brazil Ethanol Production Will Continue to Grow: IEA," Reuters, October 13, 2010, www.reuters.com/article/2010/10/13/us-iea-brazil-idUSTRE69C2VR20101013.

[31] David Pimentel and Tad W. Patzek, "Ethanol Production Using Corn, Switchgrass, and Wood: Biodiesel Production Using Soybean and Sunflower," *Natural Resources Research* 14, no. 1 (March 2005). Available at www.sehn.org/tccpdf/Energy-biofuel%20outputs%20&inputs.pdf.

best marginal energy balance earned from U.S. biofuels, Brazil could be a model for countries around the globe, especially in terms of its sugarcane ethanol program. Though critics say Brazilian ethanol is only sustainable because of its high quantity of arable land and advanced agricultural-industrial technology, it is still widely considered one of the most successful alternative fuels to date.

Meanwhile, Brazil also has a successful biodiesel program that principally employs palm oil along with castor bean, soy, cottonseed, and sunflower. Petrobras is operating five biodiesel plants with a total capacity to produce 721.4 million liters of biodiesel a year in Minas Gerais, Bahia, Caera, Parana, and Rio Grande do Sul states.

Much as the United States once enjoyed a comparative advantage in energy in the nineteenth and through the first three quarters of the twentieth century, Brazil now enjoys a comparative advantage in biofuels.

This advantage also extends to other renewable energies. As discussed in Chapter 3, Brazil is one of the world's largest generators of hydroelectric power. Some 82 percent of Brazil's electricity is produced through clean renewable sources, compared to 11 percent in the United States. Brazilian energy demand is growing 10 times faster than that of the United States, principally because it has the scope to grow.

In 2008, there were 706 hydroelectric power plants in operation in Brazil. They provided approximately 85 percent of Brazil's electricity in that year. Brazil has become an exporter of expertise in dam building and construction of hydroelectric power plants. Currently, electricity consumption per capita in Brazil stands at just 560 kWh. This is far lower than electricity demand in the leading temperate economies. The comparable figure for the UK is 1,900 kWh, and in the United States it is more than 4,500 kWh.

With Brazil's population rising and its consumer spending boom set to increase the number of televisions, washing machines, refrigerators, and air-conditioners in use, Brazil's Energy Research Company (EPE), projects that the installed potential of the national grid will jump from 110 GW in 2010 to 171 GW by the end of 2020. Large-scale hydro-power is projected to rise from an installed capacity of 85 GW currently to more than 115 GW by 2012. Much of the increase will be attrib-utable to the new Belo Monte Dam under construction on the Xingu River in the state of Pará. After it reaches full capacity by January 2019, the Belo Monte Dam alone will be capable of supplying electric power to 18 million homes housing 60 million people. It will be the world's third-largest hydropower installation.[32] Brazil's estimated hydro potential is 261 GW, or the renewable equivalent of 3.57 million barrels of oil per day.

Brazil is also a world leader in bioelectricity. One hundred percent of Brazil's sugar and ethanol refineries are self-sufficient in electricity. Many of these facilities also produce surplus power that they sell to the nearest electricity grid. In fact, sales of electricity to the grid account for 35 percent of the profit earned by Brazilian ethanol producers. Bioelectricity generated from burning sugarcane bagasse, otherwise a waste product, currently accounts for 3.1 percent of Brazil's energy output, with an installed capacity of 3,400 MW. Brazil is exporting its expertise in the technology and construction of ethanol plants to many countries in Africa, as well as India, China, and Japan, among others.

Renewable Energy World magazine notes that Brazil's wind power potential is one of the greatest on the planet, "much of its northeast is blessed with some of the strongest and most consistent winds in the world." Further, "Brazilian wind energy is the cheapest in the world (based on last year's auction prices) because its wind farms are so productive."[33] EPE projects that installed wind power will multiply 12 times over by 2020. But Pedro Perelli, executive director of the Brazilian Wind Energy Association (ABE Eolica) looks for a 22-fold increase. At that level, installed capacity would represent just 6 percent of Brazil's wind power potential, now estimated at 350 GW, or the equivalent of 4.79 million barrels of oil per day. The Brazilian utility giant Eletrobras has committed to wind power in a big way, as part of its ambition to become the world's largest clean energy producer.

Of particular interest, following an auction in August 2011 by Brazil's National Electric Power Agency, Brazilian wind power is now cheaper than natural gas. Nelson Hübner, director of Brazil's National Electricity Regulatory Agency (ANEEL), says, "The results of the energy auction represent a new paradigm in power generation in Brazil because they

---

[32] Yapp, "Brazil Soars in Clean Energy Rankings."
[33] Ibid.

confirm it is possible to produce wind energy at a price that is competitive with those of thermal plants, which are more polluting."[34]

Let There Be Light

In general terms, economically generated electricity can be an adequate or even superior substitute for hydrocarbon energy for uses that don't involve mobility. It is little remembered today that the impetus that motivated Edwin Drake to drill the 69-foot well in Titusville, Pennsylvania in 1859 that launched the world oil industry was the very high price of petroleum commanded then, primarily for use as an illuminant. Even before the first well was drilled, oil that seeped "along Oil Creek and the salt wells of the Allegheny Valley found a ready market at prices ranging from $0.75 to $1.50 and even $2.00 per gallon." Given 42 gallons to a barrel, the upper range of these prices corresponds to about $80 per barrel crude oil (in 1859 dollars) or $1,900/barrel in $2009.[35]

Within several decades, electric lighting had replaced the use of kerosene as an illuminant. Electric lighting was a superior alternative to illuminant derived from petroleum at $1,900 per barrel. One kilowatt hour of electricity costs homeowners on average $0.12 in the United States today. One kilowatt hour is equivalent to 3,412.3 BTUs. As there are 5,600,000 BTUs in a barrel of oil, there is the equivalent of 1,641.12 kWh of energy in a barrel of oil. So at $1,900 per barrel, (in $2009 equivalent) consumers of kerosene in 1859 were paying the equivalent of $1.16 per kilowatt hour for illumination.

While Brazil has perhaps the world's leading portfolio of renewable energy sources, it also has a strong portfolio of more conventional power. The huge oil finds made early in this century are obviously the headline grabbers. But Brazil also has large and growing proven reserves of natural gas.

[34] "Brazil to Invest $5.5 Billion in Renewable Energy Sources by 2013," EnergyRefuge.com, September 14th, 2010, http://blog.cleantechies.com/2010/09/14/brazil-invest-renewable-energy-sources/.
[35] Hamilton, "Historical Oil Shocks," 2.

According to *The Oil and Gas Journal*, Brazil had 12.9 trillion cubic feet of proven natural gas reserves in 2011. With additional, vast amounts being discovered in the deep offshore basins, Petrobras says that the Tupi block alone could contain 5 trillion to 7 trillion cubic feet of recoverable natural gas. With much of the country relatively unexplored, Brazil's gas reserves could be gigantic. When looking at reports from the U.S. Department of Energy's Energy Information Administration (www.eia.gov), there is a general feeling that the Amazon could hold a considerable amount of untapped natural gas.

Natural gas accounts for about 8 percent of Brazilian energy consumption, with about 85 power plants installed to generate as much as 10.6 GW of thermal electricity from natural gas.

Brazil also has some coal, with current reserves estimated at about 32,000,000,000 tons. Current Brazilian coal production is approximately 11.2 million tons annually. True to Jeffrey Sachs' characterization that "coal deposits are overwhelmingly concentrated in the temperate zone,"[36] all of Brazil's coal mines are in its three southern states—Paraná, Santa Catarina, and Rio Grande do Sul—that lie entirely within the temperate zone. Coal is used mainly for thermal generation of electricity in 10 small plants in the southern states with a total installed capacity of about 2,100 MW. The thermal generation is used to supplement hydropower rather than as a principal source of supply. The Brazilian coal industry claims that the marginal costs for purchasing coal to fuel the thermoelectric supplement to the hydroelectric power for peak loads "translates into lower rates for the final consumer."

Brazil also has a nuclear power industry along with the sixth-largest uranium reserves in the world, an estimated 309,000 tons. Brazil's first nuclear power plant was the Angra I, which came online in 1983 with a capacity to generate 657 MW. The larger Angra 2 facility has a capacity of 1,350 MW. A third nuclear power plant, also with 1,350 MW capacity, but with more advanced technology, is currently under construction. When completed, it will bring Brazil's installed nuclear power capacity to 3,357 MW.

---

[36] Sachs, "Tropical Underdevelopment," 21.

Declining Power after an Energy Transition

I am persuaded that a not insignificant cause of the decline in the fortunes of the British economy after the advent of peak coal on the eve of World War I was the lack of access to higher energy density oil in the United Kingdom.

Similarly, as we look forward to growing global supply constriction associated with peak oil it seems likely that the U.S. economy will be challenged. Just as the United Kingdom lacked the abundant oil deposits that enabled the United States to grow rapidly through most of the twentieth century, so today the United States lacks Brazil's tropical climate that provides much of its advantage in producing sugar-based ethanol, as well as the abundant, year-round sunshine that promises to make Brazil a solar energy powerhouse, as well as a leader in harnessing indirect solar energy in the form of wind. The whole or better parts of 10 Brazilian states, an area totaling more than 1.5 million square kilometers, have daily average solar radiation ranging between 5,700 Wh per square meter per day to 6,300 Wh per square meter per day.[37]

Obviously, these regions have vastly more solar energy potential than the cloudy stretches in northern Europe, Japan, and North America. Eletrobras installed Brazil's first solar power plant, the Megawatt Solar Power Plant, on the roof of the Eletrosul headquarters, with a continuation on the roof of an adjacent parking garage in Florianopolis, Santa Catarina. This is only one of numerous small-scale solar projects currently under development or already operating. Solar water heating systems have been mandatory for all new buildings in São Paulo since 2007.

The two examples cited here are both cases of Brazil adopting solar energy solutions in its temperate zone where the daily global solar radiation annual average falls between 4,500 and 4,700 watts per square meter. But a much greater solar energy potential lies in Brazil's tropical reaches, where typical annual averages for daily solar radiation are 40 percent or higher. As a predominantly tropical country with abundant sunshine all year round, Brazil is ideally placed to draw the greatest possible advantage from solar energy as the technology for doing so matures.

---

[37] Department of Energy, Federation of Industries of the State of São Paulo, "Atlas of Solar Radiation in Brazil."

In addition to its other advantages in solar energy, Brazil claims 90 percent of the world's reserves of silicon, the main raw material used for the manufacture of photovoltaic panels.

A little more than a decade since Jeffrey Sachs underscored "the possibility that differences in energy endowments might also have played an important role in the widening income gaps"[38] between temperate zone economies and those in the tropics, Brazil has gone far toward closing or even reversing that energy gap.

This success was not just a random accident, but the culmination of decades of research and the investment of billions to improve agricultural productivity and to prospect for oil and gas resources. Brazil's emerging agricultural prowess led directly to its success with renewable fuels, ethanol, and biodiesel. And the presalt oil finds, certainly the most spectacular discoveries of oil in the twenty-first century, could only have been found by a company with a mastery of deep water drilling techniques pioneered by Petrobras. As Gabrielli said, reflecting on Brazil's large new oil finds, "God hid it until Brazil was strong enough to cope."[39]

Great Britain surged to the economic leadership of the world in the eighteenth century after its entrepreneurs succeeded in mobilizing new forms of energy in the wake of peak wood. It is too soon to know whether Brazil will succeed in a like fashion in the wake of peak oil. But seven decades after Stefan Zweig said of Brazil that "no degree of imagination suffices to conceive of what this country, this world will mean to the next generation," there are stronger indications than ever that the future has finally arrived for the country of the future.[40]

Chapter 11 discusses Brazil's demographics.

---

[38] Sachs, "Tropical Underdevelopment," 21.

[39] "Brazil's Oil Boom: Filling Up the Future," *The Economist*, November 5, 2011.

[40] Stefan Zweig, *Brazil: A Land of the Future*, trans. Lowell A. Bangerter (Riverside, CA: Ariadne Press, 2000), 71.

Chapter 11

Demographic Turbocharge

Brazil's Coming Decades of Miracle Growth

. . . population dynamics could account for more than half of the miracle. A third or a half certainly isn't everything, but it makes population dynamics the most important growth determinant by far.
—David E. Bloom and Jeffrey G. Williamson, *Demographic Transitions and Economic Miracles in Emerging Asia*

One hotly debated aspect of the relationship between population and the economy is reflected in the Malthusian perspective explored earlier in this book. For many years, economists and policy analysts fretted that rapid population growth in the less developed world was a major contributing factor to chronic poverty. Specifically, observers felt that a large and growing population retarded physical capital formation. They theorized that by reducing the birth rate, developing countries could divert the resources that would otherwise be consumed by a large population of dependent children and use them for investment. Indeed, that concern figured in China's decision to adopt a one-child policy to limit population growth.

As China has enjoyed the highest compounded growth rate of any large economy in history, (growing by 9.8 percent annually since 1980, with the rate accelerating in the first decade of this century), the Malthusian move to limit birthrates may appear to have been vindicated. But look more closely. In the two centuries since the Reverend Thomas Malthus published his famous *Essay on the Principle of Population* (1798), the debate on whether a larger or smaller population is more conducive to economic progress has become sophisticated. Economists David Bloom and Jeffrey Williamson comment,

> Pessimists believe that rapid population growth is immiserizing because it will tend to overwhelm any induced response by technological progress and capital accumulation (Ehrlich 1968; Coale and Hoover 1958). Optimists believe that rapid population growth allows economies of scale to be captured and promotes technological and institutional innovation (Boserup 1981; Simon 1981; Kuznets 1967). Recent research defeats both views: population growth has neither a significant positive nor a significant negative impact on economic growth (Bloom and Freeman 1986; Kelly 1988).[1]

In keeping with the facts as summarized by Bloom and Williamson, economists have gradually refocused their attention away from gross population numbers to direct more attention to the composition of the population, or demographics, as an important variable in economic performance.

Research in recent years has shown that demographics are a considerable driver of economic growth. The larger the percentage of a population comprised of people in their prime productive years, the better the economy is likely to perform. Bloom and Williamson showed that from one-third to more than half of East Asia's economic miracle

---

[1] David E. Bloom, and Jeffrey G. Williamson, "Demographic Transitions and Economic Miracles in Emerging Asia," Working Paper 6268, National Bureau of Economic Research, 1990, 1. Please consult the original source for further information on the citations contained within the excerpt.

from 1965 to 1990 was attributable to a demographic bonus, arising solely from population dynamics.[2]

Equally, Allen C. Kelley and Robert M. Schmidt found that "core demographic variables" account for 20 percent of the variability in the relatively tame growth rate in per capita output in Europe from 1960 through 1995.[3]

One could quibble with econometric models, but there is a strong, logical foundation connecting greater economic productivity to greater contributions from persons at the most productive stage of life. Obviously, a hypothetical economy made up of 75 percent retirees, 15 percent children and 10 percent working adults would be hard-pressed to match the results of an economy with 10 percent retirees, 15 percent children, and 75 percent adults in their most productive stage of life. Of course, most countries are lucky that they do not reflect the overall age structure of either hypothetical economy as iterated above. A country without children would have very little future. Equally, a country made up of 75 percent of retirees would have huge problems. Kelley and Schmidt explain:

> The argument is straightforward. High (low) rates of population growth result in a disproportionate number of children (aged adults) who consume but who contribute little or nothing to income. Consumption by these "dependents" must be financed and this is done out of savings.[4]

The implication of demographic analysis is that an economy performs best when it has a large and growing number of well-trained workers entering the prime productive phase of life. But as the core demographics of the economy are dynamic, the sweet spots for growth, often described as a demographic bonus, depend upon the growth rates

---

[2] Bloom and Williamson, "Democratic Transitions and Economic Miracles in Emerging Asia," 4.
[3] Allen C. Kelley and Robert M. Schmidt, "Evolution of Recent Economic-Demographic Modeling: A Synthesis," *Journal of Population Economics* 18, no. 2 (2005): 275–300.
[4] Allen C. Kelley and Robert M. Schmidt, "Savings, Dependency, and Development," *Journal of Population Economics* 9, no. 4 (1996): 365–386.

of the working age and dependent populations differing. The problem is that demographic bonus phases once achieved, are almost inevitably followed by slowdowns as the workforce ages and retires. Short of an infinite expansion of the population, unlikely for obvious reasons, or a peculiar surge of mortality from a plague or pestilence, dependency ratios for the support of aged adults are inevitably destined to rise. But this waxing and waning of dependency ratios happens at different times in different economies.

It is now fairly clear that the relative performance of leading economies in coming decades will be significantly affected by the percentage of their populations destined to fall into the various cohorts over the next 20 to 30 years. Since all persons who will be in their prime working years or retired in 2030 are already alive today, demographic projections can provide useful hints about the prospects for economic growth.

Among the headline implications of demographic projections, the working age population of Russia is projected to fall by 17 million, to 101.2 million, with a further 14.2 million drop from 2030 to 2050.

Another surprising finding lurking in population statistics is that South Korea's workforce is destined to shrink by 3.7 million persons by 2030,[5] a prospect that strongly reinforces the logic of reunification between North and South Korea. In showing that the demographic bonus was responsible for as much as 50 percent of the growth of the Asian tigers between 1965 and 1990, Bloom and Williamson noted that an "important implication of these results is that future demographic change will tend to depress growth rates in East Asia."[6] Now that the demographic bonus has reversed itself, South Korea's economic performance appears destined to falter unless it can increase its workforce.

Similarly, Europe's working-age population is destined to decline by 10 percent, or nearly 50,000,000, implying an even more pronounced slowdown in economic growth. Europe's demographic decline in the

---

[5] Adele Hayutin, "Population Age Shifts Will Reshape Global Workforce," Stanford Center on Longevity, April 2010, http://longevity.stanford.edu/files2/SCL_Pop%20Age%20Shifts_Work%20Force_April%202010_v2_FINALWEB_0.pdf.

[6] Bloom and Williamson, "Demographic Transitions and Economic Miracles in Emerging Asia," abstract.

next couple of decades is destined to reduce its population by more than the Black Death.

In contrast, Brazil's workforce will add almost twice as many people as that of China between now and 2030.

China Takes a Dive?

Perhaps the most surprising projection of economic performance informed by demographic analysis is the implied slowdown in China due to a drastic fall in the growth of its workforce. China's recent economic rise has been driven by the population boom that preceded the one-child policy introduced in 1979. But demographics are fate. The downside of China's strict effort to limit population growth is the fact that it succeeded. Hence a major labor-force gap that's now only a few years away.

"China will be in deep trouble in 15 to 25 years," says Reiner Klingholz, who spent 10 years working in China and now directs Berlin's Institute for Population and Development.[7]

According to the Stanford Center on Longevity, over the next two decades, China's workforce is projected to grow by just 9.9 million persons, or about half Brazil's projected growth of 18.4 million.[8] Given that China's population is 6.5 times larger than that of Brazil, the fact that the Brazilian workforce will grow by almost twice as many persons over the next two decades may signal a sharp slowdown in Chinese growth. The other factor of note is that almost all the growth in the Chinese workforce will occur by 2015. Thereafter, the impact of the one-child policy will begin to bite.

Note that the one-child policy is more complicated and involves more exceptions than simply restricting every couple to one child, as is often supposed. When the policy was introduced, China's population comprised one-quarter of the world's people, occupying just 7 percent

---

[7] Sara Ledwith and Sophie Taylor, "From the Age of Labor to the Labor of Age," Reuters, March 25, 2010, www.reuters.com/article/2010/03/25/us-age-europe-idUSTRE62O0SO20100325.

[8] Hayutin, "Population Age Shifts Will Reshape Global Workforce."

of the world's arable land. Two-thirds of the Chinese population was under the age of 30. The one-child policy was initially introduced as a "temporary" measure. As reported in the *New England Journal of Medicine*:

> Despite its name, the one-child rule applies to a minority of the population; for urban residents and government employees, the policy is strictly enforced, with few exceptions. The exceptions include families in which the first child has a disability or both parents work in high-risk occupations (such as mining) or are themselves from one-child families (in some areas).[9]

The policy involves a set of regulations encouraging Chinese families to limit themselves to one child or, in the cases where second children or even third children were permitted, to space their births five years apart. In the rural areas where most people lived, a second child was generally permitted after five years, especially if the first child was a girl. In remote, underpopulated regions and among some ethnic minorities, a third child was sometimes permitted. Notwithstanding often heavy-handed government enforcement of the one child preference, the *New England Journal of Medicine* described China's abortion rates as "relatively low, with 25 percent of women of reproductive age having had at least one abortion, as compared with 43 percent in the United States." Among those women having abortions, one of the main reasons given was "a lack of government approval for the pregnancy under the one child policy."[10]

The number of live births per woman in China fell from 2.9 in 1979 to 1.7 by 2004. (The rate in the urban areas was 1.3 children per woman, while that in the rural areas was just a touch under 2.) According to Chinese authorities, the policy has prevented somewhere between 250 million and 300 million births.[11] This estimate of prevented births seems credible when the growth of India's workforce is compared to that of

---

[9] Therese Hesketh, Li Lu, and Zhu Wei Xing, "The Effect of China's One Child Family Policy after 25 Years," *New England Journal of Medicine*, September 15, 2005.

[10] Ibid.

[11] Ibid.

China. India's population in 2011 was 1,210,193,422, some 130 million smaller than that of China (1,339,724,852). Nonetheless, India's workforce is projected to grow by 241 million by 2030 while China's expands by only 9.9 million. If China's population were growing at the same rate as India's, its workforce would have expanded by 278 million, midway between 250 million and 300 million.

The Chinese policy of strict population control had the effect of creating an otherwise "artificial" demographic bonus, beginning in the 1990s, as there were fewer children than there would have been otherwise, reducing the dependency ratio and increasing the percentage of the population comprised of working-age adults. Demographers estimate that the demographic bonus resulting from the one-child policy was responsible for up to 30 percent Chinese economic growth since the 1990s.

Richard Jackson, director of the Global Aging Initiative at the Center for Strategic and International Studies in Washington, points out, after expanding at an average rate of 2.5 percent a year over the past three decades, China's working-age population has almost stopped growing. He states that China's working age adult population will contract by about 1 percent a year from now through the mid-2020s. Similarly, the UN projects the number of 15- to 24-year-old Chinese will fall by almost 62 million through 2025 (to 164 million) while their aging population will rise 78 percent (to 195 million).[12]

China's population growth will turn negative in 2015 according to Wang Feng, a director of the Brookings-Tsinghua Center for Public Policy in Beijing. He says the one-child policy is the opposite of what China should be doing: "It needs to think of ways to encourage young couples to have more children," Feng says.[13]

Brazil's Demographic Bonus

While Brazil's population of 203 million seems tiny in comparison with those of China and India, it is nonetheless the fifth-most-populous

---

[12] Bloomberg, "Ageing Population to Limit Growth in BRIC Countries," *Economic Times*, January 4, 2012.
[13] Ibid.

country in the world. After experiencing falling birthrates for decades, Brazil is about to enjoy its maximum demographic bonus.

A study by Professors Cássio Turra and Bernardo Queiroz, of the University of Minas Gerais concluded that Brazilian GDP has the potential to grow by an additional 2.5 percent a year solely as a result of the demographic bonus that has increased the country's most economically productive age group (between the ages of 15 and 64) to 130 million persons. A separate study by Marcelo Neri, a researcher from the Social Politics Center of the Fundacao Getulio Vargas, suggests "an increase of up to 2.7 percent per year in the average income of Brazilians" due to the demographic bonus.[14]

According to the Brazilian business magazine *Exame*, the economically productive cohort of Brazilians will expand by 17 million persons to peak at 71 percent of the population (up from about two-thirds in 2011).

The magazine projects that the demographic bonus creates an opportunity for Brazil to grow more robustly over the next quarter of a century. The peak year for Brazil's demographic bonus is calculated to fall in 2022, at which point the productive population will be supporting fewer children and elders than at any time before or after. At that point, the ratio between people who do not work and those who do will decline to 4:10 from more than 7:10 in the early 1990s. As featured in *Exame*, Ronald Lee, director of the Demography & Economics Department of the University of California, Berkeley, and a member of the American Committee on Aging Research, says:

> This is a unique chance in the history of any country. . . . Brazilians are standing before a golden opportunity, but it is temporary. After two decades, the aging of the population will invert the curve and cause the proportion of inactive people to rise. Therefore, to make the most until then, Brazil should invest heavily in the new generations, especially by providing good basic education.

Lee's message to Brazil is clear: you have 20 more years to do the homework, modernizing the economy and improving the quality of education, and thus becoming a rich nation.

---

[14] Nicholas Vital, "Twenty Years to Become Rich," *Exame*, no. 980, 2011.

At 28.9, the median age in Brazil is low enough that most of the population is just at the beginning of the consumption cycle. By contrast, the median age in the United States is 36 years. The median age in China is almost as old—35.2 years. Russia's median age is 38.5 years, emblematic of Russia's collapsing population (all numbers are from 2010).

Along with India (25.9 years), Brazil is one of the two leading economies with a young population, where growth prospects in the coming decades are not as likely to be constrained by a high dependency ratio.

But note that while growth in India is likely to surge as the Indian workforce grows by almost one-quarter of a billion persons, India has other demographic problems.

Russia has a collapsing population. Demographers project that it will plunge from 143 million today to just 111 million by 2050. It is unlikely that Russia will be able to supplement its population deficit through immigration, at least from investors seeking opportunity.

This is the opinion of Bill Browder, who distinguished himself by becoming the largest foreign investor in Russia, deploying some $4 billion in that country. The Russian government responded by trying to arrest him and steal some of his investments. Browder cannot even visit Russia. He was banned from the country in 2005 as "a threat to national security" after he exposed high-level corruption. In November 2009, his lawyer died in a Russian prison after being held for a year without charge. Browder recently told an audience at Stanford Business School that anyone investing in Russia "is out of their mind."[15]

China occasionally uses high-handed tactics in commercial disputes, as when BHP employees were arrested for "stealing state secrets" when they attempted to gauge upcoming Chinese demand for iron ore. Brazil has problems with petty corruption, (and even some not-so-petty corruption), much as you would find in dealing with the Miami City Council. But no one has ever been arrested there or banned from entering Brazil after investing billions. There is little in the record of the other BRICs to suggest that criminal mischief is commonly directed at investors.

---

[15] Maria Shao, "Don't Invest in Russia Today, Warns Bill Browder," October 1, 2009, www.gsb.stanford.edu/news/headlines/browder09.html.

However, both India and China face serious difficulties because they countenance a different form of crime—gendercide—a widespread practice of selective abortion plus female infanticide, which leaves them with a large cohort of boys and young men without potential mates. A four-year study in South India showed that "*72 percent of all female deaths were due to femicide,*" the outright murder or intentional health neglect of baby girls (emphasis added).[16]

In some provinces of China, the ratio of young men to women is 1.4:1. In addition to being morally repugnant, the mass murder of young girls has set the stage for grave social unrest because of an unmanageable bride shortage in the near future.

In Brazil, any baby murder that happens is an individual tragedy, not a cultural phenomenon. Brazilian parents do not routinely kill their daughters to escape the burden of providing them with dowries. Unlike India and China, gendercide is not the equivalent to making a deposit in a 401(k) account—a way to improve retirement prospects. Brazilian parents are just as prone to love their beautiful daughters as their sons, as witness the fact that gender imbalance in Brazil leans the other way, the natural way. There are millions more Brazilian women than men. (As mentioned, that's happy news for red-blooded guys everywhere.)

In Greece, the poster child for Europe's retirement culture, citizens over the age of 65 account for 40.62 percent of the total potential workforce according to OECD statistics. The ratio is projected to jump to 58.26 percent by 2030, another vivid indicator that the Greek debt crisis is unlikely to be resolved without default.

Currently, Japanese citizens over the age of 65 equal 38.29 percent of the total potential workforce. That percentage is expected to balloon to an astonishing 68.84 percent within 20 years. This is one reason why many analysts forecast that the Brazilian economy will surpass Japan in the first half of this century.

The expected surge in economic growth from the demographic bonus will accentuate Brazil's emergence as a global leader in a number of markets. In 2011 Brazil was already the world's third-largest market for toiletry and beauty products behind only the United States and Japan. According to forecasts from *Euromonitor*, Brazil could overtake

---

[16] Sabu George, Rajaratnam Abel, and B. D. Miller, "Female Infanticide in Rural South India," *Economic and Political Weekly*, 27, no. 22 (1992): 1153–1156.

both the United States and Japan in less than a decade to become the world's largest cosmetics market. *Exame* reports that the Brazilian cosmetics market "should reach $108 billion in 2020,"[17] almost double the size of the current market in the United States. Surprisingly, Brazilians brush their teeth, on average, more than any other people. And their passion for personal hygiene leads Brazilians to use more deodorant per capita than residents of the United States.[18] The millions of new Brazilians entering the workforce will accelerate the growth of household formation in Brazil. According to *Exame*, "It is estimated that, each year, about 1.7 million new families will be created in the country. Up to 2030, there will be at least 35 million new families, mainly from the rising class C, that will need a place to live."[19]

A Laboratory for New Products

The New Brazil is becoming a laboratory of the new world economy. As Michael R. Czinkota and Ilkka A. Ronkainen write in their book, *International Marketing*, "Some countries are emerging as test markets for global products, Brazil is a test market used by Procter & Gamble and Colgate."[20] Stephen Kanitz reports in his blog *Betting on Brazil* that, "7,000 new products were introduced in Brazil in the first semester of 2009. Nearly 6 percent of all new products introduced in the world. Why?"[21] There are several reasons, including that Brazil's consumer economy is expanding robustly as income rises.

Another factor that contributes to the decision to launch products in Brazil is low advertising costs. This is partly a feature of the fact that almost all Brazilians speak one language, Portuguese. The United States has two languages; Switzerland, four.

---

[17] Vital, "Twenty Years to Become Rich."

[18] Dean Newman, "Demographic Changes to Boost Brazil's Investment Appeal," *Interactive Investor*, July 4, 2011.

[19] Vital, "Twenty Years to Become Rich."

[20] Michael R. Czinkota and Ilkka A. Ronkainen, *International Marketing*, 8th ed. (Mason, OH: Thomson South-Western, 2007), 484.

[21] Stephen Kanitz, "Brazil: The Future Testing Ground of the World," *Betting on Brazil* (blog), November 26, 2009, http://brazil.melhores.com.br/2009/11/brazil -the-future-testing-ground-of-the-world.html.

Kanitz adds other considerations by pointing out that Brazil has remarkable demographic strengths because of its relatively young median age and the fact that many new consumers are entering markets for the first time. This enhances the prospects for growth and makes Brazil a wonderful market to try new products. If you choose Switzerland as your testing ground for a new product, where everyone is loyal to a 30-year-old brand, you may find more resistance than acceptance to new concepts. But because much of Brazil's emerging middle class has only recently gained sufficient discretionary income to participate in consumer culture, they are more open and receptive to new products and services than consumers who have had brand preferences imprinted on their consciousness for generations.

For this and other reasons, Brazilians have the same sort of brash affinity for the new that characterized U.S. consumers when the U.S. economy came of age early in the past century. Brazilians are curious, technologically bent, and will try out everything new. Brazilians have more cell phones and more people on the Internet; more than 50 percent of Google's ORKUT social network affiliates worldwide are Brazilian. They are eager adapters of new technology.

A Real Cultural Melting Pot

Another point in Brazil's favor is that it is a melting pot of many cultures, with more persons of Italian descent than anywhere other than Italy, along with lots of Poles, Lebanese, and other groupings. My former Brazilian wife is descended from Dutch, Portuguese, Italian, and German ancestors. Brazil also has a large Asian population, with more Japanese than anywhere outside of Japan. Brazil is home to more persons of African-American descent than the United States, and there are tens of millions of Brazilians of German ancestry. In short, Brazil is a true cross-section of what you will find when you go international with your product.

The United States has long prided itself as being the world's melting pot. Brazil is like the United States in that respect, only more so. As the Austrian novelist, Stefan Zweig, observed in 1940,

. . . for centuries the Brazilian nation has been established on one principle alone, that of free and unrestrained intermixing, the total equality of black and white and brown and yellow. What in other countries is only set down theoretically on paper and parchment, absolute civil equality in public and private life, has a visible effect here in the real sphere. . . . Seldom can we see more beautiful women and children anywhere in the world.[22]

Brazil is a true melting pot of many cultures from different races and backgrounds, a cross-section of what you will find when you go international with your product. Hence, Brazil will be the center of most multinational companies' marketing strategies in the decades to come because it abounds with young consumers who all speak a single language and are eager new adapters of technology and new ideas.

Every country in the world would be poorer if a global collapse dampened demand for commodities and finished products. On one level, the unfavorable demographic projections for China would appear to be problematic for Brazilian commodity exports. Because China has been such a huge consumer of commodities at the margin, a sharp drop-off in Chinese buying would have an impact in Brazil.

That said, in a collapsing world, I suspect that Brazil would survive a Chinese slowdown more easily than most. Brazil's growing middle class creates a vibrant internal market with a vast upside to expand. And its demographic bonus raises the growth target for Brazil up to the miracle level previously enjoyed by the high-growth Asian economies.

Next up, after much fawning, we discuss a few of Brazil's complications.

---

[22] Stefan Zweig, *Brazil: A Land of the Future*, trans. Lowell A. Bangerter (Riverside, CA: Ariadne Press, 2000), 10, 11, 122.

Chapter 12

Back to the Future

What Could Go Wrong

Brazil is no country for beginners.

—Antônio Carlos Jobim

Vinícius de Moraes, the Oxford-educated Brazilian poet who wrote "The Girl from Ipanema," was an unabashed lover of Brazilian women. He married seven of them.

De Moraes knew a good thing when he saw one, and he was unapologetic in his devotion to feminine beauty. He famously declared, "Ugly women, forgive me, but beauty is fundamental." Through his writing he did much to incite the imaginations of men across the globe about the allure of Brazilian beach culture. There was an actual "Girl from Ipanema," Heloísa Eneida Menezes Paes Pinto, a supermodel-beautiful 17-year-old with emerald green eyes, and a walk like poetry, whom de Moraes spotted in 1962 from his girl-watching perch at the Veloso Bar, a block from the beach at Ipanema.

"The Girl from Ipanema" won a Grammy for Record of the Year in 1965 on its way to becoming the second-most-widely-recorded popular song in history. More than any other single influence, it probably helped shape Rio de Janeiro's reputation as home to some of the world's most beautiful women. As *Victoria's Secret* proclaimed in its "The Girls of Brazil" advertisement, "No country has produced more Victoria's Secret models than Brazil."

I freely admit that I was one of many men who fell under the spell that de Moraes cast. Before I ever set foot in Rio de Janeiro, I was completely sold on the attraction of scantily clad Brazilian women cavorting on white sand beaches. Indeed, as I have previously confessed, I married a Brazilian girl who made the *Sports Illustrated* swimsuit models seem like slobs. With her as a goad and a guide, I spent much of the past decade getting to know Brazil.

As upcoming details explain, not everything I learned is good. Brazil is a complicated country. Like every country, it has its snares as well as allures. To be sure, I found myself more interested in the allures of Brazil, especially its beautiful women than in some of its less attractive features. As I got to know Brazil, however, I became excited about its economic prospects, with gratifying results. In recent years, the model portfolio I recommend to investors in *Strategic Investment* has been heavily tilted toward Brazilian equities and bonds with returns that far exceeded the "risk-free" gains you could have made in U.S. Treasury obligations, much less the U.S. stock market as measured by returns on the S&P 500.

Partly because North Americans have tended to hold a low opinion of Latin America, I have sought in this book to open eyes about the opportunities in Brazil. A Brazilian friend who went to school in the United States was literally asked by American schoolmates whether Brazilians have ever seen elevators. In trying to counter this kind of ignorance about Brazil, I may perhaps have inadvertently overstated the case for Brazil, partly by downplaying the drawbacks and difficulties that Brazil faces and that you might face in trying to do business or live there.

In this chapter, I want to take a second and closer look at some of the troubles with Brazil. Not the least of these is that Brazil seems to be following too closely in the footsteps of the United States.

Is Brazil Following the United States Too Closely?

Russia, China, and India, the other BRIC countries, have little cultural affinity to the United States. Brazil, alone among the emerging powerhouse economies, is an American economy that shares close cultural affinities with the United States. As Jim O'Neill, chairman of Goldman Sachs Asset Management points out, "Demand in the so-called BRIC economies of Brazil, Russia, India, and China is now more important to the world economy than the United States and Europe."[1]

The following main points that I bring to your attention do not contradict O'Neill's observation that Brazil is rapidly becoming one of the world's foremost economies. Indeed, I may even move there. But I do so with my eyes open. I can see that for all its strengths, Brazil also has weaknesses. For better or worse, it really is another different, less arthritic version of the United States. As it matures, many of its "American" similarities to the United States are destined to come more to the fore. Among the worrying signs I explore in this chapter are a surge in obesity, growing abuse of consumer credit, too much American-style, anticompetitive economic regulation. Topping it all is the unequivocally sorry indicator that Brazil trails only the United States among the world's countries in the number of lawyers per capita. Of course, if you can endure these drawbacks in the United States, you should feel right at home in Brazil.

Let's start with "The Girl from Ipanema." Vinícius de Moraes wrote that song about her heartbreaking beauty around the time that French President Charles de Gaulle was dismissing Brazil. De Gaulle quipped, "Brazil is the country of the future, and it always will be." I decided to look back to de Gaulle's time to see what I could learn about this beauty who allegedly sucked the air out of the Veloso Bar every time she sauntered past.

Was de Moraes telling the truth? Or did the legend of Brazilian beach culture begin with a hallucination? Was Vinícius de Moraes such a sucker for Brazilian women that he could fall in love with any Brasileira who wasn't dog ugly?

That could conceivably have been difficult to answer, but a few minutes research persuaded me that de Moraes did not exaggerate when he praised the girl named Heloísa. One of the links I discovered in my online research was to a 2003 *Playboy* featuring Heloísa Pinheiro,

---

[1] Jim O'Neill, "Panic Measures Will Ruin the BRIC Recovery," *Financial Times*, August 10, 2011, 6.

"The Girl from Ipanema," shot when she was 58 years old. There are few women at that age who would be plausible *Playboy* models, but even with the damaging effects of decades spent in the sun, Heloísa Pinheiro—once, The Girl from Ipanema, and now, The Grandmother from Ipanema—was still gorgeous in 2003.

Seeing Heloísa at 58 makes it easy to believe that she was impossibly beautiful as a 17-year-old girl in 1962. No wonder that de Moraes and his collaborator, composer Antonio Carlos Jobim, became infatuated with her. She embodies what has tended to make Brazil special: not only the legendary beauty of its women, but their ability to hold their beauty late in life. This is reflected further in Brazil's Miss Grandmother contest, which went viral on the Internet a few years ago.

Weight

Brazilian women tend to hold their looks well into middle age. And this, unfortunately, punctuates a recent and worrying trend about what is now going wrong in Brazil. Sadly, whereas the original "Girl from Ipanema" was tall, thin, young, and beautiful, her counterpart today has almost a 50 percent chance of being overweight on the way to being obese.

An unhappy side effect of the surge in real income in Brazil has been a surge of obesity. Brazil, like all the BRIC countries is getting fatter as it gets richer. A social indicator of weight gain among Brazilians is the drop in undernourishment that accelerated in the last quarter of the twentieth century. In 1975, four times more Brazilians were underweight from malnutrition than were obese. That changed as incomes grew.

Part of the issue is that poor people who reach middle class income levels tend to have status anxieties. In particular, they know that rich people seldom prepare their own food. Consequently, a surge in income can lead a formerly poor family to completely abandon the traditional diet. Rather than prepare their own meals from higher quality fresher, natural ingredients, they prefer to abandon cooking altogether and buy ready-made meals, such as store-bought breads and cakes, frozen dinners, and fast food. The move away from the traditional cooking to more processed foods tends to make people fatter.

Another reason that surging wealth may tend to make people fatter, in addition to eliminating undernourishment and deflecting people away from the traditional diet, is the effect it has in contributing to more sedentary leisure activity. In per capita terms, Brazil was by far the richest of the BRIC countries in 1970. Yet even Brazil has experienced an enormous increase in the proportion of households with TV sets, from 24 percent in 1970 to 88 percent in 1999.[2] That percentage would now be above 90 percent after a jump in real income that brought 39.5 million Brazilians out of poverty and into the middle class in the nine years ending in May 2011.[3] People who spend a greater percentage of their leisure time in sedentary pursuits like watching television tend to gain weight.

There are no doubt other factors in addition to greater caloric intake and more sedentary leisure pursuits that contribute to an unwholesome weight gain as incomes rise. I am convinced that consuming more highly-processed fast foods laden with unnatural ingredients such as trans fats and high fructose corn syrup contributes significantly to the obesity epidemic.

If you don't understand the dangers of high fructose corn syrup, it is a highly refined, unnatural product that cannot be metabolized readily into ATP for cellular energy like sucrose. Scientists and natural foods advocates believe that the 1,000 percent increase in consumption of HFCS between 1970 and 1990 is responsible for the surge in nonalcoholic fatty liver disease in the United States.[4] It turns out that drinking a lot of soft drinks loaded with high fructose corn syrup can be as harmful to your liver as swilling vodka or cachaça, the Brazilian rum that is the third most widely drunk spirit in the world.

Of course, as the world's largest and most efficient sugar producer, Brazil suffers less with high fructose corn syrup than does the United States; Brazil produces 20 percent of the world's sugar at a cost of

---

[2] Carlos A. Monteiro, "Is Obesity Replacing or Adding to Undernutrition? Evidence from Different Social Classes in Brazil," *Public Health Nutrition* 5, no. 1A (2002): 105–112.

[3] "Almost 40 Million Brazilians Climbed to Middle Class in the Last Eight Years," MercoPress, June 28, 2011, http://en.mercopress.com/2011/06/28/almost-40 -million-brazilians-climbed-to-middle-class-in-the-last-eight-years.

[4] See Dana Flavin, "Metabolic Danger of High-Fructose Corn Syrup," *Life Extension*, December 2008, www.lef.org/magazine/mag2008/dec2008_Metabolic -Dangers-of-High-Fructose-Corn-Syrup_01.htm.

production "on the order of $170 to $210 per ton," as compared to $525 per ton in the United States.[5] Presumably, the greater efficiency of Brazil's natural sugar industry will slow the substitution of industrial, high fructose corn syrup for sugar. But the temptation to substitute a cheaper, if metabolically dangerous, sweetener will eventually impinge further on the traditional Brazilian diet.

Almost every group that becomes rich enough to eat fast food quickly gains weight and puts itself on the path toward insulin insensitivity and Type II diabetes. The roughly 40,000,000 Brazilians who escaped poverty over the past decade showed a high propensity to move away from the traditional diet toward prepared foods, including store-bought breads and fast food. The alacrity with which people tend to consume products that frequently create health problems for themselves also creates investment opportunities for others. In our *Strategic Investment* model portfolio we have had a profitable holding in Souza Cruz, the Brazilian tobacco giant. Disinterested observers have known since the days of King James I that smoking is bad for your health. Yet this common-sense observation has not deterred millions of additional smokers from taking up the habit each year.

Equally, three Brazilian billionaires, among them former tennis champion Jorge Paulo Lemann, noticed the growing propensity for fast-food consumption among lower-middle-class Brazilians and decided to do something about it. They bought Burger King Worldwide Holdings for $4 billion and have subsequently announced plans to expand the number of Burger King outlets in Brazil by tenfold, from 108 to more than 1,000.[6] Presumably, they know what they're doing. They are the same shrewd investors who orchestrated a $52 billion takeover of Budweiser through an international vehicle—a fact that brings new perspective to the joke that Americans who want to use their consumption to stimulate the U.S. economy should spend all their money on beer and prostitutes, as those are the only things still made in the United States. Presumably the Brazilian Beer Barrel Billionaires who own Budweiser got a chuckle out of that.

[5] *Sugar and Sweeteners Outlook*/SSS-249, Economic Research Service, USDA, June 4, 2007, 31.

[6] Kerry A. Dolan, "The Burger King Deal Winners: Three Brazilian Billionaires," *Forbes*, April 4, 2012, www.forbes.com/sites/k2012/2012/04/04/three -brazilian-billionaires-cash-out-some-of-burger-king-stake.

In the likely event that Brazilians escaping poverty continue to lavish their higher incomes on fast foods rather than buying more fresh fruits and vegetables, you can expect to see a growing number of obese people in Brazil.

According to a 2010 report on the Reuters newswire, nearly half of adult Brazilians are overweight, and 15 percent are obese. The story quotes Brazil's health minister José Gomes Temporão, as saying, "if we stay at this pace, in 10 years, we will have two thirds of the population overweight (or obese) as has happened in the United States."[7]

Unfortunately, more and more Brazilian waistlines are bulging, betraying the country's image as a haven for buff sun worshipers. Among Brazilians between 20 and 24 years old, the percentage of overweight women has shot up to 48 percent from 28.7 percent in a previous national survey (1996–1997). Whereas a decade ago and earlier the beach on Ipanema was crowded with beauties, today about half of them look like the stereotypical overweight American.

It is a sign of the times that the Brazilian magazine *CartaCapital*, published in conjunction with *The Economist*, ran a photo of an obese woman cavorting on a sparkling, white sand beach, with a warning that a mere 50 to 100 excess calories per day can result in obesity.[8] On the lighter side, the report also emphasized that Brazil still has a long way to go to sink as far into obesity as the United States where 70 percent of adults carry excessive weight, 30 percent are obese, and 10 percent are morbidly obese. More shocking still is the projection from researchers at Johns Hopkins University that essentially all American adults will be overweight by the year 2048 if present trends continue.[9]

For a lover of Brazilian women, seeing this country move along the same trajectory as the United States in the direction of obesity is a sad sight. It is also an instructive one from an investment perspective. It suggests that Brazil is a country where the opportunities and risks may be

---

[7] "The Chubby Girl from Ipanema? Brazil Puts on Weight," Reuters, August 27, 2010, www.reuters.com/article/2010/08/27/us-brazil-obesity-idUSTRE67Q3UK 20100827.

[8] "Dieta, estilo de vida e gaanho de peso," *CartaCapital*, July 27, 2011, 65.

[9] Maryn McKenna, "A Diabetes Cliffhanger" *Scientific American* 306, no. 2 (2012): 26–28.

tending to follow a template based upon its stage of economic development, rather than being more directly informed by peculiarities of Brazilian culture, much less genetics.

Unfortunately, for lovers of beautiful women, Brasileiras are tending to get fatter in proportion to income growth. Women in the south of Brazil, the country's wealthiest region are fatter than those in the north. And obesity is growing most rapidly among those whose incomes have risen the most. Wealthier women in the cities tend to be chubbier than poor women in the countryside. The one bright spot to show up in nationwide surveys undertaken in Brazil since 1975 was a hint that the obesity among the wealthiest segment of Brazilian women in the southeastern region tended to drop as their commitment to physical exercise rose after 1989. This seems to be unique among developing countries.[10] No others seem to have any distinct demographic segments that are making countertrend headway against obesity. This may reflect the uneven development of Brazil, concentrated in the southeastern region of this vast country. The states of São Paulo, Rio de Janeiro, and Minas Gerais, encompass an area greater than seven core states of the European Union—Austria, Belgium, Luxembourg, the Netherlands, Italy, Denmark, and Germany—combined. In the immortal words of George W. Bush, "Wow, Brazil is big." Brazil's industrialized southeastern region, about one-tenth of the country, with a population of about 75 million, is more comparable to a middle-income country than to a developing economy one.

The apparently established trend for higher-income women in Brazil to counteract the slide toward obesity through exercise suggests a bright future for operators of health clubs in Brazil and purveyors of exercise clothes and equipment, like Track & Field, the high-end Brazilian brand now expanding into the United States. Its first stateside shop opened on the Upper East Side of New York close to Central Park at Madison Avenue and 77th Street.

Effects on Health Care

The growth of chubbiness also has grim implications for health care costs. It implies a future of declining marginal returns for health

---

[10] Monteiro, "Is Obesity Replacing or Adding to Undernutrition?"

care spending in Brazil, following along the lines of the astonishing plunge in marginal returns on health care spending in the United States. As you may remember from the footnotes of the debate surrounding Obamacare, the United States spends twice as much per capita on healthcare as any other advanced economy, without achieving any measurable benefit in terms of improved health outcomes. Among the grim correlates of increased consumption of high fructose corn syrup, in addition to growing nonalcoholic cirrhosis, are surging heart and kidney disease, all of which contribute to soaring health care costs.

It is notable that the stage of economic development tends to be more telling in informing the propensity to fat than apparently distinctive genetic and cultural factors. Across the G-20, North America is by far the fattest continent, with Mexico joining Canada and the United States near the top of the obesity scale. The high-income British settlement colonies also are standouts for obesity, even more than the United Kingdom itself. Canadians, Australians, the British, and Germans all have their issues with fat. Italians and French are less prone to obesity.

The Japanese are outliers. They have enjoyed the world's second-richest economy through the last quarter of the twentieth century. But just about the only fat people in Japan are sumo wrestlers who stuff themselves remorselessly in a concerted effort to gain weight.

The question is whether and to what extent other countries, such as Brazil, may have a cultural/genetic advantage that tends to obviate the impact of growing real income in leading to obesity. Approximately 1 percent of the Brazilian population is of Japanese ancestry, implying that Brazil might share to a minor degree in any genetic factors that contribute to Japanese remaining lean.

What does the record show? There is strong evidence that people of Japanese descent, as with other immigrant groups in Brazil, are rapidly assimilated as Brazilians. This was underscored late in the past century when the Japanese government, aware of the demographic problems presented by plunging population, decided to solicit Brazilians of Japanese ancestry to return to Japan. The government reasoned that because of their Japanese ancestry Japanese-Brazilians would be more readily accepted in Japan. Special legislation was passed in 1990, giving the descendants of Japanese in Brazil priority status in immigrating back to Japan.

Contrary to expectations, however, it soon became evident that the "returning Japanese" from Brazil were no longer Japanese but Brazilian. As one account put it, "Despite their Japanese appearance, Brazilians in Japan are culturally Brazilians, usually only speaking Portuguese, and are treated as foreigners."[11] While I am only guessing, I suppose that the body fat profile of Japanese has more to do with their diet and physical activity than their genome. Whether this is reflected among Brazilians of Japanese descent is complicated by the fact that Brazil's distinctive culture is likely to have played a role by thoroughly mixing the country's gene pool.

Diversity Issues

The thorough mixing of the country's gene pool first occurred to me as I began to wonder why Brazilian women have long enjoyed a reputation for great beauty. Let me explain. If you are looking for a succinct definition of beauty one of the best is the regularity and symmetry of the features. Perhaps the best way to attain regularity and symmetry of features is by thoroughly stirring and mixing the human gene pool. This is what Brazilian culture has done. As the Austrian author Stefan Zweig wrote almost three-quarters of a century ago in *Brazil: A Land of the Future*:

> . . . for centuries the Brazilian nation has been established on one principle alone, that of free and unrestrained intermixing, that total equality of black and white and brown and yellow. What in other countries is only set down theoretically on paper and parchment, absolute civil equality in public and private life, has a visible effect here in the real sphere. . . . It is touching to see even the children, who vary through all shades of human skin color—chocolate milk and coffee—come from school arm in arm. . . . this whole thing constantly mixed itself together,

---

[11] See Kaizô Iwakami Beltrão and Sonoe Sugahara, "Permanentemente temporário: *dekasseguis* brasileiros no Japão," *Revista Brasileira de Estudos de População* 23 (1) (Portuguese); available at bases.bireme.br/cgi-bin/wxislind.exe/iah/online/?IsisScript=iah/iah.xis&src=google& base=LILACS&lang=p&nextAction=lnk&exprSearch=447388&indexSearch=ID.

interbred, and was refreshed by the constant influx of new blood through the centuries. Having come here from all European countries and finally, with the Japanese, from Asia, these blood groups are incessantly multiplied and varied in innumerable crosses and hybrids within the borders of Brazil. All shades, all nuances of physiology and character can be found here. Anyone who crosses the street in Rio sees more peculiarly mixed and already indeterminable types in an hour than he would otherwise see in another city in a year.[12]

As a result, Zweig concluded, "Seldom can we see more beautiful women and children anywhere in the world."

Taking this at face value as an informing factor in beauty, there is the further question of whether high-speed "race mixing" makes for a healthier, leaner population. To my knowledge, this is a subject that has never been researched. But the fact that the United States, Canada, and Australia are among the fattest countries on the globe suggests otherwise. All three countries have populations comprised of immigrants from all over.

The United States has frequently been perceived as the great melting pot. During its dynamic period, the culture of the United States attracted immigrants to assimilate. No longer. Today's immigrants to the United States tend to segregate themselves in ethnic enclaves and continue speaking their original languages. As Zweig observed over 70 years ago, Brazil is the world's most thoroughly stirred melting pot. Genetically and culturally, Brazil is a much more integrated society than the United States. If there are health benefits from thoroughly mixing the genomes of various populations, they should be more evident in Brazil.

On the other hand, especially where obesity is concerned, it is equally conceivable that the populations that have been exposed to the traditional Western diet over the longest time may be better adapted to it. There is strong evidence that some peoples, who have only recently begun eating Western-style diets, are more prone to obesity and Type II diabetes than those of European descent. Polynesian immigrants to New Zealand, for example, are dramatically overrepresented among the ranks of the

---

[12] Stefan Zweig, *Brazil: A Land of the Future*, trans. Lowell A. Bangerter (Riverside, CA: Ariadne Press, 2000), 10–11, 122.

morbidly obese. They are disproportionately diabetic and more prone to suffer from other ailments aggravated by being overweight.

Equally, there is evidence that the general health of Brazilians has been improved in at least one sense because of the more complete assimilation of immigrant groups in Brazil. A striking example of this is provided by the different experience of Arab immigration to the United States and to Brazil. Notably, nineteenth-century Muslim immigration to both countries, mostly from the Ottoman Empire, did not lead to the formation of distinctive Islamic communities. Most immigrants were rapidly absorbed into the wider American or Brazilian society.

More recently, however, Arab immigration to the United States has led to the formation of distinctive Arab-American communities. Arab-American associations estimate that there are 3.5 million Americans of Arab descent.[13] As time has passed, they have proven ever less likely to assimilate. There are an estimated 1.8 million practicing Muslims in the United States.[14]

By contrast, as reported in the *Washington Times*, few of Brazil's estimated 10 million descendants of Arab immigrants even realize that they have Arab ancestry.[15] A recent census showed only 27,000 Brazilians claimed to be practicing Muslims. Why the very low level of identification as Arabs among Brazilians of Arab descent? Because they don't form distinctive communities. Intermarriage between Brazilians of Arab descent and other Brazilians, regardless of ethnic ancestry or religious affiliation, is very high; few Brazilians of Arab descent have more than one parent of Arab origin. Consequently, new generations of Brazilians of Arab descent show no ongoing affiliation with Arab culture. Only a few speak any Arabic. Instead the vast majority, especially those of younger generations, speak only Portuguese:

> "Assimilation and integration have been so strong that sometimes it is difficult, if not impossible, to know who in this country is of Arab descent and who is not," São Paulo State

---

[13] "Arab Americans," Arab American Institute, www.aaiusa.org/pages/arab-americans.
[14] CIA World Factbook, www.cia.gov/library/publications/the-world-factbook/geos/us.html.
[15] "Arab Roots Grow Deep in Brazil's Rich Melting Pot," *Washington Times*, July 11, 2005.

Governor Geraldo Alckmin said at a recent meeting of Brazilian and Arab businessmen. "About 10 million Arabs live in Brazil, giving it the largest Arab population outside the Middle East," said Antonio Sarkis, president of the Arab-Brazilian Chamber of Commerce.[16]

Although Brazil may have a higher representation of Arab blood in the population than the United States, the country has until recently been almost entirely free of Islamic terrorism-related events. This apparent immunity to the troubles arising from what Samuel Huntington described as the clash of civilizations, came to an abrupt end early in April 2011 when a Brazilian Muslim opened fire on Tasso da Silveira primary school in Rio de Janeiro. The shooter, Wellington Oliveira, killed 10 girls and 2 boys and wounded 12 others before committing suicide after being shot in the legs by Brazilian police. Oliveira's neighbors and relatives described him as a "nearly friendless, introverted man" who had recently converted to Islam from being a Jehovah's Witness.[17]

A good thing about Brazil has been its apparent immunity to the violence, tribulation, and social costs arising from the clash of civilizations. Now there is unwelcome evidence that even a highly integrated country with a distinctive culture cannot remain entirely aloof from the random antics of homicidal maniacs. Where such terrorism doesn't arise from ethnic groups harboring grievances, similar grievances can be transmitted to "nearly friendless, introverted" weirdos over the Internet.

Apparently, even Jehovah's Witnesses can be converted into terrorists if they have a reliable, broadband connection. One of the troubles with Brazil is that if lunacy is a modern contagion transmitted over the Internet then Brazil will be increasingly exposed as broadband coverage grows. According to Internet World Stats, 34.4 percent of Brazilian households were wired in 2010, as compared with 74 percent in the United States.[18]

---

[16] *Washington Times*, July 11, 2005.

[17] John Lyons, "Brazil Mourns the 12 Killed by Gunman," *Wall Street Journal*, April 9, 2011, http://online.wsj.com/article/SB10001424052748704843404576251182737094852.html.

[18] Internet World Stats, www.internetworldstats.com.

Heretofore, the absence of terrorism in Brazil has made it very attractive to me. I have always found it a good thing that one can generally travel within Brazil without having to deal with heavy-handed security at airports or to worry about a terrorist attack. Unless you're flying to the United States, airport security is low-key in Brazil. The way I like it. You do not have to take off your belt or your shoes or remove every scrap of lint in your pockets to board a plane. You don't even have to take your computer from your briefcase to clear security. That part of travel in Brazil can be a delight.

Infrastructure

Less delightful is the fact that Brazil needs to invest hundreds of billions in upgrading its infrastructure beginning with airports. Economists suggest that infrastructure bottlenecks cost Brazil more than 1 percent of GDP annually. I would guess that this is an underestimation.

For example, much of Brazil is comprised of unexploited iron deposits. But transportation bottlenecks prevent production of many potentially world-class deposits. Many of the transportation and port assets that are required to access the huge iron deposits are controlled by Vale, the world's largest iron exporter, and Anglo Ferrous, a wholly owned subsidiary of AngloAmerican, PLC. The Brazilian government requires Vale to share a small portion of the haulage capacity on its private railroad with other iron producers. But the demand far exceeds the capacity.

There are plans or hopes of spending vast sums to expand railroads in Brazil. Included are plans to build high-speed bullet rail links between Rio de Janeiro and São Paulo. And many more billions will have to be spent upgrading airports, freight rail links, and highways. Part of the difficulty that explains the slow development of infrastructure in Brazil is based in the country's geography. While Brazil is the world's most well-watered country (in the sense that it has more fresh water than any other country), as discussed previously, the waterways are not conveniently situated to facilitate transport. Among Brazil's major navigable rivers, only the Amazon flows to the sea. But the area it drains is mostly tropical jungle—a region of low productivity. Brazil's most productive regions, in the southeast of the country, do not have easy access to the sea through waterways. Unlike coastal regions of the United States, most of

Brazil's Atlantic Coast is defined by a high wall known as the Grand Escarpment. This is the exposed face of another difficult geological/topological feature, the so-called Brazilian or Amazonian Shield; an area where most of the rivers flow away from the sea, either north, as tributaries of the Amazon, or to the west where they eventually feed into the Paraná River system, and thus into the Rio de la Plata, past Buenos Aires and Montevideo into the Atlantic Ocean.

As discussed, the engineering required to provide infrastructure for transport of Brazilian products is much more complicated and costly than the equivalent infrastructure in the United States. Fundamental logistics obstacles help explain the slow development of Brazilian infrastructure. Another hampering factor blocking improved infrastructure in Brazil has been a tradition of astonishing, Italian-style corruption in the public sector. As in Italy, the bureaucracy in Brazil is bloated and ponderous. (Not that it is always much better in the United States.) What Brazilians get in return, like the Italians, "is mediocre secondary schooling, a lottery in healthcare, and a permit-mad bureaucracy apparently designed to impede what it cannot entirely prevent."[19] The heavy-handed bureaucracy is the handmaiden of corruption. Among the most corrupt agencies of Brazilian government is the Ministry of Transportation. As the BBC reported on July 7, 2011,

> Alfredo Nascimento stepped down after a magazine alleged staff at his ministry were skimming off money from federal infrastructure contracts.
>
> Mr. Nascimento denies any wrongdoing, and says he will co-operate with any investigation.
>
> He is the second member of President Dilma Rousseff's cabinet to resign over corruption claims in the past month.
>
> Her chief of staff, Antonio Palocci, resigned after press reports questioned his rapid accumulation of wealth. He's also denied wrongdoing.[20]

---

[19] Rosemary Righter, "Italy Is Venal, but It's Not Greece: Rome's Balance Sheet Looks Awful. There Is, However, a Bright Side," *Newsweek*, August 1 & 8, 2011, 13.
[20] "Brazil's Transport Minister Quits in Corruption Scandal," BBC News, July 7, 2011, www.bbc.co.uk/news/world-latin-america-14055768.

Setting aside the question of whether Minister Nascimento is personally part of the ring of corruption in his agency, it is easy for anyone who drives on Brazilian public highways to credit the notion that large sums are being skimmed from infrastructure projects. The public highways are always in disrepair. The pavement is wavy, curdled, and punctuated with potholes.

The bright spot for drivers in Brazil is the fact that many thoroughfares have been converted to private concessions. In general the upkeep on private toll roads is vastly better than on public highways. The private toll roads in Brazil can be very lucrative. More than 1.2 billion people travel the highways in Brazil each year. And auto sales have surged, leading Brazil to surpass Germany as the world's number four car market. Note that we have made handsome profits in *Strategic Investment* from our holdings of the public Brazilian tollroad company, CCR Rodovias. As of July 2011, we had posted an unrealized gain of 173.69 percent, equivalent to more than 1,000 years of income from constant maturity U.S. Treasury bills. As I write, Bankrate.com reports the constant maturity yield for one-year Treasury notes at 0.16 percent.[21] In a mere millennium, plus another lifetime (1,085 years), you could gain 173.69 percent in U.S. Treasury yield. Brazil has troubles. But among them is not the trouble of living with an insolvent government. Brazilians with money to invest do not face financial repression as those of us in the United States do.

But even though there appears to be a broad political consensus in favor of privatized highways, (even the left-oriented Workers Party government has pushed privatization), many members of the public resent paying the higher tolls generally charged on privately maintained roads. There is a feeling that the public gets very little return on the high taxes it pays. So you may have to keep an eye out for the danger of a backlash against private toll roads, which could eat into the high profits of CCR Rodovias. But so far, so good.

---

[21] "Treasury securities," Bankrate.com, www.bankrate.com/rates/interest-rates/treasury.aspx?ec_id=m1104762.

Corruption

The Brazilian news magazine *Epoca* published a cover story in its July 25 2011 issue "Agencia da Nacional da Propina" (National Bureau of Tips) documenting corruption in the Agencia Nacional do Petroleo (ANP). This story details the procedures employed by high officials of the ANP to transform theirs into an agency for payoffs and extortion. Transcripts of conversations, including photographs, document the bold demand for R45,000 of *propinas* to secure a meeting for clarification of the process to be followed by an oil company to register its interest in obtaining an oil concession. The story goes on to list nine other agencies that appear to be tainted by similar corruption.[22]

The *Epoca* exposé underscores the pernicious logic, familiar to everyone who does business in Brazil, that links ponderous bureaucracy to payoffs and extortion. (Think of doing business in Broward County, Florida.) It is commonplace for mayors and other officials of municipalities, much less national politicians and administrators of ministries, to grow quite rich in the course of a few years in office. Their support is so often required to expedite the approval process for licenses and permits to do anything associated with building that major contractors shower them with *propinas* (tips) as a cost of doing business. The bureaucrats may not contribute much to the productive process, but their support is essential.

I recently heard an example that starkly illustrates the fact that regulators and administrators of bureaucracies in Brazil tend to pursue their own interests rather than their ostensible purpose in promoting the welfare of the public. A tycoon in the major industrial city of Belo Horizonte proposed to build and contribute a civic center to the city at his own expense. He proposed to provide the land upon which the structure would be built, commission a first-caliber design, and pay the full construction costs. All told, he offered the city a gift worth more than R10 million. What he was not prepared to do was pay off officials in the permitting departments to accept the gift. In the end, that proved

---

[22] Diego Escosteguy, "Agencia da Nacional da Propina," *Epoca*, July 25, 2011 (Edicao 688): 40—46.

to be a fatal deficiency, as the bureaucracy rejected the proposed civic center.

The apparently cavalier rejection of this large donation to the city made good economic sense from the point of view of bureaucrats looking to optimize the value they receive in *propinas*. Obviously, they could not expect to extort large sums from a civic benefactor simply for the privilege of permitting him to proceed with his contribution.

They would much prefer to deal with the landowner trying to advance a for-profit project. By rejecting the civic center this is what they got. The tycoon still owns the land. Since he was frustrated in his endeavor to make a civic contribution, he has decided instead to try to build a for-profit concert center. Time will tell whether he will be more prepared to "tip" the bureaucracy to gain their approval of his for-profit endeavor. But as he grew quite rich doing business in Brazil it is reasonable to assume that he is comfortable doing business in the Brazilian way. This must be what the bureaucrats assumed and helps explain why functionaries allegedly working in the public interest would be only too glad to block a major civic contribution.

The bureaucracy has nothing to gain from civic benefaction. But for-profit projects, office blocks, apartment buildings, retail space, and, yes, concert venues, entail situations where time is money and well-placed functionaries can find themselves in a position to profit handsomely by helping landowners, developers, and contractors to create a more favorable equation between time and money by parting with some of the latter in the interests of saving a lot of the former.

Bureaucracy

As this suggests, one of the troubles with Brazil is that it is not an easy place to do business. A big part of the problem is that almost every step in launching a company is ponderous and heavily regulated. I have had a hand in launching companies in many countries over the past 40 years. Unlike the process in the United States, Canada, New Zealand, Australia, or in most European countries, where opening a company is quick, usually requiring no more than filling out a form or two, launching a company in Brazil is a much more drawn-out, complicated process. It takes an average of 120 days to open a new business in Brazil, compared with just under two weeks in the average OECD country. I recently slogged through a process of almost a year to launch a new company in Brazil. It entailed hours wasted at the notary and standing in successive lines in various bureaucracies. In the process, I had to apply for a Brazilian social security number or CPF. It gave me an appreciation of what Antonio Carlos Jobim may have had in mind when he warned that, "Brazil is no country for beginners."

Consider it a form of protectionism (for those already in business, the competition is lessened when would-be competitors are sidelined by red tape), or merely an expression of a peculiarly Brazilian approach to business, but unlike in most other countries, official applications in Brazil require that your name must be executed with your first name first followed by the middle names and your last name. In the United States, the United Kingdom, or Canada, any legal document that asks for your name would be answered with your last name first, followed by your first name, and then your middle names. When I filled out my application for my CPF, as an analog reaction, I automatically began with my last name as I have become accustomed to doing. In due course (a matter of more than a month), my CPF was issued. I was dismayed to discover, however, that due to my unfamiliarity with the Brazilian way to fill out applications my CPF was useless in completing the formalities for launching the company. It was issued to a man with the first name of Davidson. To remedy this, effectively required me to "change my name," a process that entails a whirlwind of visits to the notary and one bureaucracy after another.

One thing that process taught me was that it is not always preferable to handle documentation and paperwork for Brazil in Brazil. Most official documents, including the CPF, can be obtained from Brazilian consulates overseas. Dealing with them has the advantage that they are usually consolidated in one place, so you don't have to wander all over large cities visiting many different official offices as a supplicant. Also your chance of getting help in a language other than Portuguese is much higher in a consulate office than it would be in Brazil itself.

While there are certainly informing differences, if anything Brazil has a tendency to be too much like the United States. I have never been a fan of the surfeit of lawyers in the United States; there is one for every

265 Americans. Equally, it strikes me as a bad sign that Brazil follows the United States closely with one lawyer for each 306 persons.[23]

Of course, Brazil's legal tradition, unlike that of the United States, is not rooted in English common law. The common feature that Brazil shares with the United States is a tradition of high returns to pettifogging. People in both countries go into the practice of law because it pays. Unhappily, a slowdown in business development is a likely consequence of prosperity for lawyers.

Contemporary Brazil certainly provides ample evidence of stultifying bureaucracy inhibiting progress. One of the more striking examples involves evidence that foreign partners have been required to market innovations in dental practices created by Brazilians. Many residents of advanced countries would be surprised to learn that in keeping with brushing their teeth more than any other people, the Brazilian standard of dentistry is among the highest in the world. Recently the American dental supply company Ultradent, along with its German competitor KaVo, expanded their product research into Brazil:

> "It's an environment that encourages original research," says Luiz Abreu, general manager for Brazil and South America at Ultradent. . . . "Brazil always attracted our attention because it is the third or fourth country in the world in terms of numbers of articles published in orthodontic journals," he says. "But since we arrived . . . we've got closer to that reality and seen that Brazilians really contribute new ideas, especially in combining more sophisticated materials with less invasive techniques."[24]

As the *Financial Times* concludes,

Not all conditions in Brazil are ideal for innovation, however. Just as notorious as the country's inequality is its stultifying

---

[23] "What Country in the World Has the Most Lawyers per Capita?," Answers.com, http://wiki.answers.com/Q/WHAT_COUNTRY_IN_THE_WORLD_HAS_MOST_LAWYERS_PER_CAPITA.

[24] Jonathan Wheatley, "Brazil's Dentists Continue to Innovate in the Face of Stultifying Bureaucracy," *Financial Times*, January 7, 2011, 16.

bureaucracy. Ultradent's Tilos range, developed by Brazilians, is on sale in the United States, Europe and Japan but not Brazil.

"We can develop new products, but our product registration process is one of the most complicated in the world," Mr. Abreu says.[25]

Within a year or two the new technology developed by Brazilians will be available for use by Brazilian dentists.

Custo Brasil

Another of the troubles with Brazil, closely linked to the ponderous bureaucracy, is the surprisingly high cost of employing people in Brazil. A common misconception of people planning to set up business in Brazil is that the country has a cheap workforce. This is a reasonable extrapolation from the fact that slightly less than 64 million of Brazil's population, the so-called D and E social classes, working class and poor earn less than U.S. $9,880 per year (U.S. $760 per month). But while there is a lot of poverty in Brazil, that does not translate into cheap labor.

For one thing, payroll taxes in Brazil are extremely high. Your actual costs to pay someone R$10,000 per month would be more than R$20,000. Compounding that, you are obliged by law to pay every employee a bonus of a thirteenth month's salary each year. So instead of calculating your annual employment costs by multiplying a month's salary by 12, you must multiply by 13. The higher up the skills scale you go, the more expensive compensation is in Brazil. As reported by Moises Naim in the *Financial Times*, "the salaries of executives in São Paulo are higher than London."[26] The "Custo Brasil," or Brazil cost, is such that Brazil tends to be, as Joseph Leahy reported in the *Financial Times*, "a low-margin market in terms of profitability, particularly for companies in the start-up phase."[27]

[25] Wheatley, "Brazil's Dentists Continue to Innovate in the Face of Stultifying Bureaucracy."

[26] Moises Naim, "End the Party before Brazil's Bubble Bursts," *Financial Times*, June 1, 2011, 10.

[27] Joseph Leahy, "The High Price of Booming Brazil," *Financial Times*, February 20, 2012.

The employment taxes and social benefits mandated in Brazil are so steep that state and municipal governments looking to save money sometimes evade the social contributions mandated by law. By failing to pay their withholding taxes, pension contributions, and other levies, the lower levels of government can cut their current costs drastically, but at the expense of creating multiple liabilities in the future.

Notwithstanding the great strides achieved in modernizing the Brazilian economy as reflected in the acceleration of growth in recent years, Brazil's potential continues to be stunted by heavy-handed bureaucracy, endemic corruption, and the highest real interest rates in the world. Within the past few years, the surge in real incomes has lifted approximately 40,000,000 Brazilians into the new middle class, creating the basis for the emergence of consumer credit on an unprecedented scale. Per the *Financial Times*, "Mean household income has grown by 1.8 percentage points above gross domestic product (GDP) per year since 2003—the reverse of China, where GDP growth has grown above household income by two [percentage] points a year."[28]

In other words, the more rapid growth of income in Brazil shows that Brazil's economy is more dependent upon consumption and has a much lower investment rate than China's. As Shannon O'Neil, author of *LatIntelligence* observed, China's growth has been investment led:

From 2000 to 2008, China invested an average of 41 percent of GDP, a ratio more than double that of Brazil (and other countries such as the United States). In 2009, in the depths of the worldwide global downturn, investment soared to almost 50 percent of GDP, much dedicated to infrastructure. Thousands of factories, millions of miles of road, new ports, high speed railway lines, and airports have sprung up over the past decade. The country is now populated by entirely new cities and manufacturing centers that then drive growth.

Brazil, by comparison, invests less than 19 percent of GDP a year. Infrastructure is notoriously bad—which some economists estimate will curtail future growth by nearly 1 percent a year. Instead, consumption fuels Brazil's recent rise. In 2009

---

[28] Joe Leahy, "Brazil: Credit to Redeem," *Financial Times*, July 12, 2011.

a whopping 84 percent of GDP was consumption—compared to . . . just 13 percent in China. Brazil now ranks at the top of the list of the world's best shoppers led by booming credit, the expansion of foreign and domestic retailers, and the now 100 million strong middle class. The current over-reliance on consumption leads economists and policymakers alike to worry about overheating.

Furthermore, China's transformative growth has been mostly self-funded. It leads the world in internal domestic savings, which has risen steadily since the turn of the 21st century and in 2007 topped 54 percent of GDP, dwarfing the 23 percent average rate of OECD countries.[29]

Many economists who have studied Brazil suggest that "the best way to fund investment is to increase the efficiency of the public sector." While I know of no direct study estimating losses to Brazil due to government corruption, the famous *tangetopol* (or "bribesville") analysis in Italy showed losses equivalent to 7 percent of GDP. According to the Corruption Index compiled by Transparency International, Brazil is only slightly more corrupt than Italy, ranking 73rd, as compared to 69th, on a descending scale.[30] If you adopt the not-unreasonable assumption that corruption costs Brazil 7 percent of GDP, it implies an annual loss in excess of US$150 billion. Curtailing that corruption could, in theory, free enough resources to raise Brazil's investment rate to 25 percent.

One way or the other, the best opportunity for improving long-term growth prospects is to curtail corrupt and inefficient government. According to Harvard University economist Ken Rogoff (co-author of *This Time Is Different*, quoted in Leahy's *Financial Times* article, "the government has grown inexorably, which makes it less flexible. . . . That's a weakness, I think it's actually *the* weakness in the model."[31]

---

[29] Shannon O'Neil, "Why Can't Brazil Grow as Fast as China?" *LatIntelligence*, www.latintelligence.com/2011/06/24/why-can%E2%80%99t-brazil-grow-as-fast-as-china/.

[30] Transparency International, Worldwide Corruption Perceptions Index (CPI), Ranking of Countries, http://cpi.transparency.org/cpi2011/results/#CountryResults.

[31] Leahy, "Credit to Redeem."

Brazil, like the United States, is highly consumption oriented. It is, after all, an "American" economy. Although a formal rendition of "shopping center" into Portuguese would be *centro comercial*, the common term for a shopping center in Brazil is *um shopping*. They turn the American adjective "shopping" into a masculine noun.

A recent visit to a major Brazilian shopping center underscores the familiar-but-different character of Brazilian consumerism. One thing that immediately strikes a visitor is not just that a shopping center is *um shopping*, but the fact that many Brazilian retail outlets trade under English names: BrooksField, Basic Blue, Handbook, Sketch, Authentic Feet, Track & Field. These were just some of dozens of English-language brands calling to Brazilian shoppers at B.H. Shopping in Belo Horizonte.

As I entered Mr. Cat shoe store to explore sale prices on comfortable Brazilian shoes, I heard the lyrical voice of Bruno Mars crooning the unofficial anthem of consumerism everywhere: "Billionaire."

Something else you would soon notice in *um shopping* is the tremendous difference in the quality of customer service in a Brazilian shopping mall as compared to one in the United States. Decades of stagnant income in the United States have dictated a strategy of cost-cutting as a primary focus of successful retailers. Consequently, when you enter a store in the United States you can generally wander the aisles unnoticed and unmolested by sales personnel. Typically, when you select products to buy in the United States you must then stand in a long line waiting for someone to take your money. Not so in Brazil. When I entered the Mr. Cat shoe store, I was one of four customers being attended by five sales personnel. Something you must get used to in Brazil is the eager attention of sales staff now employed in record numbers in the hope of encouraging you to buy.

Credit

Surging income, along with the reform of the bankruptcy laws, has helped accelerate the boom in Brazilian consumer spending. But the fact that many of the new middle class really are new to credit creates a worrisome potential for short-circuiting the boom. For one thing, the growth of consumer credit has helped drive the surge in imports of durable goods, such as home appliances from China. Consequently, the

30 percent improvement in Brazil's terms of trade arising from the global commodity boom has been diverted into consumption rather than savings or investment.

Just as Brazilians who shift to an American-style diet tend toward obesity, so Brazilians who indulge in U.S.-style credit abuse may face considerable difficulties. The dangers of overindulgence in credit are even greater in Brazil than in the United States because Brazil has the world's highest interest rates.

As of May 2011, the average rate of interest on consumer lending in Brazil jumped from 41 percent to an astonishing 47 percent, and the average interest rate on signature loans reached 147 percent. With interest rates at that level, amounts owing double in little more than the blink of an eye. As you would expect with rates this high, however, most loans are short term. Thus the inflection point where Brazil's credit cycle turns sour figures to be much nearer the starting line than it is in the United States, where the average interest rate on consumer credit cards on July 15, 2011 was 16.43 percent.[32] With Brazilian interest rates almost three times higher than those in the United States, it is little wonder that three Brazilian banks are among the world's 10 top credit card issuers: Itau-Unibanco, Bradesco, and Banco do Brasil.

Partly because Brazil does not have a level of consumer credit reporting comparable to the United States, Brazil's consumer credit laws permit more ready garnishment of wages than do the laws in the United States. (About 60 percent of consumer loans in Brazil are secured against payrolls, cars, or property.) For this reason, the current exposure of Brazilian banks to bad consumer debt is less acute than it would be under American laws. Nonetheless, delinquencies in Brazil (in excess of 15 days) have moved up rapidly, rising from 7.8 percent to 9.1 percent of total loans in the first five months of 2011. According to a separate analysis by credit rating agency Serasa Experian, delinquencies rose at a 23 percent rate through June 2011.[33]

Of course, sky-high interest rates still being paid by more than 90 percent of borrowers provide substantial coverage against losses for the

---

[32] See credit card rates at www.indexcreditcards.com/credit-card-rates-monitor.

[33] Jonathan Wheatley, "Brazilian credit: big threat to growth," *Financial Times*, beyondbrics (blog), July 12, 2011, http://blogs.ft.com/beyond-brics/2011/07/12/brazils-credit-bubble-big-threat-to-growth/#axzz1xUnGWOJF.

banks. The most worrying aspect of the deterioration of credit indicators is that they are occurring in an economy that has remained strong and where unemployment is at a record low. As Paul Marshall observes,

> Normally credit indicators cyclically follow [read lag] the economic cycle. When they begin to deteriorate before any economic weakness, it usually represents a structural problem relating to underlying cash flow or underwriting weakness in the quality of credit—Brazil has both problems.[34]

The combination of high nominal and real interest rates in conjunction with growing delinquencies implies that Brazil's credit cycle will be unnecessarily short. Even if Brazilian families, many unaccustomed to handling credit, do not mind devoting 20 percent of their current income to pay the debts from the previous spending spree, the expansion of high interest consumer debt in Brazil is nearing its limits. This implies a slowdown ahead.

While increased consumer credit and consumption are mechanisms to facilitate popular participation in economic growth, Brazil must increase its investment to continue to grow robustly in the future. As true as this is, it would be a mistake to ignore the fact that Brazil has already made crucial investments that put it well ahead of the United States particularly in the important field of energy. As you will be well aware, American politicians have been jabbering on for decades about the importance of achieving energy independence. In Brazil, this is not a daydream, it is a fact.

Brazil is not only energy independent, it has gone much further than the United States in developing so-called alternative energy. Brazil is the world leader in biofuels. It is also right at the top with 82 percent of its electricity generated through renewables. The figure for the United States is 11.14 percent.

Speaking in support of his scheme to spend trillions to double the percentage of U.S. electricity generated from renewable energy, no less an authority than President Barack Obama proclaimed, "We know the

---

[34] Paul Marshall, "Brazil Risks Tumbling from Boom to Bust," *Financial Times*, July 5, 2011, 22.

country that harnesses the power of clean, renewable energy will lead
the twenty-first century." Wittingly or not, Obama endorsed Brazil
as the country of the future where energy is concerned. The promise that
the United States will generate a significant percentage of its electricity
through "clean, renewable energy" is reminiscent of Obama's promises to
end unemployment and balance the federal budget, but the promise of
renewable energy in Brazil is not pie in the sky. It is here today.[35]

Not only is renewable energy generation installed on a large scale in
Brazil, it pays a hefty yield. CIA Energetica de Minas Gerais (CIG;
recent price: $17.55) operates 54 hydroelectric generating facilities, in an
array of low-cost, renewable assets that includes three thermal plants and
two wind farms. While U.S. politicians talk about building the system of
the future around "clean, renewable energy," CEMIG (as it is known)
powers a state larger than France almost entirely with renewable generation that involves scarcely any hydrocarbon fuels.

Even better, as I write, CEMIG paid a dividend of 11.14 percent.
Compare this to the 3.75 percent yield (again, as I write) on the U.S. 30-
year Treasury bond. I personally don't happen to believe that President
Obama is right about very much. But I do think he hit the nail on the
head when he said, "We know the country that harnesses the power of
clean, renewable energy will lead the twenty-first century." The trouble
is that the United States is ill-positioned to take more than trivial steps
toward meeting its liquid fuels and electricity needs from renewables.
Brazil, on the other hand, will.

Looking out over the next several decades, it seems quite likely
that the return on a 30-year IOU issued by a bankrupt government is
likely to be a lot lower than the return on an equivalent investment in
one of the world's leading renewable electricity generators, especially
given that the yield on CEMIG is three times that of the Treasury bond.

While in the past, Brazil has often seemed to be disadvantaged by its
tropical climate, energy is one area where it benefits tremendously.
For one thing, in a world getting colder, Brazil is a huge beneficiary
of old-fashioned solar energy. As I write this sentence in August, the
expected high temperature in Belo Horizonte, capital of Minas Gerais, is

---

[35] See   www.whitehouse.gov/the_press_office/Remarks-of-President-Barack
-Obama-Address-to-Joint-Session-of-Congress.

77 degrees Fahrenheit. This is the dead of winter in Brazil. Because of weather like this, Brazilians do not have to spend money buying heating oil to warm their homes

All countries and economies have drawbacks and weaknesses, Brazil no less than others. The key to successful investment is to find places where life will get better and problems will be solved. No one should labor under the illusion that Brazil is paradise. It isn't. People grow as old and ludicrous and fat here as they do anywhere else, but while many wealthier economies shrank during the global financial crisis, Brazil grew 5 percent with growth surging to 7.5 percent in 2010. It grew in spite of higher real interest rates and the fickle withdrawal of hot money.

Notwithstanding high real interest rates, and the dangers of growing consumer debt, Brazil enjoys the considerable advantage of being a more deleveraged, solvent economy. While dependable data on aggregate debt to GDP are hard to come by, total debt in Brazil appears to be at least 50 percent lower as a percentage of GDP than debt in the United States. (McKinsey's 2010 study put aggregate debt in Brazil at 142 percent of GDP with aggregate debt in the United States at 296 percent.) Brazil's external indebtedness is also much lower relative to GDP than that in the United States In fact, Brazil is the fourth largest external creditor and holder of U.S. government debt.[36]

Updating the vision of Brazil that Stefan Zweig spelled out in 1940, "its development is still in its initial stages, and no degree of imagination suffices to concede that what this country, this world will mean to the next generation. Anyone who describes Brazil's present unconsciously already describes its past."[37]

For all its problems, Brazil remains, as Zweig perceived, "one of the most important, if not perhaps *the* most important future reserve in the world."[38]

If there is a future for prosperity anywhere, it is in Brazil. In the next and final chapter, we discuss taking part in Brazil's bright future.

---

[36] "Debt and Deleveraging, "McKinsey & Company, www.mckinsey.com/Insights/ MGI/Research/Financial_Markets/Debt_and_deleveraging_The_global_credit_ bubble_Update.

[37] Zweig, *Brazil: A Land of the Future*, 70–71.

[38] Ibid.

Chapter 13

On the Outside Looking In

Making the Move toward Prosperity

For us, it was like sitting on a sinking ship, waiting for it to go down.
—Scott and Mandy Harker, on why they left the
United States for Brazil

The thought that haunts the imaginations of middle-class people in North America and throughout the developed world is the fear that the new normal living standard for middle-class jobs in the future will be normalized at the income and lifestyle of the middle-class Indian or Chinese. A frightening thought for Americans in particular.

The prospect of being reduced to the living standards of the Brazilian middle class would be somewhat less daunting. Brazil's population of 203 million as of July 2011 and nominal per capita income of $12,917 (IMF 2011) are roughly those of the United States four decades ago. Since then, per capita income in the United States has soared, but the average income for males employed full time has dropped by $800.

This points toward the need to make some unsettling decisions. In a collapsing world, facing an energy transition, running away from home may be a rational response to an upheaval in prospects.

Conclusions

In his widely-hailed book, *The Collapse of Complex Societies* (1988), Joseph A. Tainter sketched out a thesis on the economics of problem solving. It is an argument with great importance for people in today's circumstances, pointing toward some sobering conclusions that the mainstream media and most investment advisors have relegated to the shadows.

One of the more crucial of these is that it is most unlikely that the United States will rapidly or painlessly recover the charmed position it enjoyed in the world economy during the nineteenth and twentieth centuries. With the United States already suffering from declining, or even negative, marginal returns from complexity, it is more likely to collapse than to prosper.

As highlighted earlier in this book, the United States seems to face a future of static or declining energy inputs. Global oil production appears to have peaked in the middle of the past decade on the eve of the global debt crisis that culminated in the subprime meltdown and the collapse of Lehman Brothers.

To repeat, with static or falling energy inputs, the United States' economy is closer to collapse than almost anyone suspects. Tainter's argument, when combined with recent developments, brings this frightening possibility into perspective. He writes:

> Energy has always been the basis of cultural complexity and it always will be. If our efforts to understand and resolve such matters as global change involve increasing political, technological, economic, and scientific complexity, as it seems they will, then the availability of energy per capita will be a constraining factor. To increase complexity on the basis of static or declining energy supplies would require lowering the standard of living throughout the world. In the absence of a clear crisis very few people would support this. To maintain political support for our current and future investments in complexity thus requires an increase in the

effective per capita supply of energy—either by increasing the physical availability of energy, or by technical, political, or economic innovations that lower the energy cost of our standard of living. Of course, to discover such innovations requires energy, which underscores the constraints in the energy-complexity relation.[1]

Tainter argues that "complex societies" are prone to declining marginal returns across a broad range of activities. As problems arise, societies try to solve them by increasing complexity ("complexity" in the sense used by Tainter usually means solutions imposed by government), in ways that make for higher costs over long periods. In other words, stable societies tend to proliferate bureaucracies, raise taxes, and deploy costly armies. As the cost curve evolves, (it "may at first increase favorably, as the most simple, general, and inexpensive solutions are adopted") then "society reaches a point where continued investment in complexity yields higher returns, but at a declining marginal rate." At such a point "a society has entered the phase where it starts to become vulnerable to collapse."[2]

Note that Tainter defines collapse as "a rapid transformation to a lower degree of complexity, typically involving significantly less energy consumption."[3] When "its easier solutions are exhausted, problem-solving moves inexorably to greater complexity, higher costs, and diminishing returns."[4]

As highlighted earlier in this book, examples of greater complexity involving higher costs and diminishing returns are almost everywhere you turn in President Obama's America. Nonetheless, it may be useful to revisit some examples, beginning with one that Tainter highlighted in an earlier analysis. He showed that the productivity of the United States healthcare system declined by 60 percent from 1930 to 1982.[5]

---

[1] Joseph A. Tainter, "Complexity, Problem-Solving, and Sustainable Societies," from *Getting Down to Earth: Practical Applications of Ecological Economics* (Washington, DC: Island Press, 1996).

[2] Ibid.

[3] Joseph A. Tainter, *The Collapse of Complex Societies* (Cambridge: Cambridge University Press, 1988), 4.

[4] Tainter, "Complexity, Problem-Solving, and Sustainable Societies."

[5] Ibid.

Healthcare

Ironically, the early 1980s was hardly a time of conspicuous stability or positive returns for U.S. healthcare. To the contrary, it appears that the productivity of U.S. healthcare may have declined more rapidly after 1980 than before. Cross-national spending comparisons based on OECD data show U.S. healthcare costs per capita skyrocketing from around $1,200 in 1982 to $7,290 in 2008.

Over the same time, the United States' standing in terms of the health indicators used by the OECD to measure the success of healthcare—including life expectancy, self-reported health status, premature mortality, death due to cancer, infant mortality, and mortality due to medical misadventure, among others—fell to 17th, dead last, among 17 wealthy countries.

The outlays are so large, and the deterioration so significant that the marginal returns from U.S. healthcare spending may actually be negative in some respects. This forewarning of collapse is underscored by a similarly startling suggestion of diminishing or even negative marginal returns from complexity in the other major undertakings of government in the United States.

Education

As reported in a University of Southern California Infographic, "U.S. Education Spending and Performance versus the World," "the U.S. is the clear leader in total annual spending, but ranks ninth in science performance and tenth in math" in a comparison with 11 other leading economies.[6]

According to the U.S. Department of Education, annual U.S. spending per school-aged child was $7,743, as compared to $1,683 in Brazil. In this respect, the United States suffers from declining marginal returns compared to Brazil. While Brazil's test results trailed the pack among the 11 leading economies selected by the U.S. Department of Education for comparison, unlike the United States, Brazil was not

---

[6] "U.S. Education Spending and Performance vs. the World," MAT@USC blog, February 8, 2011, http://mat.usc.edu/u-s-education-versus-the-world-infographic.

spending lavishly on education without obtaining commensurate results. The United States spends at least a third more than any other leading economy but the productivity of this spending is evidently meager.

Note, as well, that the U.S. Department of Education conspicuously omitted China from its comparisons. The Chinese spend even less than the Brazilians on education, but top the world in achievement test results.

Furthermore, there is good reason to suppose that the per capita spending reported by the Department of Education grossly understates actual U.S. outlays. Bill Ponath, author of *Verdict for America: Critical Issues Facing Our Nation*, argues that "the United States is spending at least $20,576 per student in elementary and secondary schools."[7] He bases this on the average of spending across all U.S. jurisdictions, ranging from $10,896 per student in Idaho to an astonishing $38,986 per student in the District of Columbia. (Washington, DC schools are notoriously among the worst in the United States, while also being the most expensive.) In addition to state spending, the federal government is laying out $1,917 per pupil toward the total national average of $20,576.

The 2009 Program for International Student Assessment (PISA) reported scores for 65 countries based on the administration of uniform tests in reading, math, and science to 15-year-old students in each country. The results showed that China-Shanghai had the highest overall average score, with China-Hong Kong the second highest, and Finland the third highest.[8] Notably, the per capita education outlays in China were $1,326 annually, or just 6.5 percent of the level in the United States.

Given the current technological frontier, it is generally assumed that healthcare and education can only be provided locally. More is the pity, because if Wal-Mart could import Chinese education at anything like its per capita cost in China, it would imply a startling improvement in the marginal returns from complexity (government spending) in the United States.

---

[7] Bill Ponath, "Um. . . . the dog ate my report card," *Verdict for America* (blog), December 11, 2010, www.verdictforamerica.com/content/um-dog-ate-my -report-card.

[8] "PISA 2009 Results: Executive Summary, Figure I., Comparing Countries' and Economies' Performance," OECD, www.oecd.org/dataoecd/54/12/46643496.pdf.

Military

An even more startling disproportion between costs and returns is evident in United States military spending. As the Ponath analysis of per-pupil educational spending in the United States implies, U.S. authorities and bureaucracies are not always eager to present clear and accurate accounts of their spending. What seems true of education is even more the case with U.S. military spending. Total Department of Defense spending for fiscal year 2010, for example, was reported at $707.5 billion. But, as I explore in a moment, this represented as little as one-half of total defense-related spending.

Outlays related to nuclear weapons, for example, comprised $21.8 billion of the Energy Department budget. Veterans' pensions took another $54.6 billion, under the budget of the Department of Veterans Affairs. Security outlays for the Department of Homeland Security entailed another $46.9 billion. At least one-third of the FBI budget, some $2.7 billion, was devoted to counterterrorism operations. The export of weapons to allies accounted for another $5.6 billion under the International Affairs budget of the State Department. A catchall category, "Other Defense-related Spending," spread among various agencies was $8.2 billion. Last, but hardly least, interest on debt incurred to fight past wars and finance other military spending totaled from $109.1 billion to as much as $431.5 billion, depending on judgment calls about which debt should be included.[9]

All told, military spending came to at least $1.030 trillion. If interest payments on all debatable debt were included, the total could be as high as $1.415 trillion, or almost precisely double the widely reported Department of Defense budget of $707.5 billion for FY 2010.

However you slice it, aggregate U.S. outlays for military purposes are staggering. The United States spends more than the next dozen highest spending countries combined, and the United States accounts for approximately half of total national security spending for the entire planet. But unlike the case of healthcare, or education, it is much more difficult to measure the marginal returns from military spending. There is no PISA test to objectively compare national security outcomes between countries.

---

[9] For an explanation of the budget shell game on military spending, focused on FY 2012 requests, see www.salon.com/2011/03/01/national_security_budget _government_shutdown.

Nonetheless, educated analysis suggests that there are declining (or even negative) marginal returns for the over \$1 trillion the United States lavishes on military spending annually. One dimension of this was suggested by William Nordhaus of, Yale University, in a paper he presented to the American Economic Association. In it, Nordhaus notes:

> One way to consider the size of our military expenditures is by comparison with other countries. Other countries face security threats, and they respond by allocating funds to security. Is it plausible that the United States faces a variety and severity of objective security threats that are equal to the rest of the world put together? I would think not. Unlike Israel, no serious country wishes to wipe the U.S. off the face of the earth. Unlike Russia, India, China, and much of Europe, no one has invaded the U.S. since the nineteenth century. We have common borders with two friendly democratic countries with which we have fought no wars for more than a century. Only one country has nuclear weapons that can seriously threaten our existence. . . .
>
> The last five major wars that the United States undertook (Korea, Vietnam, Kuwait, Afghanistan, and Iraq) were ones in which the U.S. attacked countries that had not directly attacked the United States. Four of the five are still unresolved. Whether the U.S. and the community of nations will benefit from the U. S.'s ability to undertake wars of choice will be debated for many years. But this is clearly one of the side effects of having a military establishment that has a capability far beyond its ability to defend the homeland. To the extent that Vietnam and Iraq prove to be miscalculations and strategic blunders, the ability to conduct them is clearly a cost of having a large military budget. . . . If power, secrecy, and money corrupt, then large sums, appropriated and spent in secrecy, for purposes that are unspecified, can, and in current circumstances do, corrupt absolutely.[10]

---

[10] William Nordhaus, "The Problem of Excessive Military Spending in the United States," paper prepared for American Economic Association session on "The Costs of War" January 8, 2005, 2–5. Available at http://blogs.iq.harvard.edu/sss /archives/ASSA_US%20Military%20Spending.pdf.

The possibility, suggested by Nordhaus, that U.S. military outlays entail negative marginal returns, brings into perspective the success of the Al Qaeda "rope-a-dope" strategy of engaging the United States in conflict. As detailed in the *New York Times,* "Al Qaeda spent roughly half a million dollars to destroy the World Trade Center and cripple the Pentagon. What has been the cost to the United States? In a survey of estimates by the New York Times, the answer is $3.3 trillion or about $7 million for every dollar Al Qaeda spent planning and executing the attacks."[11]

The *Times* goes on to state that the total "equals one-fifth of the current national debt." This underscores the prospect that, with economic growth stalled, growing numbers of Americans will experience highly negative returns from the "complexity" imposed upon them by the U.S. government. The apparently remorseless desire of both major political parties in the United States to increase the costs of government without respect to the marginal returns engendered by their programs brings to mind the parallels we discussed earlier that Tainter drew with the collapse of the Roman Empire.

He also points out that "as a solar-energy-based society which taxed heavily, the empire had little fiscal reserve."[12] (Not incidentally, a major part of the Roman Empire's problem as it slid toward collapse was a significant decline in solar energy inputs as the climate turned colder.) Confronted with crises, Roman emperors responded ruthlessly, putting the state's interest in extracting more resources ahead of any consideration of the hardships imposed on citizens. They debased the currency again and again,

> and the level of taxation was made even more oppressive. . . . Inflation devastated the economy. . . . While peasants went hungry or sold their children into slavery, massive fortifications were built, the size of the bureaucracy doubled, provincial administration was made more complex, large subsidies in gold

---

[11] Shan Carter and Amanda Cox, "One 9/11 Tally: $3.3 trillion." *New York Times,* September 8, 2011, www.nytimes.com/interactive/2011/09/08/us/sept-11 -reckoning/cost-graphic.html.

[12] Tainter, "Complexity, Problem-Solving, and Sustainable Societies."

were paid to Germanic tribes, and the new Imperial cities and courts were established. With rising taxes, marginal lands were abandoned and population declined. Peasants could no longer support large families.[13]

Tainter highlights the key to the future evolution of society: the wealthy in ancient Rome, as well as the poor, fled from the government. At that time, given the structure of the Roman state and its policy of imposing ruinous tax obligations collectively on the residents of towns and cities, the best and perhaps the only avenue of escape was to withdraw to the countryside.

President Obama's policies, also enacted under conditions of declining (and even negative) marginal returns to complexity at a time of declining energy inputs share similarities with those of the authoritarian emperors in the final years of the Roman Empire. As "the menacing specter of state bankruptcy" draws ever nearer, President Obama enthusiastically embraces the old remedies of "reduction in the value of the currency and increased taxation." To a degree that few Americans yet realize, President Obama has opted for the most severe "financial repression" in American history, seemingly to "squeeze the population to the last drop." To better appreciate these parallels, see the account of the fall of Rome in *The Cambridge Ancient History*, volume XI.

As I became interested in Brazil over the past few years and sought to learn its ways, I became persuaded that Stefan Zweig's often ridiculed description of Brazil as a land of the future, is true. It is, as Zweig wrote,

> extravagantly endowed by nature with space and infinite wells within that space blessed; with beauty in every imaginable power it still has the old task of its beginning to plant people from over-populated areas in its inexhaustible earth and, combining old with new, to create a new civilization . . . its development is still in its initial stages, and no degree of imagination suffices to conceive of what this country this world will mean to the next generation.[14]

---

[13] Tainter, "Complexity, Problem-Solving, and Sustainable Societies."

[14] Stefan Zweig, *Brazil: A Land of the Future*, trans. Lowell A. Bangerter (Riverside, CA: Ariadne Press, 2000), 70–71. Translated from the German by Lowell A. Bangerter.

Generally, immigrants leave poorer countries for richer ones. There is much less migration of individuals from higher-income countries to economies with higher prospects. Note, however, that is exactly the model for the early settlement of the United States, whose founding settlers left England to seek a better life in the "New World."

"Plagiarize, Plagiarize, Why Not Use Your Eyes?"

One of the legendary investors of the twentieth century was the late Nils Taube, an original backer of my financial newsletter, *Strategic Investment*. Nils achieved "an investment track record that is virtually unmatched in the world of global investing,"[15] realizing an annual compound return of more than 15 percent in almost half a century as a fund manager. He was just about the best in the business. Nils repeatedly advised me "to plagiarize, plagiarize, why not use your eyes?"

He was quoting Tom Lehrer, in what Nils took to be one of the more dependable recipes for investment success. He thought the fact that different societies have tended to reach prosperity at different times created a fantastic template for pocketing low-risk profits.

Put simply, he thought you could dependably profit by seeing what worked in the past in the then-leading economies, and doing something similar when other societies pass through similar stages of development.

I would guess that many Americans and individuals who became wealthy in other advanced economies have gained experience that they could apply to building riches in Brazil.

One of the more successful adjustment strategies to the decline of British hegemony, to cite a less antique example than the fall of Rome, was simply getting out. Those who emigrated, in general, fared far better in realizing a share of higher economic growth in the countries where they resettled. The question is: Where would you go today? This is a question that has been complicated by history.

Notwithstanding improvements in transport technology over the twentieth century, it has grown a good deal more challenging to

---

[15] Nicholas A. Vardy, "Lessons from a 50-Year Career in Global Investing," NicholasVardy.com, October 13, 2006, www.nicholasvardy.com/global-guru /articles/lessons-from-a-50-year-career-in-global-investing.

leave the fading hegemonic power than it was when the Royal Navy ruled the waves.

Coming Soon: Financial Repression

The U.S. government today—unlike the UK government then (and even now)—taxes citizens wherever in the world they choose to live. So long as you remain a citizen of the United States, you are exposed to U.S. tax liabilities anywhere on the planet.

Although it is not often noted, taxation by nationality is a form of financial repression designed to prevent you from escaping any deep crisis in the United States. In *This Time Is Different*, co-author Carmen Reinhart argues that there is a clear path of events during financial crises: governments first encourage credit expansion in turn leading to an increase in bad debt and panic. Then, governments nationalize the financial sector while revenues decrease, along with the economy across the board. In his May 24, 2010 blog, Martin Wolf comments on Reinhart's observations, asking: "What do governments do when it becomes expensive to borrow? They promise to mend their ways, of course. But, by now, it is often too late; nobody believes them. So they tell the central bank to buy their bonds, which starts a run on the currency. Pegged exchange rates collapse and floating exchange rates fall. Inflation becomes an imminent threat."[16]

At that point, governments begin forcing the financial sector to hold their bonds, and financial repression sets in; these efforts ensure that *nobody* can easily move his or her money outside the jurisdiction of the government. That's why you want to get out sooner rather than later.

Historically, as Tainter tells us, in respect to the fall of Rome, where a complex society is experiencing decline, much less negative returns from complexity, the logical solution is not to make provision for the payment of confiscatory taxes; rather it is to move somewhere you may be able to escape them.

This, indeed, is what a growing number of native-born Americans have decided to do. Faced with financial repression at the hands of the

---

[16] Martin Wolf, "How Likely Is Financial Repression?" Martin Wolf's Exchange (blog), May 24, 2010, http://blogs.ft.com/martin-wolf-exchange/2010/05/24/how-likely-is-financial-repression/#axzz1nyUh4eD8.

Obama Administration, a silent migration has been underway in which Americans are fleeing the United States at a rate of 742 per hour. *Barron's* financial weekly is almost unique in having covered this important story. "The Great Escape" by Bob Adams, reports the astonishing statistic that 40 percent of young Americans between the ages of 18 and 24 are thinking of relocating outside the United States to seek economic opportunity. The IBOB-Zogby opinion survey firm found approximately five percent of Americans between age 25 and 34 are already planning to move.[17] While this rush for the exits has apparently escaped the notice of the mainstream news media, it seems to have attracted President Obama's attention. He has decided to crack down with both administrative and legislative initiatives designed to make it more difficult for Americans to live abroad or even obtain passports for travel.

In the first instance, President Obama has sought to deprive Americans of their civil right to open bank accounts outside the United States. As a moment's reflection will confirm, it is practically impossible to live anywhere in the world at a decent standard of living without operating a bank account. In his rush to seal off the exits, Obama went for the jugular first seeking to prevent you from opening or maintaining a bank account outside the United States if you are an American. The Foreign Bank and Financial Account Report (FBAR) and Foreign Account Tax and Compliance Act (FACTA) impose onerous and costly regulatory mandates on foreign banks that have American customers. These heavy-handed regulations seem to have achieved their purpose in bullying most foreign banks and financial institutions into rejecting applications from, and closing accounts held, for United States citizens. Americans living abroad, and even those who have never lived in the United States, all reporting great difficulty in opening and maintaining bank accounts.[18]

President Obama's next line of attack in his drive to foreclose your potential lines of escape from the punishing tax hikes that lay in store was to make it more difficult to obtain a U.S. passport. Under President Obama, the application to attain a U.S. passport is to be complicated with an incredible array of niggling questions that even the most exacting citizen would be unlikely to complete in a "true and correct" fashion.

---

[17] Bob Adams, "The Great Escape," *Barron's*, November 26, 2011.

[18] David Jolly, "For Americans Abroad, Taxes Just Got More Complicated," *New York Times*, April 15, 2012.

Among other things, you would be required to list your "mother's residence one year before your birth." You would also be required to list your mother's place of employment at the time of your birth, as well as the dates of her employment, the name of her employer, and the employer's address. Good luck in assembling the information if your mother is dead.

But it gets more ridiculous. You also would be obliged to declare whether your mother received prenatal or postnatal medical care. If so, you would have to provide the name and address of the doctor who administered these procedures, along with the name of the hospital or other facility and the dates of your mother's appointments. You would also be requested to provide a description of "circumstances of your birth including the names (as well as address and phone number, if available) of persons present or in attendance at your birth."[19]

The proposed form would also require you to list all of your residences inside and outside of the United States starting with your birth until the present as well as "all your current and former places of employment in the United States and abroad." Equally, you'd be required to "list all schools that you attended inside and outside of the United States with the dates of school attendance."

In addition, you would have to provide excruciating detail about your family, "living and deceased," including the full name, place and date of birth, and date of citizenship for a whole array of your relatives.

Perhaps most astonishing of all is the proposal that would require you to specify details of your circumcision if you're a circumcised man. Mercifully, most of us cannot recall details of our circumcision, but that ignorance might provide President Obama's bureaucrats with the pretext they seem to be looking for to deny you a passport. In a step away from the rule of law and toward arbitrary, high-handed government, a passport application replete with demands for superfluous information in excruciating detail all but assures that your passport could be denied on grounds that you filed "an incomplete application." Whether the "Passport Application From Hell" is proposed to take immediate effect in an election year, or perhaps delayed until later, it clearly betrays the

---

[19] Caroline Costello, "The Passport Apllication From Hell: Coming Soon?" Independent Traveler.com, April 25, 2011, http://www.independenttraveler .com/blog/?p=1792

Obama Administration's disposition to frustrate the ambitions of millions of Americans planning to relocate abroad.[19]

Not content to overload the passport application with a battery of pettifogging questions that would be impossible for the average person to answer, the Obama Administration has also sought *de jure* powers to cancel your passport, thus preventing your escape.

"Revocation or Denial of Passport in Case of Certain Unpaid Taxes"

Apparently, with that in mind, the Obama Administration included a provision (section 40304): "revocation or denial of passport in case of certain unpaid taxes" in a highway bill. If this provision, which already passed the Senate by a vote of 74 to 22, sails through the House as well, you can add the United States to the list of countries like the former Soviet Union, North Korea, Cuba, and the former East Germany (all rightly called "police states") that explicitly limited their citizens' right to travel. The bill would give the IRS the right to revoke your passport if they merely allege that you owe $50,000 or more in taxes (including interest and penalties that the IRS can multiply more or less at will).

If you want a good chuckle, try to imagine what Thomas Jefferson would have thought of these current events.

From the Empire Settlement Act to Unsettling Choices

The obstacles to getting your money out, much less emigration from the United States, are far steeper than they were when Britain began to fade as the world's leading economy a century ago. Far from blocking UK citizens from leaving, the British authorities actually subsidized their passage in many cases. After World War I, discharged British soldiers were given assistance to emigrate as a veteran's benefit. Some 26,560 gained assisted passage to Canada, and almost 60,000 more steamed off to Australia and New Zealand, among other destinations. All told, the scheme to resettle decommissioned servicemen (and women) in overseas dominions accounted for 12 percent of the total number of British emigrants who settled in the Empire between 1919 and 1922.

The scheme for subsidized emigration assistance was widened significantly in 1922, when the British Parliament passed The Empire Settlement Act. This provided for training and financial assistance to emigrants. The Act empowered the British secretary of state,

> in association with the government of any part of His Majesty's Dominions, or with public authorities, or public or private organizations either in the United Kingdom or in any part of such Dominions, to formulate and co-operate in carrying out agreed schemes for affording joint assistance to suitable persons in the United Kingdom who intend to settle in any part of His Majesty's Overseas Dominions. An agreed scheme under this Act may be either (a) a development or land settlement scheme, or (b) a scheme for facilitating settlement in or migration to any part of His Majesty's Overseas Dominions by assistance with passages, initial allowances, training or otherwise.[20]

Part of the motivation for training emigrants as they left the UK was to counter criticism in Canada and Australia "about the number of ex-imperials who arrived physically unfit and unable to undertake employment of any kind," as Stephen Constantine wrote in *Emigrants and Empire: British Settlement in the Dominions between the Wars*.

Setting aside the option of subsidized relocation that hundreds of thousands of Britons enjoyed in moving to Australia, Canada, and New Zealand, many thousands of others took advantage of cultural and language similarities to migrate from the UK to the United States.

In some cases, trade unions in Britain helped to pay for members to emigrate to the United States. Union leaders thought that by reducing the number of workers available, they could increase wage rates of those still in the UK. Many of those receiving subsidized passage from unions had been blacklisted for militancy, and were therefore more comfortable moving outside the British Empire.

The English-speaking settlement countries were all attractive destinations where economic growth during the twentieth century significantly outpaced that in the UK. All told, nearly 1.5 million people left

---

[20] Stephen Constantine, ed., *Emigrants and Empire: British Settlement in the Dominions between the Wars* (Manchester, UK: Manchester University Press, 1990), 17.

the UK. between 1919 and 1939 to settle in what were then known as the "white" settlement countries.

Looking at BRICs

Today, the situation for an American or Canadian looking to migrate to a more promising venue is more complicated than it was when the leading candidates to enjoy rapid growth and future prosperity were the Anglo-Saxon settlement countries. All the countries that would now be candidates to realize substantially higher growth in the coming decades are less familiar to most North Americans than Australia, Canada, New Zealand, and the United States were to the British in the past century.

For reasons detailed throughout this book, I am convinced that Brazil will be the twenty-first century refuge for the American Dream. I believe that Brazil will be the United States of the twenty-first century, while the United States seems destined to become this century's Argentina.

Stefan Zweig suggested seven decades ago that Brazil is a country that should appeal to both the young and the old; to the young especially "because there is a future in this country . . . it is a good country for older people who've already seen much of this world and now long for quiet and privacy in a beautiful, peaceful landscape so that they can think about and evaluate their experience."[21]

Beyond the many themes developed earlier in this book, there is yet another unorthodox market test of the most attractive destination if you seek to "outsource" yourself. As reported in "Brazil as an Outsourcing Destination," "The Brazilian passport is the most expensive passport in the black market, as anyone can pass for a Brazilian. How this translates into the outsourcing arena: it makes the Brazilian culture a boundary-less one."[22]

Untapped Resources

From previous chapters, we know Brazil has more arable land and fresh water than any other country. Brazil has the largest reserve of productive

---

[21] Zweig, *Brazil: A Land of the Future*, 149.

[22] "Brazil as an Outsourcing Destination," Brazil Exports IT, November 26, 2008, http://brasilexportati.com/artigos/brazil-as-an-outsourcing-destinations.

land still available in the world. The biggest producer of food in the world today, the United States, can't expand production because all the technology available to enhance production on existing acreage is already being employed by American farmers, and there are no new frontiers of arable land in the United States to exploit.

Likewise, in Europe, almost all useable land is already taken. India, Russia, and Canada, three other countries with large land areas, face climatic and geographic limitations to expanding farm production. China has 10 percent of all the agricultural area in the world, but also has to feed 20 percent of the human population. India, in spite of being the seventh-largest country on earth, is intensely crowded, with 328.59 persons per square kilometer—almost two and a half times the population density of China and 15 times that of Brazil.

Brazil is the only country in the world with large areas of fertile land already mapped and available for immediate use. Estimates of Brazil's unused arable land range as high as 350 million hectares (865 million acres) that still can be used for farming—an area more than two and a half times as large as the land area of the United States dedicated to farming.[23] This good land is available cheaply.

While the United States currently produces more agricultural products by volume and weight, Brazil's agro sector is the world's most profitable. Brazil's free-market farmers make more money from their crops than heavily subsidized U.S. farmers.

Climate: Brazil Stays Warm in the Little Ice Age

Elsewhere in this book, I spell out reasons to suspect that alarms about global warming are overbought. My politically incorrect view is that climate change is driven by solar physics rather than trivial additions to global CO_2 from use of carbon-based fuels. Temperatures have fluctuated cyclically over the centuries in conjunction with sunspot activity. The recent downturn in solar output presages a turn to colder weather, perhaps akin to that which characterized the Little Ice Age.

---

[23] United States Department of Agriculture, National Agricultural Statistics Service.

While the exact directions that climate will take are still to be seen, the possibility of distinctly cooler weather during this century should be a matter of attention for every thinking person. It would be a development that could prove disastrous as the human population soars above 7 billion.

Of particular note, the average summer/winter temperature gradient in the farm belt of the United States is 59 degrees Fahrenheit. Cooler temperatures could drastically slash food output in North America. Already, the Canadian Wheat Board has warned of a drop in the length of the growing season by 10 days in recent years.

A return to Little Ice Age conditions could find food in scarce supply almost everywhere—except Brazil. With more than three-quarters of a billion acres of fertile land unused for farming, the one economy that will be able to feed itself and quench its thirst, given the probable range of climate change over this century, is Brazil.

The average summer/winter temperature gradient in Brazil is less than the average temperature difference between day and night. Hence, even if winter temperatures prevailed year-round in a spate of global cooling, growing conditions in Brazil would be little changed.

But if cooling resulted in winter temperatures lingering into spring or coming early in autumn, growing conditions in North Atlantic temperate economies could be seriously impaired. Remember also, that Brazilian farmers can bring in up to two crops a year.

U.S. Farmers Lead the Migration to Brazil

This is only one reason that farmers are leading the parade of opportunity seekers emigrating from the United States to Brazil. Young families who could only afford a few thousand acres in the Midwest are acquiring tens of thousands of acres of cheaper, Brazilian land. As reported in *U.S. News*, they are realizing gains in operating income as well as capital appreciation of land:

> "What we're doing here isn't all that different from what my great, great-grandfather did," says Matthew Kruse, a native of Royal, Iowa.

He now directs operations on three farms totaling 23,000 acres for an outfit called Brazil Iowa Farms. He first visited Brazil in 2001, then moved here permanently in 2004. He has a Brazilian girlfriend, and out on the farms he manages between 90 and 150 workers, depending on the time of year. When he first visited rural Brazil, he says, "it seemed like we were looking at something in National Geographic. We had fallen off the planet. Now, I call it home."[24]

Among the growing numbers of American farmers who have sold out and moved to Brazil for better land and a better life, are Scott and Mandy Harker, formerly of Idaho, where they struggled to make a profit. They told *U.S. News*, "For us, it was like sitting on a sinking ship, waiting for it to go down." They sold everything in Idaho and moved to Brazil.

Brazil is already the world's largest producer of beef and poultry. It is also a leading producer of coffee, sugar, soybeans, corn, orange juice, tobacco, and almost every other farm product.

The question is whether Brazil's middle class is destined to stall out at roughly the same level as that of the middle class in the United States or whether Brazil can continue to grow. As indicated, I believe that a crucial element informing growth in the future will be the ability of an economy to increase energy inputs.

As explored earlier in this book, Brazil is perhaps better situated to increase energy inputs than any other leading economy. Not only does Brazil enjoy a net surplus of petroleum, with many tens of billions of untapped reserves in the presalt fields, but Brazil is also the world leader in renewable energy. Brazil has the factor endowments to continue growing in the face of the challenges that beset the leading temperate zone economies. If you have human capital, you may be able to put it to better use in Brazil than you can wherever you currently call home.

---

[24] For more tales of American immigrants making good in Brazil, see Thomas Omestad, "American Farmers Try Their Luck in Brazil," *U.S. News & World Report*, June 25, 2008, www.usnews.com/news/world/articles/2008/06/25/american -farmers-try-their-luck-in-brazil.

Making the Move

The very fact that Brazil is a rising power where about 40 million people have emerged from poverty in the first decade of the twenty-first century, augurs well for the prospects of social stability. As canvassed throughout these pages, Brazil has vast scope for continued growth because of its diverse energy resources and position as the emerging, tropical agricultural powerhouse. Brazil has food, water, and power for better living. But the fact that the prosperity of Brazil is destined to increase, while that of the advanced temperate economies crumbles away, implies that the Brazilian state may not be as weakened as nation-states elsewhere that face crises of growth. Consequently, there is a better-than-even prospect that the Brazilian government will impose legal restrictions further complicating the ability of non-Brazilians to profit from Brazil's future prosperity.

If you are persuaded by my argument about how the world is changing now, one of the better strategies for taking advantage of that change may be to secure a foothold in Brazil for yourself and your family. Obtain Brazilian residence, or even a Brazilian passport, to assure that you will always be welcome in the country of the future.

How do you obtain Brazilian citizenship? As is usual in things Brazilian, there is no bright-line time requirement for obtaining Brazilian nationality. There are various avenues open to you.

The slowest and perhaps least exciting way is to become a permanent resident of Brazil for 15 years and avoid creating a criminal record during that time. If you can handle that, you qualify. However, the process can be shortened to just four years if you can learn to read and write Portuguese and you can gain employment or show proof that you have sufficient capital to support yourself and family. It can be further reduced to three years if you own property or a business in Brazil with a certain value. If you have certain professional, scientific, or artistic abilities, time requirements can be reduced to two years. And the wait can be shortened to a single year if you have a Brazilian wife or child. As is usual in such matters, you also have to be in good health and show good conduct.

Equally, if you are a citizen of Portugal, your wait for Brazilian nationality may be minimal. According to Paragraph 1, Article 12 of the Federal Constitution of Brazil, Portuguese citizens with permanent residence in Brazil have the same rights as Brazilian citizens.

This is an advantage that is being exploited to the full, as record high unemployment in Portugal has led some 330,000 Portuguese to legally immigrate to Brazil, up from 277,000 as recently as 2010. As a matter of interest, the Portuguese government, unlike the U.S. government, is actually encouraging its citizens to leave so they can find work where the prospects are better. In late 2011, Prime Minister Pedro Passos Coelho advised unemployed teachers to search for jobs in Brazil.[25]

Given the choices, and the various positives I've discussed throughout this book, it probably wouldn't hurt to try and secure a Brazilian wife or child.

My experience with my Brazilian son has been a delight. This may not seem likely to translate very well to your circumstances, but perhaps it may. One of the strong points of the joyous Brazilian culture is the strong family relationships that tend to prevail. If you are an American, you have no doubt heard loose talk about family values; Brazilians really mean it. They have a lot of fun with their families. If you become involved with a Brazilian spouse, it will not be a one-to-one relationship, but a relationship of one to many. If my experience is any indication, you will be welcomed at every turn, fed prodigious quantities of Brazilian BBQ, and lubricated with your choice of wine, beer, and cachaça.

In general, Brazilians have a lot of fun. Where else would the Minister of Health call for more sex and dancing?[26] In a world reeling from grim economic disappointments, you could do a lot worse than to join in with those who are enjoying upward mobility in numerous economic spheres, including agriculture, aviation, biofuels, commodities, energy, medicine, music, and television. Not to mention the warm weather and a party culture that few other countries can match.

---

[25] Mariana Barbosa, Catalina Sousa, and Naomi Westland, "Recession Has Portugal Urging Citizens to Leave to Find Work," *USA Today*, February 21, 2012, 5A.
[26] "Brazil Health Minister Urges More Sex, Dancing," CBSNews, April 26, 2010, www.cbsnews.com/2100-204_162-6434221.html.

About the Author

J ames Dale Davidson edits "Strategic Investment," a well-regarded newsletter which predicted the Japanese Crash, the fall of the Berlin Wall, and the collapse of the Soviet Union. He was a founder of Agora with Bill Bonner and also a founder of the media outlet, Newsmax. He founded the nonprofit National Taxpayers Union, whose 300,000-plus members work for fiscal restraint and lower taxes. He is author of five previous books, including three with Lord William Rees-Mogg, former editor of the *Times* of London: *Blood in the Streets: Investment Profits in a World Gone Mad; The Great Reckoning: Protecting Your Self in the Coming Depression* (1994); and *The Sovereign Individual.*

Davidson is the chairman of Ouro do Brasil Holdings. He is a current or former director of a number of companies, including Anatolia Minerals Development, Ltd.; California Gold, Inc.; Sibcoal; Core Values Mining & Exploration; Banco Comafi, Buenos Aires, Argentina; Plasmar S.A., La Pax, Bolivia; Martinborough Vineyard, New Zealand; and the Pembroke College (Oxford) Foundation.

Index